Jesus
the
Holy Fool

Jesus the Holy Fool

by Elizabeth-Anne Stewart

SHEED & WARD

Franklin, Wisconsin

As an apostolate of the Priests of the Sacred Heart, a Catholic religious order, the mission of Sheed & Ward is to publish books of contemporary impact and enduring merit in Catholic Christian thought and action. The books published, however, reflect the opinions of their authors and are not meant to represent the official position of the Priests of the Sacred Heart.

1999

Sheed & Ward
7373 South Lovers Lane Road
Franklin, Wisconsin 53132
1-800-266-5564

Printed in the United States of America

Cover design: Karen Jones
Interior design: GrafixStudio, Inc.
Cover and interior art by Ansgar Holmberg, C.S.J.

Library of Congress Cataloging-in-Publication Data
Stewart, Elizabeth-Anne, 1951–
    Jesus the holy fool / by Elizabeth-Anne Stewart.
      p. cm.
    Originally presented as the author's thesis (Ph.D.)—
University of Malta, 1999.
      ISBN 1-58051-061-2 (alk. paper)
      1. Jesus Christ—Person and offices. 2. Fools and jesters—Religious aspects—Christianity. 3. Folly—Religious aspects—Christianity. 4. Holiness. I. Title.
BT205.S857   1999
232—dc21   99-34131
                                    CIP

1 2 3 4 5 / 02 01 00 99

Dedication

This daring caper into Holy Foolishness was made possible by the loving support of three wisdom figures: Dr. Ewert Cousins, Fordham University; Dr. Marie-Henry Keane, O.P., Blackfriars, Oxford University; The Rev. Dr. Peter Serracino-Inglott, University of Malta. As I struggled with my own brand of Holy Folly, it was only their encouragement and prayers that allowed me to see this project through to the end.

About the Art

O Sapientia, quae ex ore Altissimi prodisti, attingens a fine usque ad finem, fortiter suaviter disponensque omnia: veni ad docendum nos viam prudentiae.

O Wisdom,
who proceeds
from the mouth
the breath
of the Most High
reaching
stretching
from end to end
of space
of time
courageously,
(that is with heart)
and delightfully
arranging everything,

Come and teach us
the way of Prudence
of foreseeing in advance
what our actions will bring.

—Ansgar Holmberg, C.S.J.

Contents

Introduction 1
Jesus, Lord and Fool 3
The Christ of Many Faces 7
Approaching Jesus 11

Part 1: Jesus and Human Folly 15
Psychological Archetypes 15
  Christ as Archetype of the Self 18
Plain Fool versus Holy Fool 27
  The Holy Foolishness of Jesus 33
The Fool as Archetype 35
  The Trickster 37
The Fool as Professional 39
The Fool as Scapegoat and Sage 45
The Fool as Spiritual Quester 48
Biblical Precursors of the Holy Fool 51

Part 2: Jesus and Divine Folly 55
The Foolishness of God in Creation and Election 55
The Foolishness of Jesus' Actions 67
  The Infancy Narratives 67
  The Embarassing Baptism 73
  Rejection in Nazareth 74
  Jesus in Bad Company 75
  Jesus' Folly and Conventional Wisdom 77
  Jesus and Shabbat 79

Jesus and Torah 82
Jesus and the Temple. 84
The Foolishness of Jesus' Teachings. 90
The Consciousness of a Child. 91
The Sermon on the Mount 95
The Parables. 104
The Way of Paradox. 113
Jesus and Prayer 120
Jesus and Healing 122
The Price of Holy Folly 130
Name-Calling. 130
To His Family, Jesus Was Mad. 131
To His Opponents, Jesus Was a Sinner. 133
To the Religious Establishment,
     Jesus Was a Blasphemer. 134
To Many, Jesus Was Possessed 135
The Outcome of Holy Folly. 136
The Passion Narratives 136
Jesus Is Mocked by the Religious Powers 137
Jesus Is Mocked by the Secular Powers. 139
Possible Sources for the Passion Narratives 142
Jesus Is Mocked by Spectators 144
The Last Laugh 147
The Foolishness of the Holy Spirit 149
The Spirit as Intoxicator 149
Pentecost and Inspired Speech. 151
The Spirit and the Early Church. 154
The Effects of the Spirit. 157
Costly Grace. 159
The Folly of Baptism 164
The Foolishness of the Trinity. 166

Part 3: Christian Faith and Folly 171
Holy Foolishness and Inculturation 171
Relationship with Jesus the Holy Fool 175
The Russian Holy Fool 184
   Fools for Christ's Sake 184
   Holy Fools and Russian Piety 187
Holy Foolishness and the Church Today 194
   Holy Foolishness and Christian Spirituality 194
   Holy Foolishness and Worship 205
   Holy Foolishness and Justice 211
Holy Foolishness and a New Ecclesiology 223

Conclusion 239

Notes 243

Topical Bibliography 263

Index 277

Introduction

Can folly be holy? At first glance, folly and holiness might seem diametrically opposed. Folly suggests willfulness, stupidity, rashness, immorality, spiritual shortsightedness, the inability to foresee consequences. . . . Holiness, on the other hand, indicates the desire to walk in God's ways, even if this means going against one's own inclinations. Can a fool be holy? we might ask. Conversely, can one who is holy act like a fool? Through an archetypal examination of the fool motif and of the gospel Jesus, this book will attempt to reconcile folly and holiness, firstly, to offer new insights into Christology and, secondly, to explore the pastoral ramifications of this Christology.

Jesus. Jesus the Christ. Jesus the Word. Jesus the Savior. Jesus the Messiah. Jesus the High Priest. Jesus the Suffering Servant. Jesus the Son of God. Jesus the Son of Man. Jesus the Lord. Jesus the Holy Fool. . . . To link the name of Jesus, that name above all other names, with the seemingly offensive title of "Holy Fool" is an act of daring and of piety. It

1

might suggest to some an iconoclastic approach to that which is sacred—namely, the person of Jesus. One's immediate response could well be outrage, for the title itself—unlike other christological titles—seems to indicate both mockery and blasphemy. To designate Jesus as Holy Fool, might—if one ignores the modifier "holy"—imply that Jesus is essentially foolish in the sense of being stupid or morally deficient. Inherent in this title, then, is the risk of causing misunderstanding and deep offense.

Because of its complexity, the motif of the Holy Fool cannot be confined to the discipline of theology. As an archetype—that is, as a pre-existing pattern of being which forms part of the psychic inheritance of all the human race—the Holy Fool exists in many of the world's religions and cultures. It is found in literature from all times and in all places; it surfaces in the findings of psychologists and anthropologists; it is present in the foundational myths of many peoples. Again and again, the motif of Holy Fool crops up in the lives of saints and martyrs everywhere—those who choose integrity over security and are willing to pay the price for their choices, those who abandon the world to live the life of the Spirit more fully. At all times, however, my concerns will transcend the insights and examples upon which this study depends. The focus will always be the person of Jesus; the purpose will always be to arrive at a more intimate knowing of who he is; the expectation will always be that knowledge will lead to deeper loving.

The risks involved are warranted. To understand the Holy Foolishness of Christ can lead one into a deeper contemplation of the mystery of God. If Jesus is truly God and if Jesus is truly Holy Fool, then whatever we say about Jesus the Holy Fool also becomes a statement about the Trinity; if this were not the case, then the very oneness of God would be at stake, for what is true about one Person must be true of all Three. This study, therefore, will also involve an exploration of the nature of God and this, too, stretches and challenges expectations. To name the Divine Foolishness is a prophetic act precisely because it forces us to abandon all preconceived—and limited—notions about God, all our assumptions about how God acts. Instead we find ourselves in new territory, encountering God where we might least expect to find anything of theological relevance. As we explore Holy Foolishness, we will discover that the wisdom of the world has little to do with God's wisdom and that the foolishness of humankind is less than holy. Our way of seeing is not God's way of seeing; our way of thinking is not God's way of thinking. What we consider holy God may deem foolish, and what we deride God may consider wise. Accordingly, the concept of Holy Foolishness offers an indispensable lens for examining holiness itself, both in human and divine terms. It is a characteristic way for God to act, and so provides us with a clear mandate for Christian living. Salvation history is replete with examples of God's Holy Foolishness. If we ignore these examples, we not only miss a theme of the Hebrew and Christian Scriptures, but we also immunize ourselves against the breath of the Holy Spirit. Implicit within the title Holy Fool, then, are ramifications for the people of God and for the institutional church.

What we learn about the nature of God invites us to consider new ways of approaching God and of living in deeper fidelity to the gospel. Theology, however, has accorded almost no attention at all to either the Holy Foolishness of Christ or to the Holy Foolishness of the Trinity. By exploring a Christology of the Holy Fool, this work seeks not only to offer fresh insights about the person of Jesus, but also to suggest how these insights might translate into spirituality, ecclesiology, pastoral ministry, and Christian participation in the human community.

Jesus, Lord and Fool

Jesus Christ. Jesus the Lord. . . . But why add Holy Fool? That name above all other names—Jesus Christ—is complete in itself. It means everything and contains everything; it is the embodiment of holiness. That name beyond all other names invites us to contemplate the mystery of God's presence among us, the mystery of the incarnate Godhead. That name beyond all other names challenges us to behold the locus of real   power—the power of goodness and truth, the only power by which the world is healed of its infirmities and by which the cosmos is renewed. That name beyond all other names is the very name of God which God conferred on Jesus, together with all authority, because of his obedience. Jesus, then, exalted as *Kyrios,* is the recipient of all divine functions, including that of creator.[1]

Why, one might ask, would anyone link that name beyond all superlative titles with the concept of foolishness, albeit, Holy Foolishness? If that name before which all creation bends is complete in itself, why add anything which might diminish it? The answer is implied in the letter to the Philippians:

> His state was divine
> yet he did not cling
> to his equality with God
> but emptied himself
> to assume the condition of a slave . . .
> he was humbler yet,
> even to accepting death,
> death on a cross.
> But God raised him high
> and gave him the name
> which is above all other names. . . . (Phil 2:69).

Far from clinging to divine status, Jesus allowed himself to be an image of utter absurdity—not only a wretched slave, but an outcast who suffered the most humiliating of deaths, abandoned not only by his followers and by the fickle crowds, but seemingly by God. To die on a cross, was tantamount to being a fool of the most depraved variety. After Jesus encountered rejection and was publicly shamed, God "raised him high." The very moment of scandal, of mockery, of ridicule was precisely the occasion of Jesus' surprising elevation to glory. Implicit within the title Kyrios, therefore, is also the title Holy Fool; the Crucified One—the Holy Fool—is also Lord. The starkness of the cross is what makes the resurrection a possibility—and, one might add, an inevitability. It is the resurrection, after all, which validates the Holy Folly which precipitated his death. Unquestionably, then, it was not as a political or nationalistic messiah that Jesus was exalted but as Holy Fool—in fact, as O. Cullmann demonstrates, Jesus showed "extreme reserve" toward the title messiah and actually considered political conceptions of the messiah as satanic temptations.[2] His words of rebuke to Peter for objecting to the first prophecy of the Passion show how strongly he felt on this topic: "Get behind me, Satan! You are an obstacle in my path, because the way you think is not God's way but the way of humans" (Mt 16:23).

Peter, having just proclaimed Jesus as the Christ . . . "the Son . . . of the Living God," must have been perplexed indeed. For him and for the other disciples, there was evidently a gaping discrepancy between their concept of Jesus' lordship and Jesus' own self-understanding (Mt 16:17). Jesus' words to Peter indicate that he saw this discrepancy as demonic: if Jesus considered himself to be the messiah it was a "foolish" messiah whose mission was to walk towards Jerusalem, that is, towards certain death (Mt 16:21). Moreover, since this death would come at the hands of the establishment—that is, at the hands of the elders, the chief priests and scribes—it would, by necessity, make Jesus a social outcast, scapegoat, and public spectacle. The Holy One of God would be tried and sentenced by the upholders of tradition, religious mores, and spiritual values. Even though the execution was actually carried out by the Romans, the absurdity of this situation is hard to fathom.

The synoptic Gospels suggest that Jesus most identified with the figure of the Son of Man—not only as eschatological judge, the one who would come again, but as the one in whom God's work was already being accomplished. Here, again, however, the theme of Holy Fool is implicit; Jesus not only used the title "Son of Man" in a way familiar to his audience, but also in a more original way that points to humiliation and debasement:

> We conclude that, apart from one or two passages
> in which the term may designate all men, Jesus
> used the title Son of Man to express his conscious-
> ness of having to fulfill the work of the Heavenly
> Man in two ways: 1) in glory at the end of time—a
> thought familiar to the expectation of the Son of
> Man in certain Jewish circles: 2) in the humiliation
> of the incarnation among sinful men—a thought
> foreign to all earlier conceptions of the Son of Man.[3]

Moreover, Jesus' consciousness of himself also included the role of *eved YHWH* or Suffering Servant. He did not expressly designate himself as Suffering Servant, but applied to himself "the idea of vicarious suffering and death, and the idea of the *eved*'s restoration of the covenant between God and people."[4] While his disciples hoped he would assume the political messiah's "glorious kingly role," Jesus took upon himself the expression of deepest humiliation, the willingness to die a shameful death for the sake of the people:[5] "For the Son of Man did not come to be served but to serve, and to give his life as a ransom for the many" (Mk 10:45).

In his very person, in his very function, then, Jesus was both a sign of majesty and of humiliation, a sign of contradiction, a sign of scandal. Seen in this light, the disciples' flight following his arrest was not merely human cowardice, but a reflection of embarrassment and disappointment. It was one thing to stand in awe on Mount Tabor, overwhelmed by the splendor of the Transfiguration; it was quite another to stand on Mount Calvary, subjected to the jeers and cruel jibes of the mob. They ran the risk of being labeled fools for following one who, judging by external criteria, seemed so eminently foolish. The one for whose sake they had left everything no longer had anything to offer them; the one upon whom they had staked all their dreams and expectations had allowed himself to become a public spectacle; the one who might have rewarded them with status and glory was himself stripped of everything. No wonder they ran—not from the Christ but from this Holy Fool whose very foolishness made them appear ridiculous.

Their fears, of course, were entirely justified by the crucifixion. As he hung upon the cross, Jesus was both king and felon, both savior and victim. In his death agony, he was a king without a kingdom, a guru without followers, a man of prayer without God. Despite promising beginnings, he had come to a fool's end, and with him, all who believed in his "fooldom." Battered and bruised, he hung between heaven and earth, a naked "foolosopher" whose fool's errand had led him to a fool's paradise. . . .

The Christ of Many Faces

About fifteen years ago I began to reflect upon the possibility of a many-faceted Christ. It struck me that the "Amen" we proclaim upon receiving the eucharistic bread and wine is intricately connected to *who* Jesus is for us. Jesus is clearly greater than any personal definition that we might have, but because we ourselves are limited, such a personal definition becomes essential in terms of our relating to him. Although we cannot begin to comprehend the fullness of his humanity, let alone his divinity, it is helpful to focus on those aspects of his reality which most attract us.

This is not to say that we are limited to a one-dimensional understanding of Jesus. At times, however, a particular facet of who he is becomes more important than other facets; or expressed differently, a particular Christology may somehow be more relevant to our own lived experience. Understanding this frees us to relate to Jesus out of the context of our lives. It might be difficult, for example, for someone living in dire poverty to relate to Jesus as king; or for someone in need of comfort and reassurance to relate to Jesus as judge. What is more helpful is to identify with the Christ who speaks to us in the immediacy of our unique circumstances. Through this identification, we find the courage to transcend our situation and to *be* as he would be, to *do* as he would do. In this way, our imitation of Christ is not based on idealized norms but on the authentic ground of our experience.

To the extent that we have a communal memory, we assent to much the same as everyone else: to be the salt of the earth, the light of the world, a crucified people, a risen people, a redeemed people, inheritors of the reign of God. However, what we "remember and honor" also has individual variations. If we regard Jesus primarily as healer, for example, we pledge to become healers ourselves; if Jesus is primarily teacher, by saying "Amen"—so be it, "yes"—we pledge to be like him and to do likewise. Obviously, there are some facets of Jesus which are more appealing than others and which are easier to integrate into our spirituality; Jesus the Holy Fool is not one of them. If we say "Amen" to the Holy Foolishness of Christ, we are stating our readiness to take risks and to appear foolish in the eyes of the world; in effect, we are expressing our willingness to be taunted for the sake of Christ and his gospel and to submit to whatever suffering comes our way.

The richer and more multifaceted our understanding of the presence of Christ, the more profound will be the meaning of our "Amen." Just as there are innumerable portraits of Christ, each reflecting some facet of his identity, so, too, there is a multitude of Christologies. Each Christology reflects something essential about the personhood of Jesus; each Christology provides a challenge for us to emulate.

The *Faith and Culture Series* published by Orbis Books reflects the issues of christological diversity which are arising as the Church attempts to respond to a new global reality. In *Faces of Jesus*, for example, we learn that the traditional African worldview is sympathetic towards the gospel presentation of Jesus. H. Sawyerr suggests calling Jesus "the elder Brother," the founder of the "Great Family," the church. J.S. Pobee, a member of the Akan people from Ghana, sees Jesus as "the Great Ancestor," the one with the power to judge, reward and punish, while A.T. Sanon views him as the "Head and Master of Initiation." Similarly, Aylward Shorter takes healing as the perspective for his Christology, interpreting Jesus in light of the healing traditions of African medicine men.[6]

R.S. Sugirtharajah, in his introduction to *Asian Faces of Jesus*, describes the "misgivings and ambivalence Asian Christians feel about the images of Jesus that were first introduced to them by foreign missionaries and still dominate their thinking"; he also articulates the desire of many Asian Christians to discover for themselves Jesus' place among the other saviors of the continent.[7] Ironically, it was Indian Hindus who first reflected on Jesus from the perspective of Asia's religious traditions. Sugirtharajah lists a variety of images emanating from different philosophical strands within Hinduism:

> Jesus as Supreme Guide to human happiness . . .
> Jesus as true Yogi and Divine Humanity . . . Jesus as
> Jivanmukta (one who has attained liberation while
> alive) . . . Jesus as the Supreme Satyagrahi (lover
> and fighter for truth) . . . Jesus as Advaitan (one
> who has realized destiny with Brahman/ God).[8]

Influenced by such indigenized portraits of Christ, Indian Christians developed images of their own: Jesus as *Prajapati* (Lord of Creatures), Jesus as *Cit* (Consciousness); Jesus as *Avatara* (Incarnation), Jesus as *Adi Purusha* (the first person), Jesus as *Shakti* (strength), and Jesus as Eternal *Om* (logos).[9]

Clearly, however, while it is appropriate—and desirable—to work towards the inculturation of the Gospel, some portraits of Jesus have greater validity than others because of their timeless wisdom. Some christological interpretations have been influenced by the intellectual trends of a particular era—by Marxism or Freudian analysis, for example. Interpretations which are grounded in the testimony of the four Evangelists carry a "higher" authority—the authority of the earliest faith statements about Jesus and about the decisive events in his life. Although there are differences among the four Gospel portraits, they collectively present aspects of Jesus' life which are foundational for Christian theology, ecclesiology, liturgy, and piety. It is very different, for example, to name Jesus the Ché Guevara of the first century than to name him as Holy Fool. The first case suggests a romantic freedom fighter in Cuba whose courageous exploits caught the imaginations of liberals in the 1960s and 1970s; the second designation is implicit within the Gospels and therefore needs to be accorded the attention that is its due. One designation could be regarded as a subjective projection with a limited historical context; the other represents the timeless truth of God.

Just as there is a face of Christ for each individual and every national group, so, too, there is a face for every era. If artists and writers capture the spirit of an era, then a brief examination of the works of Georges Rouault (1871–1958) will reflect the validity of proposing that the face of Christ as fool is particularly appropriate for the current age.

Taking seriously Jesus' words, "I tell you solemnly, tax collectors and prostitutes are making their way into the reign of God before you" (Mt 21:31–32), Rouault chose as his subjects the derelicts and victims of society, a motley array of clowns and prostitutes whose features and demeanor bear striking similarity to his depictions of the humiliated Christ. Evidently, he was captivated by Jesus' Holy Foolishness and could see the wisdom underlying this seemingly perplexing saying: that the most hated and despised members of society were more worthy of being in the presence of God than those who held places of rank and privilege.

Rouault, who identified with both clowns and prostitutes because of their ability to "take on the shape of all that is perishable and transient in human nature," saw in Jesus the face of suffering humanity.[10] Though it is unlikely that he would have ever used this title himself, it would seem that Rouault therefore had an intuitive grasp of the meaning of *eved YHWH*. Thus such works as *Head of a Tragic Clown* (1904), the paintings of *Prostitutes* (1906), *Tragic Clown* (1913), *Benito* (1937), and *The Injured Clown* (1932) are not unlike *The Holy Countenance* (1932), *Passion* (1937) or *Christ Mocked* (1939).

In these works, we find the rawness of human flesh—not glamorized or softened but presented in all its starkness. Even when the subjects are clothed, we see the nakedness of despair and hopelessness, and suffering. We see women who are neither attractive nor seductive, and clowns who have forgotten how to laugh; their make-up camouflages nothing. Whether Rouault is depicting clowns or the suffering Christ, we find the same downward curve of the lips, the same elongated features, the same immense pain emanating from eyes like cavernous pools, the same overwhelming poignancy—in short, the tragic countenance of all humanity.

Rouault's critics accused him of being irreligious and of taking a leap "into utter darkness";[11] in truth, his concern was to reveal God in the heart of pain, even in the hearts of the damned.

> I saw clearly that 'the clown' was myself, ourselves . . . almost all of us . . . that this rich, spangled costume is given us by life, we're all of us clowns, more or less, we all wear a 'spangled costume,' but if we are caught unawares, the way I caught that old clown . . . who would dare to claim that he is not moved to his very depths by immeasurable pity . . . King or emperor, what I want to see in the man facing me is his soul, and the more exalted his position, the more misgivings I have about his soul.[12]

Rouault was able to distinguish between the world's wisdom and God's wisdom; the exalted, as he suggests, are perhaps more foolish than those the world deems foolish. Those with nothing may ultimately be more spiritually healthy than their wealthy counterparts. Through Rouault's portraits of the humiliated Christ, the soul we see is simultaneously the soul of suffering humanity and the anguished soul of God made manifest in him; in his portraits, we find a Christ for our times.

Approaching Jesus

We have seen that there are many valid ways of looking at Jesus. There is one Lord, yes, but a multiplicity of viewpoints on this one Lord. To the extent that we are willing to embrace these multiple perspectives, the richer our understanding becomes. It is not as though we can ever fully nail down the reality of Christ; many have tried—including those who crucified him—but he is always too elusive, too indefinable. Neither staunch defenders of the faith nor the most devoted of artists have succeeded in presenting anything more than a fragment of the truth, a glimpse into the kaleidoscope of his being. Even if their efforts have been exercises in overreaching—rather like Icarus' ill-fated flight towards the sun—each has its own significance.

Doctrina Patrum de Incarnatione Verbi, a Greek florilegium redacted about the end of the seventh century, presents an extensive list of names for Christ. Some—"Son of God," "Light of the World" and "Bread of Life"—have come into contemporary usage. Others—like "Chosen Arrow," "Unicorn," "Poor Youth," "A Worm," and "Apple Tree"—are obsolete.[13] Though these highly unusual titles are not ones which most of us today would associate with Jesus, they must at one time have had appeal and relevance. Derived from Scripture and endorsed by popular culture, these terms once expressed profound theological insights. A worm, for example, captures the poverty Jesus embraced through the Incarnation—the poverty of limited physical "being." Psalm 90, with its references to the dust of human origins and to the brevity of life, expresses some of the sentiments behind this title: we are all worms by virtue of being human; one could argue, however, that Jesus' sufferings intensified his lowliness (Ps 90:3–90:6). Psalm 22, so often accorded a christological reading, says this of the Suffering Servant:

> 7 But I am a worm, hardly human, despised by all, mocked by the crowd.

> 8 All who see me jeer at me, sneer at me, shaking their heads. . . .(Ps 22:7–8)

In contrast, Apple Tree, a title derived from a christological reading of The Song of Songs expresses a mystical consciousness of Christ. Just as the apple tree is a source of sweet fruit and longed-for shade, "so is my Beloved" (Song 2:3). As the apple tree, prized among other trees, offers delight, comfort, and restoration, so does the Beloved. The term Apple Tree, then, is no mere whimsy but a term charged with intimacy, desire, and sexual undertones. It is a christological title from which most theologians would run, precisely because it is too charged with connotative power.

Explorations in Christology provide new lenses, new possibilities for approaching Jesus. Each theologian's effort provides a crucial insight from which others might not only learn but also grow in faith. At the same time, a theologian's effort is limited by his or her perspective—whether this is formed by gender, culture, age, personality, or socioeconomic background. At its best, then, Christology is a discipline which presents a variety of perspectives on how to approach the Jesus of faith, some of which are more useful than others.

This study of Jesus the Holy Fool explores a Christology which has been largely neglected—or more precisely, avoided. Grounded in insights I have gained through my own lived experience, it stretches the boundaries of christological territory. Whether out of fear of stating the outrageous or of being considered sacrilegious, theologians have refrained from naming Jesus as Holy Fool. The rich insights to be derived from this Christology have been ignored, to the impoverishment of the Church. One has to wonder whether the prospect of highlighting the "absurdity" of Jesus was simply too much for those who preferred to venerate Jesus as "Christ the King"; after all, the regality of this Jesus reflects on his subjects, as surely as does the absurdity of a foolish Christ and, given a choice, most would choose to be followers of an imperial Jesus.

Nevertheless, if it is valid to approach Jesus as the Historical Jesus or as Jesus the Servant, it is equally valid to approach him through the archetype of the Holy Fool. As will be seen, a Holy Fool is not a foolish fool or a buffoon, but a fool rich in God's wisdom—a fool who, like Jesus, places truth above security, faithfulness above control, and love above self-gain. This folly, of course, does not lead to accolades or to an overwhelming awareness of the holiness of the Most High, but to the experience of being mocked, laughed at, scorned. Jesus, by embracing Holy Folly, opens himself up to ridicule that is directed at his teachings, his actions and his very person. All that he stands for becomes game for others' jokes and irreverence, not because he is deserving of ridicule but because it is contrary to the ways of the crowd, that is, to conventional wisdom.

As Holy Fool, Jesus scorns the world's wisdom and lives out of the wisdom of God. God's wisdom, we will see, is also essentially foolish by the world's standards, and so Jesus' folly is not unique to him but expresses the life of the Trinity. Foolishness, then, or to be more precise, Holy Foolishness, is a divine quality. It leads both to the folly of the cross and to the comedy of the resurrection—"comedy" here meaning the restoration of the common good, and God's having the final laugh.

By imitating Holy Foolishness, Christians can find courage and meaning in their own lives—the boldness to stand outside the social circle of acceptability and to name what is, no matter what the price; the single-mindedness to place the love of God before all else; the daring to take great leaps of faith when everyone else asks, "Where is the safety net?" Jesus the Holy Fool is one who empowers the weak and the vulnerable. He lays the mantle of prophecy upon the voiceless and calls the marginalized to lead others to heroic stands. When the world laughs, ridiculing those who dare march to a different drummer, Jesus the Holy Fool applauds, inviting them to share the circus ring with all the holy clowns of history. Holy Fools, then, are those "made mad and merry by their faith in a God 'silly in the crib' and 'foolish on the cross,' a God whose sage folly alone can save us from the raving lunacy of the princes of this age."[14]

 *Part One*

Jesus and Human Folly

Psychological Archetypes

Before exploring notions of God's foolishness, the foolishness of Christ and the implications for the Christian journey, it seems appropriate to approach the Holy Fool with Carl Jung's concept of psychological archetypes. There are some aspects of Jungian thought which lend clarity to our topic, and others which clearly have no place in this discussion. Moreover, while the archetype of Holy Fool was operative in the life of the Gospel Jesus, Jesus also functions as the archetype of the Self (that is, as the paradigm for what it means to be human); this complicates our use of the term archetype and calls for elucidation.

For Jung, archetypes must always be seen in the context of the collective unconscious. While our immediate consciousness is of a "thoroughly personal nature," the collective unconscious is not something that develops individually but is inherited.[1] Related to Plato's idea of pre-existing ideal forms which determine the shape of the

15

material world, psychological archetypes are characteristic patterns that "pre-exist in the collective psyche of the human race, that repeat themselves eternally in the psyches of individual human beings and determine the basic ways that we perceive and function as psychological beings."[2]

Archetypes of the hero, the sage, the trickster, the magician, the divine child, the dying and rising god appear in dreams, myths, literature, and art. Jolande Jacobi explains that while Plato's ideal forms represent perfection "in the luminous sense," Jung's archetypes are "bi-polar, embodying the dark side as well as the light."[3] If we believe in divine perfection, however, we cannot allow for the possibility of a shadow side in the person of Jesus.

In *Awakening the Heroes Within*, Carol Pearson demonstrates that every archetype not only has positive energy but also a negative dimension. The benign ruler, for example, can become an ogre tyrant; the magician who holds all things in balance can degenerate into an evil sorcerer; the sage can be an unfeeling judge; the caregiver can control others by making them feel guilty; the trickster can resort to cruel and gruesome strategies.[4] Pearson explains that it is the addictive quality of each archetype that leads us into being possessed by the shadow. Addicted to relationships or to sex, the lover can develop intimacy problems; addicted to independence or perfection, the wanderer can be self-centered; addicted to work and creativity, the creator can become obsessive.[5] Precisely because of this dark side, archetypes must be taken seriously or they can erupt in neurotic or psychotic disorders, "behaving exactly like neglected or maltreated physical organs or organic functional systems."[6] They reflect aspects of ourselves which can possess us, empower us or which need development or modification.

Numerous archetypes are active in our lives and the more we recognize how they tend to play themselves out, the greater the possibility of integrating them in ways which are spiritually and psychologically healthy. Both in spiritual direction and in other counseling contexts, for example, I sometimes encourage clients to examine the archetypes which have them in their grip. Men are sometimes so firmly under the control of the warrior archetype that they are constantly in combat, seldom taking out time for reflection or for nurturing their inner lives or developing meaningful relationships; concepts such as "surrender" or "letting go" strike them with terror for they represent a way of being which is in complete opposition to all they have learned to strive for. Women, on the other hand—particularly women in mid life or older—are often gripped by the archetype of martyr, for their training has been a lifetime of learning to yield to the wishes of others and of offering selfless service. I have worked with individuals so strongly under the power of the shadow side of an archetype that the effects are akin to "demonic possession."

For some it is the absence of an archetype that is problematic. In Western culture, it seems that many of us suffer from an insufficiency of "fool" in our lives. Frenetic and uptight, we take ourselves too seriously, trying so hard to conform to a world which promotes workaholism, efficiency, and productivity that we might as well be cogs in a machine. Forgetting that playfulness is a basic human need, we shackle ourselves to our calendars, doing nothing for ourselves unless it is scheduled. Wondering why we so easily become bored and exhausted, we lose all capacity for spontaneity, authenticity, and passion. The antidote to all this would be to give the fool archetype some space, without moving into excesses of debauchery, irresponsibility, or inappropriate levity.

To be in balance, we need to be both sages and fools, both creators and destroyers, both martyrs and warriors. Sages are truly wise if they recognize the limits of their knowledge and if they can laugh at themselves every now and again; fools save themselves from wild excesses by cultivating wisdom, even as they romp and frolic across the stage of life. Creators—the artists and visionaries among us—can mature in their craft only when they learn to jettison works and ideas which may not be fully representative of their talents; destroyers, on the other hand, that is, the critics and "quality regulators" in our midst, only serve a useful purpose if their work of destruction leads to new opportunities and possibilities. Warriors need to imitate the giving spirit of martyrs while martyrs need to pursue their own dreams with all the energy of warriors, finding a voice strong enough to articulate their deepest desires.

All this involves careful discernment and involves paying attention to the patterns operative in our lives. These patterns reveal who we are, providing clues as to how we might live more fully, more intentionally. Because of this, Jung cautions against treating archetypes as "part of a mechanical system." For him, they are "pieces of life itself—images that are integrally connected to the living individual by the bridge of the emotions."[7] When we look at the Jesus of the Gospels, we will see that one archetypal pattern which manifests itself over and over again is that of Holy Foolishness. This pattern—when balanced by other healthy archetypal patterns—offers a way of being fully human, fully alive. Jesus the Holy Fool demonstrates that folly (of the holy variety) can be a path of wisdom leading to transformation of ourselves and of the world in which we find ourselves.

Christ as Archetype of the Self
Jacobi defines the Self as "the last station on the path to individuation."[8] Having explained how the acceptance of legitimate suffering can be a source of spiritual enrichment, she goes on to quote Jung's explanation as to what follows the diminishment of the personal unconscious:

> There arises a consciousness which is no longer imprisoned in the petty, over-sensitive, personal world of the ego, but participates freely in the wider world of objective interests. This widened consciousness is no longer that touchy, egotistical bundle of personal wishes, fears, hopes and ambitions which always has to be compensated or corrected by unconscious countertendencies; instead, it is a function of relationship to the world of objects, bringing the individual into absolute,

binding and indissoluble communion with the world at large.[9]

This new center of consciousness is the Self, the kingdom of God within, the image of the "ideal human"; as such, the Self is fittingly represented by the person of Christ who is himself a paradigm of the individuated ego:

> When Jung speaks of Christ as the exemplification of the archetype of the Self, he is referring to an event in the life of the soul. This Christ-Event not only 'speaks' to the soul; it 'acts' upon it, awakening, reviving, cleansing, nourishing, resurrecting.[10]

Christ as humanity made perfect, as the primordial sacrament of God, replaces the "I" by which most of us define ourselves. Rather than allowing ourselves to be "I" driven, reacting to life out of the lens of "I," we find our true center, our true self in the person of Jesus. All that is not of Christ within ourselves is part of the old self which needs to die. We might be fools, but from a Christian perspective, we are only Holy Fools if we are fools in Christ.

When seen from the perspective of other faith traditions, the Self represents the core of who we are, the self each of us was destined to be. In theistic traditions, the Self is that place where we encounter the divine spark within, where *Atman* (individual soul) and *Brahman* (world soul) are one. The world's traditions also teach that this Self-realization is only possible when our baser selves are purified through radical detachment. The spiritual quest thus becomes a quest for the elusive Self—a terrifying journey of ego-abandonment diametrically opposed to the path of worldly wisdom.

The twelfth century Persian Sufi mystical poem, *The Conference of the Birds,* illustrates this point. The poet, Farid Ud-Din Attar, has created an allegory about the search for the *Simorgh* or the real Self; along their journey to find the true king, thirty birds learn that it is the finite self that is the greatest obstacle to achieving their quest. At first, they are reluctant to embark upon the journey. It is a fool's quest, after all, demanding that they leave behind all that is dearest to them:

the love-sick nightingale will have to leave behind the rose in whom he has invested ultimate reality; the duck will have to abandon the comfort and security of her familiar stream; the hawk will lose the place of privilege on the royal wrist of his king. . . . Each of the birds, then, is called to embark on a dangerous journey, leaving behind all self-interest, self-definitions, self-fulfillment, and self-aggrandizement. It is the quintessential fool's trip into uncertainty, a brilliant paradigm for spiritual adventuring. Their leader, the Hoopoe, advises them:

> ". . . reject the self,
> That whirlpool where our lives are wrecked;
> As Jesus rode his donkey, ride on it;
> Your stubborn self must bear you and submit—
> Then burn this self and purify your soul. . . .
> . . . You will be gone, and only God will be."[11]

At the journey's end, exhausted, wretched, and broken, the pilgrims do indeed find that which they have been seeking: bathed in celestial light, they discover the mystery of the True Self:

> There in the Simorgh's radiant face they saw
> Themselves, the Simorgh of the world—with awe
> They gazed, and dared at last to comprehend
> They were the Simorgh and the journey's end.[12]

Ironically, the word *Simorgh* represents the pilgrims who survive to the journey's end: "only thirty (si) birds (morgh) are left at the end of the Way, and the si morgh meet the Simorgh, the goal of their quest."[13] The end of all their journeying is to discover that the treasure they seek lies within themselves; worldly wisdom, however, clouded their eyes with spiritual foolishness making them oblivious to this reality.

What is clear from sages, mystics, biblical writers, Jungian analysts, and pop psychologists is that suffering can be a prelude to holiness or "wholeness" or "individuation," that is, "the conscious coming to terms with one's own inner centre." Marie-Louise von Franz, states that this journey to self-discovery "generally begins with a wounding of the personality and the suffering that accompanies it."[14] This wounding is no trivial matter but a self-shattering process which plunges us into existential terror. It forces us to confront questions of meaning and purpose; it demands that we acknowledge our own vulnerability and powerlessness; it breaks all our idols and all our attempts at establishing control over our circumstances; it proves the shallowness of our ways of thinking and the limitations of our worldview. In the end, however, it is a soul-event which leads to transformation.

The journey of purgation, then, is a journey to which all are called but few respond. The stakes are simply too high; too much folly—the folly of self-abandonment—is exacted from those who respond to this invitation. When one desires to move away from the narrow confines of ego gratification and to allow the Higher Self a place in one's life, there is no telling what will be involved in this process. In the Hebrew Scriptures, Job provides an example of what can happen to those who embark on the journey of purgation. Job, it is true, does not choose the harrowing events which befall him, but he does provide a powerful depiction of suffering humanity; he is at once himself, a unique individual, and "Everyone"— a representative of every person who, by virtue of being human, will encounter some form of purgation in the course of life. As Everyone, Job encounters not only his fragility but also the mystery of "Why?" Why, we might ask ourselves, should any righteous, God-fearing person blessed with prosperity have to suffer the complete loss of wealth, family, and health in a moment?

Job, of course, wrestles with this question, cursing the day he was born and accusing God of senseless cruelty. Affronted by the shallow explanations offered by his "sorry comforters," Job experiences what it is to become a laughingstock, an object of derision. In his culture —as is still the case in certain cultures to this day—misfortune was regarded as the consequence of sin. Job, beset by so much tragedy, must therefore be responsible for what has befallen him. Insisting upon his innocence, he says "I am the butt of mockers" (Job 17:2);

his loss of reputation, then, accompanies all the many other losses which he has to endure. In the eyes of his friends and of his society, he is a "sinner," the recipient of God's justice. This man who was at one time the refuge of the poor and the oppressed, the lord of the city, has become a loathsome outcast, reviled by all. The only comfort that comes his way consists of insults, pious speeches, and scorn.

Writing on the drama of Job, Edward Edinger shows that Job's ordeal is applicable to all; just as we tend to scream out the universal question, "Why must this happen to me?," so Job—the most blessed and upright of people—has to face the question of why misery has befallen him; as he ponders over why God has made him a laughingstock, he eventually arrives at one conclusion: "The answer that emerges from the Book of Job is so he may see God":[15] "I knew you then only by hearsay; but now, having seen you with my own eyes, I retract all I have said, and in dust and ashes I repent" (Job 42:5–6). From this we may conclude that in order to reach the Beatific vision—in order to behold God—we must be stripped of every vestige of pride, entitlement, and self-righteousness; only then will the veil of worldly foolishness be lifted from our eyes.

This journey of purgation is powerfully presented in *La Divina Commedia*. Like Dante, at some point in our lives we find ourselves lost in the Dark Wood and in need of the purgatorial flame, if we are ever to become worthy enough to enter the mystical White Rose. Dante mirrors what the journey entails. Only by learning to despise the fruits of sin and to move from pity to outrage at the perpetrators of evil is Dante the Pilgrim able to encounter his own sinful nature. Ascending from the inferno to the Mount of Purgatory, he has to face the three terrifying beasts which appear in the first Canto of the Commedia —the Leopard, the Lion, and the Wolf—not as external realities but as parts of his own flawed nature from which he must be redeemed. Through the sufferings of Purgatory, he is cleansed of the Leopard's lust for pleasure, the Lion's pride, and the Wolf's terrifying ego-greed. But unlike Job, this purgation is not something he experiences passively; rather, his will—indeed, his whole being, must assent to the process.[16]

To let go of the ego and all that feeds it, to let go of the flawed aspects of our personality upon which we have depended for our identity, to change our habitual patterns of behavior is to undergo a death—the death of all we thought we were. In submitting to the process of conversion, Dante agrees to embrace suffering that is no less all-encompassing than that faced by Job. Job may lose oxen, flocks, and children, but it is not difficult for most of us to find symbolic equivalents in our own experience. And just as Job's material losses are a source of great anguish to him, so the attitudinal losses we have to face can be equally devastating.

Often beginning in an experience of being lost—the Dark Wood experience—the purgative stage of the spiritual journey refers to a time of desolation during which senses and spirit are stripped so radically that God becomes the only concern. Frequently, the stripping process is accompanied by an anguished sense of God's absence; suffering is intensified by feelings of abandonment, unworthiness, and the desire for God. God's love is experienced as "wounding" and "afflicting," seldom as comfort, though the darkness may be punctuated by brief moments of joy. Painful as this may be, however, it is a process which turns foolish fools into Holy Fools. All that is not of God is burned away.

John of the Cross distinguishes between two phases of the dark night, that experience of purgation about which many talk but which few actually know. The dark night of the senses is that phase of the spiritual journey during which one is not only stripped of material objects but of the very desire for them. Anything to which we cling for security, anything which we grasp for comfort, anything we crave to distract ourselves from suffering is an obstacle on the path to union with God. These "things" include all appetites and gratifications, all goals and desires, all attachments to creatures and possessions:

> It makes little difference whether a bird is tied by a
> thin thread or by a cord. For even if tied by a

> thread, the bird will be prevented from taking off
> just as surely as if it were tied by a cord.[17]

This need to "let go" is consistent with the teachings of Jesus, who over and over again invites us to take the existential risk of releasing ourselves from all illusions and deceptive investments. His mandate is the foolish recommendation that we step into the unknown, relying only upon our God.

Nobody is exempt from suffering. Buddhism, founded on the premise that "all life is suffering," offers the path of detachment (The Noble Eightfold Path) as the "solution" to illness, decrepitude, and death. By following this path to the extinction of self, that is, to *Nirvana*, one finds liberation from "life's crippling disabilities."[18]

To be "set free" in Buddhist terms is to be open to all possibilities, to live fully, without clutching on to anything; it is this practice of "mindfulness" that leads to enlightenment, or "right seeing." One cannot move beyond the imprisonment of the senses if one imagines possessions or desires have ultimate significance; clear vision comes when one is wise enough to abandon the false wisdom offered by the world. But this wisdom does not come cheaply. . . .

Freedom and right seeing are also the goals of the Christian spiritual journey. In Dante's world, letting go has much to do with abandoning illusions about the self: the wayfarer, having witnessed the horrors of the *Inferno,* having undertaken the long, hard climb to self-knowledge, having been cleansed of the Seven Deadly Sins, finally reaches a moment of supreme consciousness: ". . . beyond up and down, dark and light, he sees the entire universe in the Centre, and, finally, in a flash of awareness knows the truth of Incarnation—nature, humanity and God as one."[19]

According to Christian understanding, illumination is the fruit of purgation which comes from divine grace; it is not something we can accomplish on our own. Dante learns to "see" because Heaven takes pity on him; without the intercession of the three blessed ladies (Mary, St. Lucy, and Beatrice), he would surely have perished in the Dark Wood, devoured by his own propensity for evil (the

Leopard, the Lion, and the Wolf). Here again, spiritual gain depends upon material loss —upon "playing the fool," if you will.

But the purpose of the Christian journey goes beyond illumination for illumination's sake; it transcends the desire for freedom or for an escape from the suffering brought on by inordinate attachments. For Christ to reside fully at the center of self, for Christ to become the self, there is a still more terrible journey of purgation. Painful as it may be, the dark night of the senses is less intense, dry and empty than the dark night of the spirit. Just as the first dark night involves the denial of self in worldly matters, so the second demands the denial of self in matters of the spirit. "Few there are," John of the Cross warns us, "with the knowledge and desire for entering upon this supreme nakedness and emptiness of spirit."[20] It is a path of absurdity along which one must willingly divest the self of every spiritual consolation and "spiritual sweet tooth" for the love of God; what is necessary is total self-denial, both exterior and interior, and this involves the annihilation, eradication and purification of everything that is not God. It involves fidelity when God is seemingly absent; it demands trust when there are no indications that anything will change; it asks for love when one's Beloved has seemingly withdrawn all affection.

Terrible as this dark night is, its fruit is reorientation—a new, more conscious, more intuitive, more loving self that clings to nothing but God, and that even in this clinging, expects nothing, desires nothing but God alone.

Suffering cleanses the soul of "habitual ignorances and imperfections, natural and spiritual"; moreover, it is this purging and illumining which prepare the soul for union with God.[21] The illumined self experiences joy, sometimes rapture, and may well think it has reached the end of its journey. This conviction may not only be reinforced by a sharper external vision, but also by a sharper way of viewing internal reality. Ultimately, as Meister Eckhart states so poetically, illumined human seeing and God's seeing become indistinguishable: "The eye with which I see God is the same eye with which God sees me; my eye and God's eye are only one eye and one seeing and one knowing and one love."[22]

The eye is no mere representation of physical sight— though the illumined soul does have a heightened appreciation for the wonders of the created world—but it is primarily a symbol of consciousness. It is the filth of self-love which blinds us; it is the filth of all our ego-drives which distorts our vision so that we can no longer see our moral inadequacy. Thus it is that in Canto I:94–97, Cato, guardian of the Mount of Purgatory, instructs Virgil to wash hell's filth from Dante's clouded eyes in preparation for his ascent into purgatory;[23] eyes, especially the luminous eyes of Beatrice, become a symbol of clear vision, of right seeing, spiritually speaking. "The real distinction between the illuminative and the unitive life," writes Evelyn Underhill, "is that in illumination the individuality of the subject—however profound his spiritual consciousness, however close his apparent communion with the infinite—remains separate and intact."[24]

In time, however, the illumined self is so consumed with the desire for God that it longs for complete union; that is, for nothing less than full participation of the human in divine mystery. Here, we are indeed in the realm of the ineffable, that place where " . . . the tongues of flame are infolded / Into the crowned knot of fire / And the fire and the rose are one."[25]

"Becoming Christ," then, or allowing Christ to be the Self, is a far more costly process than mere imitation of the sayings and actions of Jesus. Jung holds that to imitate Christ "literally" is to misunderstand his symbolic significance:

> Are we to understand 'the imitation of Christ' in the sense that we should copy his life and, if I may use the expression, ape his stigmata; or in the deeper sense that we are to live our own proper lives as truly as he lived his in its individual uniqueness? It is no easy matter to live a life that is modeled on Christ's, but it is unspeakably harder to live one's own life, as truly as Christ lived his.[26]

It is transformation not imitation that is called for here. To say that one is pursuing wholeness or complete individuation is not enough. Allowing Christ absolute centrality is the primary calling of Holy Fools in the Christian context; all other accomplishments are empty in comparison.

As we examine the archetype of Holy Fool as it applies to Christ, the implications for each of us will depend on the unique circumstances of our particular journey; moreover, we will need to remember that many other archetypes were operative in the life of Christ and to slavishly "imitate" one, to the neglect of others, will lead to spiritual diminishment, not enrichment. In other words, in addition to being a Holy Fool, Jesus was also a teacher, a healer, a sage, a liberator, a radical, a servant, a storyteller, a person of prayer. . . . Moreover, to complicate matters, there are many facets to the Holy Fool archetype. Jesus not only allowed himself to be mocked, but he also "took on" the loneliness of the fool, the suffering of the fool, the nakedness of the fool, the madness of the fool, the wisdom of the fool, the darkness of spirit of the fool, the tears of the fool. . . . Through his life, death, and resurrection, he demonstrated that the "fruit of the fool" is reorientation, vindication, the final laugh in the comedy of life. . . . Ultimately, what is important for the Christian is that the path of individuation increasingly becomes a "death to self" so that the Christ-Self may become the totality of who we are—a concept articulated in Colossians: "There is only Christ: he is everything and he is in everything"(Col 3:11).

Plain Fool Versus Holy Fool

Fool. Jester. Simpleton. Clown. Madman. . . . Traditionally, the fool has often been associated with images of stupidity. The Latin root of "fool" is the word *follis* or "windbag," while the French "fou" suggests an insane person or one who is mentally deficient. The *Oxford English Dictionary* offers three definitions for "fool": 1) a person deficient in judgment or sense who therefore behaves stupidly; 2) one who professionally counterfeits folly for the entertainment of others; 3) one who is made to appear a fool.

While it would be offensive to describe Jesus as deficient of judgment, it is important to ask why he evoked the hostility and contempt of the establishment. Much of what he said made no sense at all to his audience; to them, many of his actions were incomprehensible. They heard with their ears and saw with their eyes all that he was about, but their hearts remained unmoved: he was merely the unschooled son of a carpenter from the cultural backwater of Nazareth. For them, he was indeed a "windbag," for to admit he was anything more would be to admit their own ethical limitations, their poverty of imagination and hardness of heart. If we identify any deficiency of judgment, it is in those who perceived him and saw only what they wanted to see. We could say that foolishness then—as it is now—was "in the eyes of the beholder."

However, Jesus' words and actions in no way indicated intellectual inadequacy, even if his own relatives were convinced he was "out of his mind" (Mk 3:21). Though the Gospels present many examples in which Jesus' actions provoked the wrath of authorities or defied conventions, they do not suggest thoughtlessness or the inability to see consequences. On the contrary, the Jesus of the Gospels knew what he was doing and precisely how others would react. In fact, he frequently anticipated the response he would receive, speaking and acting with this in mind, thus having the upper hand in dealings with his opponents. What Jesus demonstrated more than anything else were skills of verbal repartee and quick thinking. There was nothing of the simpleton about him.

We must also distinguish Jesus from those who use folly merely for the sake of entertainment. In some ways, Jesus was a professional entertainer of sorts: he could spin parables which mesmerized the crowds, and he knew how to exploit the drama of a situation for pedagogical effect. But Jesus was not an attention-seeker like the fool-clown who sought power in court; nor was he a show biz man, anxious to draw attention to himself. While Jesus used elements of the comic to keep his audiences enthralled, his primary goal was to spread the Gospel. Like the prophets before him, who themselves resorted to ludicrous tactics, he was about the business of transforming consciousness; like the prophets, he sought to bring human hearts into alignment with the heart of God. For Jesus, entertainment served as an illustration, as a method rather than an end in itself. In fact, to suggest otherwise would be to downplay the danger to which Jesus exposed himself by speaking truth and exposing hardness of heart. He defied the establishment not by *playing* the fool but by insisting upon *being* Holy Fool, an icon of the presence of God.

The third definition of "fool" that appears in the OED clearly applies to Jesus: Jesus was made to *appear* a fool. During his public ministry, his opponents made several unsuccessful efforts to humiliate him. Take, for example, the episode of the woman caught in adultery. Here, Jesus seemed caught between two possibilities: either he could agree that the woman should be stoned (thereby denying his own teachings on love and forgiveness) or he could insist that she be set free (thereby undermining Mosaic law). Either possibility would have "made a fool" of him. Instead, he chose neither option but turned the tables on those who would mock him: "If there is one of you who has not yet sinned, let him be the first to throw a stone at her" (Jn 8:7).

Like the trickster of Native American traditions, Jesus turned an impossible situation into one from which he emerged as "winner." As trickster, he resorted to enigmatic behavior (writing in the sand) and unnerved his audience with his self-confidence. Instead of becoming flustered or desperate, he seemed completely unruffled and in control of events. What was going on beneath the surface, of course, we have no way of knowing, but despite any interior anxiety there may have been, he coolly called the bluff of his antagonists. So effective were his strategies, in fact, that he convinced them that he knew their inventories of sins; it was fear of exposure that made them put down their stones, not a change of heart.

We see similar dynamics in Luke's Gospel where his enemies posed the trick question about tribute to Caesar: "Is it permissible for us to pay taxes to Caesar or not?" (Lk 20: 20–26). Jesus quickly saw the danger lurking beneath a seemingly benign question: an affirmative answer would have endorsed Caesar's right to rule the Jews and to exact loyalty from them, often in violation of their religious sensitivities; it would have undermined the Jewish spirit of nationalism as well as the Mosaic prohibition against idolatry, for "emperor worship" was one facet of being a Roman subject. A negative answer, on the other hand, would have been a statement of rebellion and a punishable offense against Rome.

Jesus let his opponents answer their own question. In Mark's account, he says "Hand me a denarius and let me see it" (Mk 12:15–16). The *denarius* was the actual coin used to pay taxes; as Stuhlmueller points out, "the irony is that in producing it (i.e., having it in their possession) they themselves acknowledge the propriety of the taxation."[27] Once again, Jesus' responded to trickery with trickery of his own, cleverly putting his antagonists in their place. His enigmatic response put the burden on those who sought to trick him: "Give back to Caesar what belongs to Caesar—and to God what belongs to God" (Lk 8:25). Without defining what is God's or what is Caesar's, Jesus effectively silenced them. Mark tells us that his reply "took them completely by surprise" (Mk 12:17).

But if Jesus were skilled at avoiding outcomes in which his own words could undermine his authority and make a fool of him, he did not resist the mockery of his passion and death. In the end he took upon himself the role of servant, permitting himself to be treated as sinner and to be ridiculed as a fool. Ironically, this mockery focused on his "kingship." Jesus—the "king of kings"—submitted to the cruel jokes and jibes of his guards, allowing himself to be humiliated as an impostor king and to be crucified as a violent criminal. This submission marks a significant difference between the way in which he was mocked and the ways in which others are typically treated as fools. Often, those who become the butt of jokes and objects of mockery have something comical about them—whether their physical appearance, their naiveté, their inflated sense of self, their way of walking, speaking or gesticulating. . . . In Jesus' case, it was not his personal characteristics upon which his enemies focused, but on all that he represented—that is, everything about him which challenged their world order and exposed their spiritual bankruptcy. Thus we can say that Jesus was made a fool of, but he was not intrinsically a "fool" in the usual sense of the term.

Nor was Jesus a "fool" in the scriptural sense. The Psalms identify the true fool as that person who turns from God and from God's law:

> 1 Fools tell themselves,
> "There is no God."
> Their actions are corrupt,
> none of them does good.
>
> 2 The Lord looks down
> to see if anyone is wise,
> if anyone seeks God.
>
> 3 But all have turned away,
> all are depraved.
> No one does good,
> not even one. (Ps 14:1–3)

In their folly, such fools imagine that they are only answerable to themselves. Instead of acknowledging God's presence in their lives, they invest ultimate authority in themselves alone, pursuing that which is expedient rather than that which is ethical.

The fool is also one who fails to grasp God's goodness and God's wonders. Instead of being filled with awe in response to all that God has done, instead of being filled with delight, instead of uttering heart-felt songs of praise, fools understand nothing. Lack of understanding leads to erroneous ways. The implication of Psalm 92, for example, is that fools and the enemies of God are one and the same; they lack spiritual grounding and moral sense:

8 Scoundrels spring up like grass,
flourish and quickly wither.

9 You, Lord, stand firm forever. (Ps 92:8–9)

The Book of Proverbs has much to say about fools. In Proverbs 10, we learn that fools are the grief of their parents. Gabbing incessantly, uttering slander after slander, they head for ruin and poverty; their joy is to do wrong. All are sluggards, evildoers; all are wicked and godless. Proverbs 14 describes fools as "rash and presumptuous"; suffering from delusions, wearing the diadem of folly, they have no room for wisdom in their hearts. Accordingly, their mouths spew only folly and folly is their own punishment (Prov 15:2; 16:22). Completely lacking in reflection, they air only their own opinions (Prov 18:2). Moreover, they are incapable of exercising self-control and gobble up precious treasure and oil (Prov 20:3; 21:20). Fools scheme nothing but sin and "As dog returns to its vomit, so fools revert to their folly" (Prov 24:9; 26:11). This portrait of the fool is summarized in the Book of Wisdom: "Naturally stupid are all . . . who have not known God" (Wis 13:1).

Precisely because fools are completely self-satisfied and therefore resist the truth, they are "a more dangerous enemy to the good than evil."[28] Spiritual blindness leads to self-justification, to denial of one's sinful behavior and to projection of that behavior on to others. Instead of holding up the mirror of truth to themselves, fools blame others for the vicissitudes of life, seeing themselves—like King Lear in Act III sc.2:59—as "more sinned against than sinning."[29] There is no reasoning with fools; on the contrary, because they allow themselves to be used and exploited, fools become passive instruments, "capable of any evil and at the same time, incapable of seeing that it is evil."[30]

How foolish to be an unholy fool! God promises to lavish all good things upon creation and yet sinfulness leads fools to become so preoccupied with mere survival that they fail to believe the promise. Instead, they settle for little of consequence, squandering themselves on what is worthless, selling themselves for that which will never satisfy. Self-willed and self-delusional, fools are ridiculous creatures who strut across the stage of life as if they owned the world and the heavens above it. Patiently, God invites all unholy fools to leave behind their farcical existence, and to take their place at the rich feast of God's presence. But sin blocks them from responding to this invitation; sin prevents them from seeking God and, instead, propels them on a destructive course of serving their own petty whims and desires.

Fools turn from God; God pities them and offers forgiveness. Fools bring suffering upon themselves by their actions; God offers an alternative way of being —a way of freedom and contentment. The implication here is that fools are incapable of understanding God's wisdom. Because God's wisdom is so far beyond their comprehension, fools prefer to cling to that which they already know—that is, to their own stupidity and all the dreadful repercussions it brings upon them. Fools may hear the invitation but, more often than not, they refuse to respond, failing to believe its good news. Limited by their own lack of forgiveness and lack of imagination, fools cannot accept the good things God dreams for them. Ironically, they perceive God's love and compassion as "foolish." In short, the medieval notion of the devil as a comical figure aptly captures the supreme folly of sinful humans defying their Creator and marring the Divine image within themselves. Sin—in any shape or form, then—is laughable, the stuff of bitter comedy and wry amusement.

The Holy Foolishness of Jesus

While Jesus was made to *appear* as a fool through the actions of others, his foolishness in no way mirrored the foolishness of the godless as presented in the Psalms, in Wisdom Literature and elsewhere in the Scriptures. Jesus was grounded in his relationship with God, as was everything he did. Unlike the fool in Psalm 14, he was the paradigm for the truly upright person in whom God delights. The paradox, however, is that his fidelity to God is what made him appear foolish in the world's estimation. Just as the prophets aligned themselves with God's way of seeing, so Jesus saw as God saw—and acted accordingly. Instead of pursuing power, status, privilege, control, and security—hallmarks of egotistical behavior—Jesus relied entirely on God for his strength, allowing God's Spirit to lead him. We can conclude, then, that if Jesus exhibited any folly it was the folly of God.

For Jesus, the only path was the path of God's law which, to evildoers, is a path of absurdity. With the psalmist, he could say:

> 97 How I love your law!
> All day it fills my thoughts.
>
> 98 I am wiser than my foes,
> your judgment is always with me.
>
> 99 I outstrip my teachers,
> for your laws have tutored me.
>
> 100 I surpass my elders,
> because I keep your precepts. . . .
>
> 103 Your promises are sweet to taste,
> sweeter than honey.
>
> 104 Because your decrees give wisdom,
> I hate all evil. (Ps 119:97–104)

By biblical standards, it would seem that Jesus was the quintessential sage rather than a fool; far from being godless, he was the embodiment of holiness. But like "the Just One" referred to in The Book of Wisdom, he was "obnoxious" because in his obedience and humility, in his patience and compassion, he highlighted the sins of the evil ones:

> Let us beset the just one, because he is
> obnoxious to us;
> he sets himself against our doings,
> Reproaches us for transgressions of the law
> and charges us with violations of our training.
> (Wis 2:12)

Blinded by malice, the evildoers plot to do away with the Just One. Their intention is to subject him to cruelty, torture, and a shameful death to see if God will take his part. Human instinct wants to eliminate all that challenges depravity. It is this principle that led Jesus to his own shameful death. Ironically, those who condemned him condemned themselves. In doing away with Goodness, they exhibited their own lack of tolerance for virtue; in mocking all that was sacred, they allowed their jests and curses to rebound upon themselves.

Fool as Archetype

The fool, as archetype, has ancient roots and many cultural manifestations; it is also known by many names—clown, trickster, jester, buffoon, joker. . . . It springs up in oral traditions, in the earliest sacred texts, in legends, folklore, and fairy tales with such regularity that one might ask, "What is so quintessentially appealing about this figure? How has it succeeded in grasping the imaginations of peoples everywhere? How can this archetype reveal anything significant about the person of Jesus? As we explored the concept of psychological archetypes, we saw that "archetypes pre-exist in the collective psyche of the human race."[31] The fool, then, is a familiar figure in whom we recognize some truth about our own humanity. Often existing outside the norms of society, the fool is not far from the center of human experience. Richard Boston sees the fool as one whose role is to be the focus of laughter and who, in turn, makes us laugh, often becoming, like Jesus, a scapegoat figure.[32]

Through the antics of the fool, we find vicarious release for much we have repressed within ourselves. When we dare to "put on" the fool, the release is, of course, more complete though it is possible to cross the boundaries of ethical behavior into excess and debauchery. It is infinitely safer to watch the clowns in the circus ring than to put on a clown's costume and all the license this represents. Again, there is a need to stress here that it is the *redeemed* side of the fool which is applicable to this study of Jesus as Holy Fool. Though Jesus was a breaker of rules and taboos, an agent of chaos, his intent transcended the desire to be a catalyst of laughter and his behavior never degenerated into lewdness or cruelty. Boston lists the attributes of the typical fool as "gluttony, erudition, stupidity, sexuality, cunning, shiftlessness, malice, deceit, and truth-telling";[33] It is the wisdom of the fool and the truth-telling of the fool which are relevant here.

Fools can exhibit a depth of wisdom that seems incongruous. Given the professional fool's task of entertaining others and of being the butt of others' jests, it is startling to realize how close to the mark the fool's observations can be. It is as though the outwardly outrageous dress and behavior obscure from the casual observer the fool's ability to perceive, critique, and speak truth. One is left wondering if the fool is really a sage *incognito,* and if the trickster is the shadow of the fool. Who is really wise? The jester dressed in motley or the king who wants to be humored, in every sense of the word? Jesus—wearing the simple garb of a Mediterranean peasant—spoke the truth to those who thought he was possessed; ironically, they themselves were emotionally, imaginatively, and morally deficient, in spite of their claims to status and religious monopoly.

Fooling can also be existentially dangerous. Who would trade places with the circus clown catapulted across the ring from a fiery cannon? Or with the clown whose clothes catch fire while he or she is attempting to save a burning house? Or with the clown riding high above us on the high-wire, bravely peddling a dilapidated unicycle in serious need of wheel alignment? Or with the clown who enters the lions' cage, grasping only a mop and bucket as security? While we may laugh at the *auguste,* victim of slapstick humor, or at the white-faced clown who argues with ring master and public, while we may be mesmerized by equestrian comedy or acrobatic comedy, the truth is that the dividing line between the comic and the dangerous is thin. The illusion before us may seem to be carried out with the sleight of hand of a magician, but one false step, one error of judgment and the "near miss" could well become tragedy. Sitting in the safety of our seats, we feel the thrill of the drama unfolding before us, but seldom know what risks are being taken in the name of entertainment. In the passion narratives, Jesus the Holy Fool submits to slapstick which is ultimately death-dealing: for him, there is no safety net, no last minute reprieve, no deus ex machina, no standing ovation. There is only the laughter of mockery and the silence of the tomb.

The Trickster

Sometimes, the fool takes on characteristics of "trickster," turning assumptions and expectations upside down, promising one thing while delivering another, making the whole world topsy-turvy. As we have seen, Jesus would sometimes turn tables on those who would trap him; he also used storytelling as a device to undermine normal assumptions about life and about God, thereby demonstrating the inadequacy of these assumptions. For him, trickery served as a means of survival and a pedagogical tool.

But the trickster does not always have benign manifestations; in fact, he or she can lure others into mischief, even disaster. The serpent in the Book of Genesis, for example, seduces Eve with empty promises. This most subtle of beasts promises that if they eat of the Tree of Knowledge, Adam and Eve will know good and evil and will be like gods; in fact, their eyes do open, but it is their nakedness of which they become aware, not their divinity. This new knowledge begets embarrassment and fear; when God calls, they hide. Adam blames Eve, while Eve blames the serpent. Trickster serpent has turned Eden upside down and destroyed primordial innocence (Gn 3:13).

There are other less than praiseworthy moments of deception in Genesis. In Gerar, Abraham pretends Sarah is his sister rather than his wife, believing that Abimelech, the Philistine king, will be more likely to give them safe passage if he does not have to contend with Abraham for her sexual favors (Gn 20); years later, in time of famine, Isaac also visits Gerar and adopts the same strategy about his wife,

Rebekah, much to the consternation of Abimelech (Gn 26:7–11). Then there is Jacob the trickster, stealer of his brother's birthright—who, incidentally, was born grasping Esau by the heel (Gn 25:26). Jacob, in turn, is deceived by Laban who gives him his daughter Leah instead of Rachel after pressing him into seven years of service (Gn 29:20–30). Later, Jacob gains ownership of Laban's livestock through trickery, while Rachel steals her father's household idols and conceals them through deception (Gn 30:25–43; 31:35). Then there is the treacherous revenge Simeon and Levi exact on the Schememites over the rape of Dinah, their sister, through a mock marriage alliance involving the circumcision of all the males of the town, followed by their slaughter (Gn 34:1–24); or the cruel joke Joseph's brothers play on Jacob when they dip Joseph's multicolored coat in goat's blood and present it to their father, deliberately leading him to imagine that the wild beasts have torn his son to pieces (Gn 37:31–35).

Describing the trickster in Native American tradition, Paul Radin writes:

> Trickster is at one and the same time creator and destroyer, giver and negator, he who dupes others and who is always duped himself. He wills nothing consciously. . . . He knows neither good nor evil yet he is responsible for both. He possesses no values, moral or social, is at the mercy of his passions and appetites yet through his actions all values come into being.[34]

This trickster, often identified with specific animals such as the raven, coyote, hare, and spider and possessing exaggerated sexual attributes, is a laughter-maker. Sometimes teased and outwitted themselves, tricksters are adept at getting the best of others and of tricking them into situations in which they maintain the advantage; at the same time, they also seem to lack survival skills. Able to change gender and form at whim and to imitate the actions of other animals such as the muskrat, snipe, and woodpecker, the trickster literally shatters others' perceptions of reality: what is, is not; what seems to be has never been; all is an illusion. The parables, as we will see, are effective precisely because they shatter the worldview of Jesus' audience, leaving no assumption   or expectation unchallenged.

And yet there is a dark side to this comical mythical figure which clearly has nothing to do with Jesus the Holy Fool. In one of the episodes from the Winnebago Trickster Cycle, the trickster lures two women away from their children by telling them of a wonderful plum tree laden with fruit. In their absence, he kills the children and boils them, justifying this because he needs a good meal. Then, if this were not outrageous enough, when finished "he cut off the head of one of the children, put a stick through its neck and placed it at the door as though the child were peeping out and laughing."[35]

Jung suggests that the trickster is a collective shadow figure, "an epitome of all the inferior traits of character in individuals. And since the individual shadow is never absent as a component of personality, the collective figure can construct itself out of it continually."[36] The trickster, then, while most commonly expressed in aboriginal cultures, represents parts of ourselves that rely on intrigue, cunning, deception, and mockery to achieve its own ends. In the case of Jesus, the trickster was not shadow material but a capacity for "savvy" that relied on reversals. As trickster, Jesus dealt back what he received without losing his dignity or compromising his integrity. It was the trickster in him which allowed him to have the final word when the "best and brightest" found themselves defenseless in his presence. With masterly skill, he punctured the balloon of the ego, making a point which could neither be easily overlooked or ignored.

The Fool as Professional

A brief "history of professional fools" will highlight the complexity and multifacetedness of the fool archetype. The Roman Saturnalia, for example, was an annual fertility festival of license and revelry remarkable for its "misrule," that is, for the complete chaos that overtook society from the seventeenth to the twenty-third of December. Sir James Frazer describes how freemen cast lots for the privilege of being elected "mock king" and for being able to impose ludicrous commands on his temporary subjects. The fun was short-lived, however: at the end of his reign, this representative of Saturn became a sacrificial victim on the altar of the god he impersonated, no doubt as an offering to woo back the sun and to ensure a new harvest.[37] Thus the one who could make fools of others with apparent impunity ultimately was fooled himself; it was as though the entire festival became "trickster," bestowing kingship with one hand and a death sentence with the other. The illusion of privilege was stripped from the Lord of Misrule, along with life itself.

Raymond Brown finds no evidence that anyone was put to death as part of this feast, but points instead to the Sacean Feast, an ancient Persian festival during which a condemned prisoner "was set on the king's throne, given royal apparel, and allowed licentious behavior. After that, he was stripped, spat upon and killed."[38] Brown also refers to the Kronia, a Roman feast in honor of Kronos/Saturn, which likewise may have included elements of "orgiastic buffoonery and of a king or master for a time"; apparently, physical abuse and the execution of the mock king "seem later and much less certain."[39] Regardless of what actually "happened" at the Saturnalia and other feasts, it would seem that mocking the office of king and then mocking the king's representative provided a communal form of foolery in antiquity. The mockery of Christ as king during the passion narratives fits into this very pattern.

The origins of the professional royal jester—another "fool type" who both played the fool and was made a fool of—also stretch back to ancient times. William Willeford tells us that the earliest known jester was the dark-skinned dwarf in the court of the Pharaoh Pepi I while the research of Enid Welsford earlier this century suggests that the history of the court fool actually began "with the arrival of a mysterious little pygmy called the *Danga* at the court of Dadkeri-Assi, a

Pharaoh of the Fifth Dynasty."[40] A religious invocation found in the pyramid of Papi I (sic) suggests that the pharaoh, by identifying with Danga, hoped that he could claim a welcome in the after-life as a celestial court buffoon: "Papi is the Danga who dances the God (Bisu), and who rejoices the heart of the God (Osirus) in front of his great royal palace."[41]

Danga figures, then, were more than entertainers. It seems that they were directly in communication with the gods. As people who not only knew the divine dance of mystery but who also delighted the divine heart, they could serve as intermediaries between the human and the divine. Accordingly, they had specific court functions in terms of offering protection and humoring the gods. Welsford writes:

> The Danga was no doubt an agile and amusing little fellow, but his chief attraction was that he was mysterious, that he came from the land of shades, that he knew the dance of an exotic God.[42]

The entertainment offered by the fool in the Egyptian context, then, was connected with an "inner knowing." Whether this "knowing" was innate or learned, it was revered by pharaoh's court as a means of encountering the powers of the divine—whether beneficent or hostile. This, in itself, suggests that the gods had a comic dimension to them—or at least, an appreciation of the comic. Knowledge, in this manifestation of the fool, was not so much the wisdom of the sage as the wisdom of the one who had been initiated into the sacred mysteries. We will see that inner knowing is also characteristic of the gospel Jesus. It was not book learning but attention to God's presence that allowed him to read hearts and to proclaim God's word. He knew the sacred dance and embodied the divine mystery.

Traditionally, the fool has often been associated with images of promiscuity and stupidity. Early degenerate prototypes of the fool include the shameless parasites of Greek and Roman society who invited themselves to dinner in the homes of the wealthy, earning their keep by providing a little levity. Ergasilus, a stock character in Plautus' *The Prisoners*, describes his occupation as follows:

> "My name—that is, the nickname given to me by our young people is The Harlot. Why? Because at their tables I am employed, not invited. . . . When a lover throws the dice after dinner, he employs the name of his harlot to bring him luck; so you can say she is employed. And the term certainly applies to us professional table companions; nobody ever invites us—nor, for that matter, do they call upon us to bring them luck! No, we're like mice, always nibbling at other people's food. When the vacation comes and everybody goes off to the country, then our teeth have to take a vacation, too."[43]

This soliloquy goes on to explain that life as a parasite has its lean times and its fat times; there are times of having one's ears boxed or pots broken on one's head and times when flattery brings royal treatment. While Gabba, the buffoon of the Emperor Augustus had a position in the royal household, most parasites lived from hand to mouth, sacrificing self-respect for a precarious mode of existence.[44] And yet, the fact that parasites survived at all or that they had an accepted role within society indicates a certain innate intelligence. Whether we dismiss this as survival instinct or as quick-wittedness, it is apparent that parasites knew how to take care of themselves—most likely, with some of the trickster's skills of deception and manipulative strategies.

The parasite—emerging, as it does, from the unredeemed shadow—is not an image that can be applied to Jesus, but this stock figure does provide a useful counterfoil to the gospel portraits. Jesus, as the Bread of Life, as the host of the heavenly banquet, as the one who presides over the Last Supper, and, finally, as the one who gives of himself in the Eucharist, offers food to all who would feed on him. Like the pelican who is reputed to feed her young from her own flesh rather than let them starve, Jesus is the food upon which all of us are invited to feast. While we might be parasites, however, what we receive we receive freely; there is no need for tricks, witticisms, or other humor-producing tactics to earn our bread at the table. The comedy is that everyone is welcome; no one will be turned away.

Like the parasite, medieval court fools served to delight their aristocratic owners. In addition to being talented jugglers, tumblers, and practical jokers—much like contemporary circus clowns—court fools would also allow themselves to be the butt of their own jokes. One typical example is the story of the fool who tried to teach his horse to live without food; upon the horse's death, he concluded that the experiment would have succeeded had not the horse died first. Another jester carried around a brick from his house in order to show his audience what the building looked like; yet another clung to a ship's anchor for security while the ship was sinking.[45]

The humor typified here is a far cry from the foolishness of Christ. In the medieval courts, laughter-making was typically at the expense of someone's dignity—usually the jester's, and was directed at deformity, humiliation, and physical violence. In contrast, even when Jesus was himself center of the comic stage, nailed to a cross, he did not become ludicrous, though others laughed at him. His crucifixion was no self-defeating act but a complete outpouring of self in love and obedience to God. Bystanders imagined they were looking at a fool, but behind the visible degradation was the wisdom of God made manifest in apparent folly. Nor did Jesus ever use any form of humor that diminished anyone. He may have ridiculed ego-driven attitudes and behaviors, but he did not shame others; rather, his audience took on their own shame as their eyes were opened to their unholy folly.

Like the trickster, many medieval fools and clowns had exaggerated sexual attributes. They wore asses' ears or cocks' combs as part of their attire. There were "natural fools" or those fools who were born with marked mental deficiencies, therefore requiring warders for them to function at all; and there were also "artificial fools" like Piculf who received feudal honors for his folly, and Grant-Jehan who was salaried. But whether natural or artificial, the fool was frequently a source of social disruption.[46] Commenting on Fra Mariano Felti, a buffoon at the court of Leo X who delighted the pope with his inordinate appetite, Welsford describes his tricks as "childish":

> He hunts live poultry across the dining-hall table, catching and killing them and smearing his face with gravy; he leaps onto the supper tables, jousting with lighted torches and threatening the beards of fellow buffoons; he organizes a battle worthy of Tweedledum and Tweedledee, where the combatants fight with dishes, pots, washtubs, and all kinds of terra-cotta instruments. . . . [47]

Gluttonous tendencies, disgusting behavior, and the laughter-making skills of the parasite also found communal expression in certain ecclesiastical customs based on memories of the ancient Saturnalia.[48] Occurring between Christmas and the New Year in dances of priests, lower clergy, subdeacons, and children, the rites included the election of an *episcopus puerorum* (children's bishop). Dressed in pontifical robes, this "bishop" would pay a ceremonial visit to the archbishop's palace where he would bless the crowd from one of the windows. While this may initially have been harmless enough, by the end of the twelfth century, the celebration had become a *festum stultorum* or feast of fools. Jung cites a report from the year 1198 C.E. in which so many abominations were committed in the Cathedral of Notre Dame, Paris, on the Feast of the Circumcision, that the holy place was desecrated "not only by smutty jokes, but even by the shedding of blood."[49] Apparently such festivals included masqueraders with grotesque appearances disrupting the Mass with their dances, indecent songs, dice games, stinking incense, and greasy meals.[50]

Communal liturgical fooling was also exhibited in the *Feast of the Ass*, celebrated in Beauvais, France. This featured a burlesque re-enactment of the *Flight into Egypt*, which began with a procession led by a donkey throughout the town and culminated in a mass at the Church of St. Etienne, during which the people brayed instead of giving the traditional Latin responses. Like the *festum stultorum,* this feast offered the people the opportunity to burlesque the sacred. Again, this behavior stands in marked contrast to Jesus' approach to the sacred. While the Gospels provide startling images of Jesus cracking his whip in the temple, scattering tables, chairs, sacrificial animals, and money-changers, the Evangelists show that he had a higher agenda than the creation of comedy and chaos. As Son of God and Savior, he resorted to the sensational to create a teachable moment; he was not debunking the sacred but the false piety of hypocrites.

But more may have been going on beneath the surface of medieval liturgical fooling than wild antics and irreverent jesting; the Native American clown societies devoted to clowning during public ceremonies provide an invaluable lens for viewing the seeming excesses of medieval foolery. During the Navaho Night Chant, for example, clowns get in the way of the sacred dancers and even attempt to usurp the leader's role by giving directions; the Zuni Ne'wekwe clowns joke with the gods in Spanish and English, using a mock telephone to reach the heavens. Ostensibly mocking what is considered holy, the clowns are in actual fact supporting the connection with the sacred, thereby making the invisible world accessible to the people. Burlesque, then, by no means indicates lack of respect.[51]

The Fool as Scapegoat and Sage

The medieval fool's role was not limited to entertaining the well-to-do by breaking rules and allowing an outlet for repressed thoughts, attitudes and antics. In many a court setting, the fool as jester functioned symbolically as "mascot, decoy and scapegoat." One principle that still has popular support in Mediterranean countries is that "misshapen, ugly, abnormal people are immune from the Evil Eye," and that contact with them brings good luck.[52] The presence of fools, then, helped deflect "ill winds" from the court; moreover, their jesting was another way of diverting threats to the kingdom from outside sources.

Above all else, the fool's function was to foster psychological wholeness, especially in the person of the ruler whose ego he or she consistently punctured. Often, artificial fools served as insightful commentators on the actions and policies of their employers, speaking the truth about the people around them; in fact, courageous court jesters often offered the only checks on a monarch's power. In Shakespeare's *King Lear*, for example, king and fool share the same stage so that the wisdom of the sage-fool can help the audience interpret the action. If Lear were capable of listening to his "all-licensed fool," he would see his own folly mirrored before him; far from being "more sinned against than sinning" (Act 3, sc.2, 1.159), he is, in fact, responsible for all that has befallen him.[53] Foolishly, the king had disinherited his youngest daughter, Cordelia, for refusing to flatter him, dividing his realm between two worthless daughters who soon, in turn, drive him away. The wise fool puts it succinctly: "Thou hadst little wit in thy bald crown when thou gavest thy golden one away" (Act 1, sc, 4, 1.177).[54] Lear, however, clings to his illusions about himself, to his vanity and his rage; precisely because he cannot face himself in the present moment, his condition degenerates until his worst fear—the fear of becoming mad—is actually realized.

It takes little effort to make connections between the fool as scapegoat and truth-speaker with the gospel Jesus. It was precisely Jesus' insistence upon speaking the truth—whether directly or through parable—that intensified the hostility directed towards him. Like the jester, he punctured the egos of the "rulers" (most frequently, the leaders of the religious establishment), thus providing a check to their power. In Mark's Gospel, for example, he responded to the Pharisees' critique of his disciples for not observing ritual laws of purification by accusing them of setting aside God's commandments to follow merely human traditions (Mk 7:8). Then, further emphasizing his point, he told the crowds,

"Nothing that goes into you from the outside can make you unclean; it is the things that come out of you that make you unclean" (Mk 7:15).

When he was finally punished for truth-speaking, Jesus became the scapegoat figure, the one upon whom the sins of the people were projected. All the repressed rage, hatred, cruelty, and spiritual blindness of the mob hounded him to his death as he was driven beyond the city limits, to Golgotha, the place of forsakenness. There, mocked and spat upon like the goat dedicated to Azazel, the demon of the desert, on the Day of Atonement, Jesus bore the transgressions not only of the house of Israel but of the whole world (Lev 16). The danger confronting the fool—and by extension, Holy Fools in general—is that of plunging into existentially threatening situations and having to pay the price, however steep.

"Jesters and fools rush in where angels fear to tread," writes Edward Hays. Commenting on the fool's propensity to play the prophet, he links the court jester with the saint, explaining how each lacks the prudence to "bow humbly before those in power."[55] Ironically, Henry VIII, "whose personal life wasn't exactly a joke," abolished the position of court jester, while Elizabeth I had them classified with "Ruffians, Blasphemers, Thieves and Vagabonds."[56] Perhaps both royal personages knew, too well, what professional fools have always known about themselves: that they appear "at the edges of our religious understanding . . . (so) that we discover ourselves in our ignorance and sin."[57] From the perspective of power—especially of *threatened* power—the only good fool is a silent fool; and as Herodias insisted, it is better to place the fool's head safely on a platter than to leave it bothersomely fixed in place (Mt 14:8).

The fool is also an archetype which invites us into the freedom of authenticity, aliveness, and delight, and into the experience of ourselves in the here and now. Pearson writes:

> When the Fool is dominant in our lives, we explore the world out of innate curiosity, creating for the simple joy of creation and living life for its own sake without thought of tomorrow and with little

> or no concern with convention, traditional moral-
> ity, or what the neighbors will say . . . only the Fool
> knows how to be "here and now."[58]

As such, the fool liberates us from "mechanistic" living, reminding us that there is more to life than statistics, categories, facts, and push-button ease. Leading us into deeper dimensions of the spiritual quest, the fool teaches us to laugh when we begin to take ourselves too seriously, helps us to see our "smallness" in terms of the cosmos, and energizes us to deal with life's absurdities and to get up—again and again—with all the resiliency of a circus clown. While its shadow side can lure us into debauchery and irresponsibility, the fool can lead us to holiness if we dare to live out of its wisdom. "When there is too little Fool in our lives," claims Pearson, "we may become priggish, repressed, uptight, anorexic, bored, depressed, or lacking in curiosity."[59]

The Fool as Spiritual Quester

The fool's relevance to the universal spiritual quest is embodied in the figure of Perceval—Parsifal, in Wagner's opera—unlikely hero in some versions of the Grail legend. In this ancient spiritual fable, one of the Fisher Kings, as a descendant of Joseph of Arimathea, is keeper of the Holy Grail, the vessel Jesus used at the Last Supper. Wounded in the side or genitals by the same spear which pierced the side of Christ, the Fisher King lies mortally wounded, unable to live fully, incapable of dying. All, save the Fisher King, can drink from the Grail; only when he is healed, only when fertility is restored to the land will the king be worthy of receiving holy food. Desperate as the Fisher King's plight may seem, there is hope: long ago, the court fool had prophesied that the king would be healed when a wholly innocent fool would arrive at court to ask a specific question concerning the Holy Grail.

In Wagner's *Parsifal*, this coming hero is described as "a blameless fool," one "made wise through pity." Parsifal, raised without a name as a simple fool, arrives at court giving ample evidence of his folly when he kills a white swan for no other reason than the fact that he is used to shooting at "all things that fly." There is expectancy in the assembly, but Parsifal, upon seeing the Holy Grail, neither partakes of the sacred meal nor asks the necessary question: "Whom does the Grail serve?" Robert Johnson comments that this is the "most profound question one can ask":

> No sooner is the question asked than the answer comes reverberating through the Grail castle walls —the Grail serves the Grail King. Again, a puzzling answer. Translated, this means that life serves what a Christian would call God, Jung calls the Self or . . . the many terms we have devised to indicate that which is greater than ourselves.[60]

In the Grail legends, Perceval, like Wagner's Parsifal, blunders into the court —the realm of the spiritual—before he is ready to understand what life is asking of him and how he must respond. In spite of this failure, his innate goodness and his ability to learn compassion for the suffering of the king bring him back to the same spot after twenty years of adventuring. As "blameless fool," he has the necessary purity to respond to this most important of tasks; the spear wound is healed because he is humble enough to try again, in spite of all odds, and because he recognizes his sin in missing the first opportunity. In spite of his naiveté, Perceval demonstrates that transformation of consciousness and heroic deeds have more to do with the heart than with one's level of intelligence: the fool succeeds when great knights and sages have failed.

The film *The Wickerman* also highlights the holiness of the fool, and reflects certain aspects of the fool in antiquity.[61] The protagonist in *The Wickerman*, a police sergeant from mainland Scotland, is summoned to a coastal island renowned for its wonderful produce to investigate the disappearance of a little girl named Rowan. Upon arrival, he finds the islanders overtly hostile, completely uncooperative and, from young to old, sexually promiscuous; gradually, he comes to realize that, having abandoned Christianity, the people, under the leadership of Lord Summerisle, are practitioners of the old pagan ways. Led by riddles and clues, he comes to the horrific conclusion that the missing child is to be sacrificed at the approaching midsummer festival because the previous year's harvest failed. Since his plane has been sabotaged, thereby preventing him from returning to the mainland for help, he decides to rescue Rowan by himself. Carried away by his own goodness, heroism, and naiveté, he falls into the very trap the islanders have set for him, amusing them with his antics while he follows every conceivable lead in his efforts to save the child. In fact, precisely because of this trap-setting, it would not be inaccurate to name the islanders as a collective "trickster." Finally, dressed as Punch, the very embodiment of the fool, and carrying a mock scepter, he joins the costumed procession of mummers, led by the Bessy and high priest (Lord Summerisle), only to discover that he was the intended victim all along. As in ancient festivals, the "make-believe" fool is the real fool. As virgin (he triumphs in one graphic seduction scene), man of courage and representative of the crown (police officer), he is a worthy victim whose death will appease the gods of fertility. There is no deus ex machina: the film ends with the chilling scene of the sergeant being burned alive in an enormous wicker cage, screaming out curses from the Hebrew prophets and then the name of Jesus, while the islanders—Rowan among them—dance and sing on the sea shore.

The protagonist is simultaneously clown, sacrificial victim, and naive fool-saint. His frantic chasing after Rowan, interpreting clue after clue in the mad paper-chase trail set by the islanders, makes him an object of derision, though he himself is unaware of it. Naively, he imagines that he lives in an ordered world in which belief in God and loyalty to the monarchy bestow some form of protection. Aware of his symbolic significance as representative of the queen, he does not for a minute think that this status will make him a worthier victim; nor does he realize his chastity will also prove to be a liability. Ironically, the very qualities which make him upright and God-fearing are the qualities which lead to his death. He, like other fools for Christ, never stops to consider his own safety but simply does what he considers to be his duty. And like the Christ he follows and whose name he invokes, he meets an absurd ending. "You and I are invited to be fools," writes Hays, "followers of the Great Fool, the Clown Christ."[62] Taking seriously St. Paul's words to the Corinthians—"Here we are fools for the sake of Christ" (1 Cor 4:10). Hays reminds us that the example Jesus set was to reject the oppressive systems of his day and to model a new paradigm of loving service; in so doing, Christ "played the fool," consciously stepping out of culturally accepted patterns of behavior and often causing outrage and scandal. Hays cites the example of Jesus washing his disciples' feet at the Last Supper, suggesting that he was playing "the classic clown."[63] Certainly, for the Teacher, Lord, and Master to place himself in the role of a humble servant was an act of comic reversal. "What better way," writes Hays, "was there to make his disciples see how comical was their desire for the sort of muscle exercised by the power brokers of the world?"[64]

In this one act, Jesus showed by his example that it was humble servanthood and not power and privilege that counted in God's reign. To those who pursued status, he became a sign of contradiction, the embodiment of obedience and self-emptying, a reminder that "in some way, every disciple is ordained to servanthood and to foolhood, ordained to be a jester to the world."[65] For if he, the Son of God, could stoop low enough to wash his followers' feet, then the logical conclusion is that they, in turn, should wash the feet of others. "God's foolishness is wiser than human wisdom and God's weakness is stronger than human strength," writes St. Paul (1 Cor 1:25). Christ, the Divine Fool, exemplifies the path of folly; to reject this path is to reject Christ.

Biblical Precursors of the Holy Fool

At this point, it is important to state that Jesus follows a line of many other biblical Holy Fools and that he was not the first of his kind. In the Hebrew Scriptures, we find Holy Foolishness exemplified in Abraham and Sarah's journey from Haran to the land of Canaan, a journey undertaken against all logic; to leave the familiar and the comfortable in one's old age, to journey across rough terrain in time of famine, to believe in God's promise that a great nation would be born of this adventure—all this was the stuff of Holy Foolishness, indeed. And the story has other elements of the ludicrous: Sarah's laugh of incredulity when the Visitors at the Oak of Mamre predicted that she, a postmenopausal woman, would bear a son; Sarah's laugh of gratitude at the birth of her son whose very name, Isaac, is a form of the Hebrew, "God has laughed"; the dark, dark comedy of the near sacrifice of Isaac when Abraham believed God was instructing him to sacrifice his only son, the one from whom the great nation was destined to spring—and was willing to follow instructions! (Gn 18:1–15; 21:1–7; 22:1–19).

We also find Holy Foolishness manifested in the Hebrew prophets who consistently put themselves at existential risk by proclaiming God's word to those who did not wish to hear. This risk not only originated with the reactions of the establishment but also with the fact that God so often made of them a laughing stock. Take, for example, the case of Jeremiah, forced to proclaim war, famine, and pestilence to the people of Judah because of their apostasy. Spurned and maltreated by the people, he resorted to foolish antics—at God's direction—to make his point; chapter 13, for example, in which he is instructed to buy a loin cloth and wear it, then to bury it near the Euphrates, then to dig it up again, has elements of the circus ring, with Jeremiah functioning as clown. The passage demonstrates that the House of Judah was no better than the spoiled loincloth, even though God originally had other plans: "For just as a loincloth clings to a man's waist, so I had intended the whole House of Judah to cling to me . . . to be my people, my glory, my honor, my boast" (Jer 13:11).

Or take Hosea who was instructed to marry a prostitute to demonstrate how deeply the House of Israel had offended God through her infidelity; Hosea's own painful marital situation not only symbolized the corruption of his people, but also was a reminder that God is a God of forgiveness, ready to embrace the children of the Covenant, in spite of their sins (Hos1:2–9). To this day, in the patriarchal world of the Mediterranean, one who is cuckolded or betrayed by his wife is regarded as a fool. For Hosea to marry a prostitute must have suggested he was out of his mind. What man in his right senses would set himself up for public humiliation by marrying a woman who was not only of poor repute but who would certainly betray him in the future? And what man, having made this grievous error in the first place, would take back his wife, over and over again, continuing to have children with her? No doubt his friends and family considered him to be deranged.

Then there is Isaiah who for three years walked barefoot and naked as a sign that it would be foolish to place trust in an alliance with Egypt: " . . . so will the king of Assyria lead away captives from Egypt and exiles from Cush, young and old, naked and barefoot, their buttocks bared, to the shame of Egypt" (Isa 20:4). Ezekiel, also commanded to absurdity, lay on his left side for 190 days, bearing the sins of the House of Israel, and then for a further forty days on his right side, bearing the sins of the House of Judah (Ezek 4;1–8). Following this, God commanded him to eat defiled food, baked over human dung, for "This is the way the Israelites will have to eat their defiled food, wherever I disperse them among the nations"; to this, however, Ezekiel, understandingly objected, and God allowed him to bake his millet cake over cow dung instead (Ezek 4:12–17). John Saward concludes: "In a world gone mad, the guardian of truth is invariably dismissed as a raving lunatic. This is the lot of every prophet."[66]

The Hebrew Scriptures are filled not only with images of Holy Foolishness, but also with other forms of absurdity. There is Jonah, swallowed by the great fish after running away from God; and there is Jonah again, after being liberated from the belly of the fish and after having accomplished his mission to Nineveh, rejoicing in the shelter of a castor oil plant, only to have it wither away when God sends a worm to attack it; and there is Jonah, lamenting over the death of this plant while he has been completely indifferent to the fate of 120,000 Ninevites and their animals (Jon 1–4). There is Job the Upright, sitting on his dung heap, reduced to an object of derision, while his friends—evidently way out of their spiritual depth— try to lecture him on the causes of his misery; and there is the boy David, the keeper of sheep, elevated to king in spite of his youth and inexperience (Job; 1 Sam 16:1–13). There is Joseph concealing his identity from his brothers when they come to Egypt to procure food and there is Moses protesting to God that he lacks the eloquence to lead his people; then there is Jacob the Trickster —aided and abetted by Rebekah— vesting himself in Esau's best clothes and covering himself with animal skins to deceive the now blind Isaac into giving him his blessing (Gn 42–45; Ex 4:10–17; Gn 27:1–29).

Absurdity, foolishness and Holy Foolishness are evidently are integral part of our biblical legacy, but, for the most part, these elements have been neglected because of our unwillingness to risk possible irreverence. Francis Landy, in his article, "Humour as a Tool for Biblical Exegesis," suggests that the excessive reverence accorded to the Bible is a form of idolatry and a hindrance in breaking open the meaning of the texts. For Landy, the tendency to read the Bible as an entirely solemn text "has created an impression of a stiff and serious document that never relaxes into a smile, so that many sensitive readers have closed their minds to its comic possibilities."[67]

It will become apparent that the deepest meanings are sometimes to be found precisely in those moments of folly and absurdity which are traditionally read without even the trace of a smile. As Holy Fool, Jesus is both the master of comedy and the victim of absurdity. He knows how to allow human foolishness to rebound on the heads of the vindictive and he is adept at using comedy as a pedagogical tool. At the same time, he is not afraid to allow himself to become the object of derision, the butt of others' cruel jokes. Understanding the comic, then, is essential for anyone who wishes to explore a Christology of Holy Foolishness.

 *Part Two*

Jesus and Divine Folly

The Foolishness of God in Creation and Election

There is a marked distinction between human foolishness and God's foolishness. If human folly in a biblical sense represents straying from the path of righteousness, then folly, when ascribed to God, must mean something entirely different: God, after all, cannot stray from God for, as Aquinas asserted, "all defect is absent from God: He is therefore universal perfection."[1] As humans, we can participate in God's perfection, but because of our limited abilities, only imperfectly. While it is therefore possible to claim that we are like God in a limited way, the converse statement would be inappropriate, for if God were like us, then God would be imperfect. Accordingly, we must tread carefully as we try to ascribe any attributes to God. At best, we can only go by way of analogy, by similitude and metaphor, especially since the essence of the Divine Substance is beyond the comprehension of our senses; "objects beyond sense," writes Aquinas, "cannot be grasped by human understanding except so far as knowledge is gathered of them through the senses."[2]

To ascribe Holy Foolishness to God is fraught with difficulties. As Aquinas points out, even angels cannot comprehend God's understanding of God's Self. Because human nature itself is flawed and prone to presumption, it is safest to approach God through what Aquinas terms as *negative differentiation:*

> For the divine substance, by its immensity, transcends every form that our intellect can realize; and thus we cannot apprehend it by knowing what it is, but we have some sort of knowledge of it by knowing what it is not.[3]

An appropriate starting point, therefore, is to say that God's folly is not like human folly; in fact, God's Holy Foolishness offers us an ethical system that is completely different than our own. It turns human expectations and assumptions upside down, establishing seeming curse as blessing and seeming blessing as curse. Nothing is as it appears to be. The Holy Foolishness of God is neither an aberration, nor a defect, nor a source of the ridiculous; nor is it a limitation, an expression of selfishness, or a manifestation of irresponsibility. Clearly, God's foolishness is of a very different order. If human folly is curse, than God's folly must *not* be curse. If human folly is destructive, then God's folly must *not* be destructive. We could, of course, cast this in the positive by saying that God's folly is creative blessing but this would be to go beyond negative differentiation.

This brings us back to the matter of analogy. For Aquinas, some terms can be applied to God literally (as for example, "God is good"), but others have metaphorical application only. Brian Davies distinguishes between the literal and the metaphorical by using the example of a rock:

> Rocks are firm and stable, as God can be said to be. But God is not made of the substance of which a rock is formed . . . So Aquinas would say, 'God is

not really a rock,' it makes sense to deny that he is a rock, and to call (God) a rock is to indulge in metaphor.[4]

Applying this to the Holy Fool, we could say that God manifests God in ways which are reminiscent of the Holy Fool; by studying this archetype, we thereby develop a vocabulary by which we can approach the reality of God. Our purpose, then, is not to define God as Holy Fool, but to learn how God acts like the redeemed Holy Fool.

We only know God in so far as God reveals the Divine Self to us. There are no names, no images, and no attributes which could ever convey more than a fleeting insight into the nature of God. The Ninety-nine Beautiful Names of Allah celebrated within Islam, the 330 million divine images found within Hinduism, the Oneness of God so foundational to Judaism, the Threeness of the Christian Trinity—these all provide us with a framework for approaching God, pointing to the very nature of God, but they are not God. God cannot be defined, categorized, limited, understood, described, assigned gender, or named. "I Am who I Am," is God's way of identifying the Divine Self to Moses (Ex 3:14). God is elusive mystery who offers us hints and guesses about Godself—a blazing bush that is not consumed, a guiding pillar of cloud, and pillar of fire, a voice calling in the night, the sound of a gentle breeze, a cloud filling the sanctuary of the Temple, a vineyard keeper, a jealous and wrathful avenger, a mother teaching her child to walk, a lover seeking the beloved. . . . [5] All we have to go by, then, are God's words and God's deeds; they alone make it possible for us to speak of "God's foolishness."

Even when we focus on God's words and actions as revealed in the Scriptures we can only judge their "foolishness" from our own flawed perspectives: what appears to be foolish from a human vantage point is, in reality, wisdom at work. However open-minded we might be, however perceptive we are, human judgments are always based on partial knowledge, bias, self-interest, and the inability to grasp "the whole picture." We can only be wise within the limitations of being human; humbly, we must acknowledge that we do not possess the gifts of perfect seeing, perfect understanding, perfect planning, perfect interpreting, or perfect predicting. Isaiah 55 clearly distinguishes between human ways and God's ways, between human folly and divine wisdom. This beautiful text begins with an invitation to leave behind all that is destructive to the quality of human life, both on a material and spiritual level:

> Oh, come to the water all you who are thirsty;
> Though you have no money, come!
> Buy corn without money and eat,
> and, at no cost, wine and milk.
> Why spend your money on what is not bread,
> your wages on what fails to satisfy?
> Listen, listen to me, and you will have good things
> to eat and rich food to enjoy.
> Pay attention, come to me;
> listen, and your soul will live. (Isa 55:1–3)

This text offers a powerful statement about what life could be like if we were to leave behind our preoccupation with survival and instead allow God to lavish us with all good things. We settle for so little, squandering ourselves on what is worthless, selling ourselves for that which can never satisfy. How foolish we are and how generous of God to invite us to leave behind such folly, so that we might take our places at the rich feast of God's presence and taste the many blessings awaiting us. Sin, however, clouds our vision to the point where we no longer recognize our folly.

The biblical record of God's folly begins with the story of creation and with God's gift of free will to humankind. By examining archetypal persons, actions, places, and things— that is, by looking at those symbols which represent universal patterns—we will find a rich body of biblical evidence to support our theme. In the first place, it does not take much for Adam and Eve to yield to the temptation of wanting to be like God; a subtle serpent, and the proverbial apple do their work, effortlessly. The Fall happens—a free fall from grace—

and the rest is history, a *commedia* with its profoundly dark moments, punctuated by moments of dazzling light. In spite of human pride, disobedience, and egocentricity, God continues to invite men and women to participate in the divine life. And, in their absurdity, men and women continue to pursue their own paths.

Surely, we ask, wouldn't an omniscient God have seen the outcome of allowing freedom of will? Wasn't this an act of supreme folly? Wouldn't God have been wiser to establish some controls over humankind? The outcome of free will is clear—evil perpetrated in one generation afflicting succeeding generations so radically that human nature itself became intrinsically flawed, as Augustine concludes. Examining his own life with a rigor which may seem curiously dated to the contemporary reader, Augustine looks back on his earliest years and observes, "I was a great sinner for so small a boy."[6] His analysis of his own disposition towards sinfulness seems excessive, particularly when he refers to his greed at his mother's breast, commenting that the only reason babies are innocent "is not for the lack of will to do harm, but for the lack of strength."[7]

While we may have difficulty appreciating Augustine's remorse over his sins as an infant, his emphasis on his own disordered will and on the choices he made as he moved into adulthood does reflect the outcome of freedom of will. Perhaps Augustine's focus on the sins of infants is intended to highlight the absurdity of the human condition; perhaps his account of his early years is meant to produce the laughter of recognition in his readers as we, too, acknowledge our own frailty and pettiness. For Augustine, it is only size and age which distinguish the greedy baby from the adult who lusts after sex and knowledge. Aquinas, some nine centuries later, names this disordered will as "the will of Adam," that is, a disposition towards sin and a movement away from God's own intellect and will.[8]

Free will abused has passed on its legacy as surely as generations have received the physical, psychic, and behavioral legacy of their ancestors. The hands that stretched out to take the forbidden fruit taught generations of hands to grasp and clutch for power; the mouths that tasted the fruit found the bite was bitter, and their toxic experience unleashed millennia of suffering. The hands which killed Abel left the mark on *all* peoples, not just the descendants of Cain. The hands which clutched at security, proudly constructing the Tower of Babel in an attempt to reach to the heavens, bequeathed confusion and the inability to communicate to their descendants. The hands which turned to deeds of wickedness let loose a flood of destruction of catastrophic proportions, sullying the very earth. How bitterly amusing these examples are! How tragically comical are human attempts to compete with God for knowledge and control! The archetypes in these stories—archetypes of willfulness, murder, overreaching and catastrophe—show how clownishly undignified we become when, ignoring the Creator of the Universe, we attempt to deify ourselves!

Just as Family Systems therapists have found links between the unhealed issues of previous generations and the issues which manifest themselves in family members yet unborn, so we can conclude that the poor exercise of free will is a burden carried by all humankind. The whole human family has been affected by the decisions of those who walked before us. We no longer walk in the Garden, that archetype of innocence, with our God because our first parents chose to walk alone. Eden was lost because Adam and Eve chose self-gratification over pleasing their Maker; the Garden was spoiled because they preferred to grasp forbidden knowledge to resting contentedly in God's wisdom. We are indeed "post-Fall" people, even if we are simultaneously "post-Incarnational."

And yet, the very gift of free will says something about God's capacity for love. God's plan for creation did not involve forced conformity at the strings of a feared puppeteer, but rather, the freedom to choose love. Though this seemingly flawed blueprint for humanity has let loose a Pandora's box of suffering, yet it has also allowed for the free response of the heart, that is, for humans to respond to God's love so fully and utterly that they indeed become that which

God dreamed them to be in the first place. Suffering, then, is a given; sin is unavoidable, but passionate commitment to the God of love is a possibility for all. How wise of God, we might say, to give us the opportunity to love. How wise of God to expand our hearts through the trials and joys of our lives. How wise of God to love us into *choosing* to love. God had two options: to choose tyranny or foolishness—how wise of God to choose folly.

But this very choice of foolishness meant that God could not be a mere deus ex machina, a God who would conveniently rescue humans from their mistakes or extricate them from their misery. By bestowing free will, God, in effect, renounced this power. The Scriptures tell us that God remained passionately present to the children of Israel, intimately concerned in their affairs, offering comfort, providing warnings, but always allowing their choices to play themselves out. By bestowing free will, God also chose to be powerless in human affairs and to open the Divine Self to the affliction of the whole human comic-tragedy. Were God to have a heart, then, God would have allowed it to be shattered by humanity's cruelty, greed, hatred, deceitfulness, violence, and pride. In giving free will, God became vulnerable.

How foolish of God, we might say, to invest in a creation which would go its own way, turning its back on its Maker; how foolish of God to choose a people which would betray the covenant of love, over and over again. The Hebrew Scriptures present countless stories of human faithlessness: though God delighted in creation, noting how all things were "very good," though God chose Israel to be the Beloved, the biblical record offers a tragic account of human behavior (Gen 1). Through the haunting voices of the prophets, we gain insight into the divine view of things:

> I reared children, I brought them up,
> but they rebelled against me.
> The ox knows its owner
> and the ass its master's crib,
> but Israel understands nothing,
> my people understand nothing. (Isa 1:3)

Though God has given humans the gift of intellect, they use it only to plot *against* God, to defy God and to attempt to usurp God's place in their lives. Creatures that we assume (perhaps too readily) have *not* been endowed with intellect— the ox and ass, for example—understand more about their place in the universe than God's "children." They know to whom they owe gratitude, while those who have been made the very stewards of creation turn their backs on the God who strung the stars and foolishly resort to the making and worshipping of golden calves and the like. Absurdly enough, these graven images, often dressed in clothes like human beings, cannot protect themselves from dust, tarnish, or woodworm; completely useless, they can neither prop themselves up nor do much shining on their own, let alone offer protection to their devotees (Bar 6).

As the prophets testify, God is neither indifferent to the wickedness of humankind nor to human ingratitude. The intensity of God's grief is like the labor pains of a woman in childbirth (Isa 42:14); Israel's affliction is God's affliction (Isa 47:6). From his analysis of prophetic utterances, Abraham Heschel concludes that "the typical prophetic state of mind is one of being taken up into the heart of the divine pathos."[9] The prophets, concerned as they are with issues of injustice and with Israel's infidelity, are ones who hear God's voice and feel God's heart.[10] Out of this *hearing* and *feeling,* they then speak to the people, uttering words through which "the invisible God becomes audible."[11] Their anguish is God's anguish; their outrage is God's outrage; their pathos is God's pathos. On the basis of biblical evidence, then, we can say that God suffers, profoundly saddened by the desecration of the Garden and by the hardness of hearts. The exploitation of the poor, the marginalization of widows and orphans, cruelty towards aliens, cheating in the market place, the worshipping of idols—all these offenses strike the heart of God to the core.

While Hellenistic thought has influenced traditional Christian theology to maintain the Creator's incapacity for suffering, the Jewish Scriptures reveal a God who suffers.

God's folly is to be vulnerable. Through the prophets, God rages, speaking words of agony, denouncing profanity, demanding justice. God, the Creator of the universe—is desolate. In the Book of Jeremiah, we hear the voice of a brokenhearted God whose people have made their inheritance an abomination: God, the source of all goodness, the source of all love, is cast off by the people, betrayed, cut to the heart—hurt so deeply that we who are flawed in our loving cannot comprehend the terrible mystery of God's anguish. Forsaken by priests and prophets, abandoned by the people, God laments, naming Israel's ingratitude and forgetfulness:

> What shortcoming did your ancestors find in me
> that led them to desert me?
> Vanity they pursued,
> vanity they became.
> They never said, "Where is God,
> who brought us out of the land of Egypt
> and led us through the wilderness,
> through a land arid and scorched,
> a land of drought and darkness,
> a land where no one passes
> and where no one lives?"
> (Jer 2:5–6)

The anguish in the text is palpable. Knowing full well the people's weakness and infidelity, knowing full well that their allegiance will be short-lived and that they will be preoccupied with their own needs, God reaches out to deliver them from the bondage of Egypt. And God leads them to safety, protecting them with the pillar of cloud and the pillar of fire, parting the waters of the Sea of Reeds, throwing Pharaoh and his charioteers into confusion, feeding the people on manna, providing water when they are thirsty, and renewing the covenant at Sinai. Through the prophetic voice, God reminds the people of the fertile country they have received, of its rich produce and blessings; upon entering this land, however, they defile the land. The priests never ask, "Where is God?"; lawmakers have no knowledge of God; rulers rebel against God's law; prophets speak in Baal's name, instead of in the name of the Most Holy One, *HaShem*. . . . God seems filled with disbelief, confusion, outrage:

> Does a nation change its gods
> —and these not gods at all!
> Yet my people have exchanged their Glory
> for what has no power in it . . .
> they have abandoned me,
> the fountain of living water,
> only to dig cisterns for themselves,
> leaky cisterns that hold no water. (Jer 2:13)

By bestowing free will and by choosing an unfaithful nation, God has set Godself up for rejection, allowing the Divine Self appear ridiculous. Israel's heart is divided (Hos 10:2); the people call on Baal, turning their backs on the One to whom they are bound by the Covenant. Instead of relying on God, they turn to foreign powers such as Egypt and Assyria. Instead of offering God loving obedience, they can only offer holocausts and libations empty of meaning. Instead of paying God homage, they scorn God and make idols for themselves out of their own silver and gold. But, protests God through the prophetic voice, "A workman made the thing, this cannot be God!" (Hos 8:6).

This pathos is even more tangible in the Book of Hosea. The relationship between the prophet and his unfaithful wife mirrors God's relationship with Israel. Just as Hosea is the loving and forgiving husband of Gomer, a prostitute, so, too, God is the faithful spouse of Israel whose apostasy is harlotry. What a ridiculous alliance, we might say to ourselves; could not God have found a more suitable partner? Here marriage becomes the symbolism through which we can approach God's sufferings over the iniquities of Israel. Hosea's own marriage experience, however, goes deeper than the symbolic: his personal fate is nothing less than "a mirror of the divine pathos," a parody of the Sacred Marriage, and his sorrow echoes "the sorrow of God."[12] In his own life, Hosea lives what God experiences in relationship to

Israel; his marriage educates him "in the understanding of divine sensibility."[13]

Dennis McCarthy points out that Israel not only turned to the cult of the fertility gods of Canaan, but also contaminated the worship of God with Baalism: "He (Hosea) understandably characterized this religion as harlotry. Israel had forsaken its true lover to give itself over to the Baals."[14] Moreover, the sexual imagery is not merely figurative, for the cults of Baal included "grossest sexual abuses, which were not forgotten in the characterization of Israel's attitude as harlotry."[15] Ironically, Hosea's central complaint is that Israel does not know God. Knowing, in most Semitic languages, "signifies sexual union as well as mental and spiritual activity."[16] Israel's sin is therefore compounded by the fact that it is incapable of intimate relationship with God, even while it engages in acts of ritual prostitution.

As though the heart-wrenching grief over a flawed creation and an unfaithful people were not enough, God sets up the Divine Self for further abuse and disappointment, for further folly. The Incarnation is God's decision to enter the world as a powerless participant—as one who will transform the created order, not through the might of armies, not through the intervention of throngs of angels, but through Divine surrender. The extent of this foolishness involves nothing less than placing the Divine Self in the cruel grasp of very foolish hands:

> God does not become an ideal, so that man achieves community with him through constant striving. He humbles himself and takes upon himself the eternal death of the godless and forsaken so that all the godless and forsaken can experience communion with him.[17]

The Incarnation leads us into the place of pathos—that place where God suffers pain, rejection, and indignity. But this pathos is not just for the sake of suffering in solidarity with humanity; rather, it is the supreme act of generosity whereby God invites all of us foolish, fallen ones to share in the divine nature, for as Athanasius states, "God became human in order that human beings might become God."[18] By participating in our sufferings, God raises human anguish to the sphere of divine activity; as a result, in human suffering we not only encounter God but can become God-like. No condition is too wretched or too hopeless; nobody is excluded from this process of "divinization" through pain.

The Incarnation also reveals a God of humility. Varillon, basing his premise on the fact that with God one cannot separate act and being, writes, "The Incarnation is an act of humility because God is a being of humility"; the author of creation becomes "of earth" (*humus*) for the sake of love.[19] Because of God's humility, the divine breath once again animates humankind, transforming clumsy clods into things of beauty made in the divine image. Through the Incarnation, human flesh is delivered from dust and decay to become the very temple in which God resides; through the Incarnation, in the person of the Divine Child, God becomes the promise that we will never again be left orphaned. But the drama of the Incarnation cannot be separated from the drama of the Passion; birth and death, as part of the human condition, are God's condition in Jesus. As Leo Lefebure writes, "The very notion of putting to death the author of life seems absurd. Yet the drama of the crucifixion is that the author of life enters into death and death itself is transformed."[20]

And yet, supremely foolish as it was, the birth of Christ, together with all the circumstances surrounding this birth, was only the beginning of God's foolishness as exemplified in the life of Christ. Jürgen Moltmann sums this up succinctly: "Jesus was folly to the wise, a scandal to the devout and a disturber of the peace in the eyes of the mighty. That is why he was crucified."[21] In Jesus, God's "foolishness" is fully enfleshed; in Jesus, God's wisdom fully manifests itself; in Jesus, the pathos of God is visible, tangible—and completely incomprehensible. . . . Jesus is the God-Archetype in all its holiness and in all its vulnerability:

> For God so loved the world
> that God sent into the world

God's only Son
that we could have life
through him. . . . . (1 Jn 3:16–17)

The Foolishness of Jesus' Actions

The Infancy Narratives
Written at a later date than the stories of the Passion or
accounts of Jesus' ministry, the legendary material surrounding the events of Jesus' birth is more important than its
length suggests.[22] In *The Birth of the Messiah,* Raymond Brown
explains the significance of these narratives:

> For orthodox Christians they have helped to shape
> the central doctrine of Jesus God and man. On the
> one hand they leave no doubt that Jesus was the
> Son of God from the moment of his conception; on
> the other hand the portrayal of physical birth (plus
> the Lucan references to the manger) has under-
> lined the true humanity of Jesus' origins.[23]

But if the stories surrounding Jesus' birth have been
shaped by post-resurrection reflection on the meaning of his
life and death, then they must also be infused with the spirit
of comedy—that is, the knowledge that all will be well—for
the Evangelists knew "the happy ending." Replete with
archetypal elements, the stories can, of course, as scripture
scholars have suggested, be read as a microcosmic passion
play: there are epiphany moments, fear and resistance from
the establishment, plots to kill the child, the massacre of the
Innocents, the flight into Egypt. . . . At the same time, however, there are moments of the absurd, of the surreal.

Take, for example, the Annunciation. Like the miraculous
conception stories of heroes from antiquity, the story of Jesus'
conception stretches one's sense of what is probable and possible. A peasant girl agrees to bear "the son of the Most High"
(Lk 1:32) and her fiancé, an upright man of little imagination,
assumes she has been unfaithful. Then, this same practical
man, encountering an angel in a dream, completely

reassesses the situation, agreeing to take on both mother and child, regardless of the danger and inconvenience. How seriously we read this story! How dull it becomes when our proclamation is flat and factual because we miss the humor. John the Baptist turns somersaults in his mother's womb, but we listen to the text as though it were an excerpt from a history book, rather than the living Word of God. Perhaps we fear that we, like Zechariah, might be struck dumb for responding inappropriately to God's Good News. Zechariah's problem, however, is not laughter but disbelief. In the following poem, I try to capture something of God's "sense of humor" in dealing with Zechariah:

Apophatic

Old Zeck was alone when it happened:
chosen by lot, he hunched over the brazier,
muttering before the Holy Place
in his thin, age-cracked voice,
when the angel popped into view
and rudely interrupted.

Outside, the congregation prayed,
hoping their words would rise
like the sweet-smelling incense
burning within.
Zeck trembled,
distraught at the disturbance,
but the angel persisted in absurdity,
promising a son, an infant prophet
to bring joy to the geriatric pair.
Skeptical but restrained, Zechariah
followed sacred tradition
by demanding a sign,
and mighty Gabriel,
burning bright at the right side
of the altar, silenced him.[24]

The infancy narratives are filled with absurdity. One would imagine that a Divine Child would be born in the most elevated of circumstances, surrounded by pomp and pageantry, by the symbols of wealth and power; such a child would not only be attended by an entourage of loyal dignitaries, but would also have rows of bodyguards. Instead, Jesus was born into illegitimacy, poverty, and exile. Not only could Mary have been stoned to death for conceiving him out of wedlock, but both mother and child could have perished in the cold of night for want of shelter. Then, having survived the odds, the family had to flee Herod's destructive plans and head for Egypt, that land where generations before, the Hebrew people had been kept in bondage. Events such as these point to the birth of a Holy Fool, not to the birth of some great king or divinity.

Traditionally, however, the births of great mythical and historical heroes are frequently surrounded by amazing events, threats to the child's life and some degree of absurdity. In an original inscription, Sargon I, King of Babylon, makes the following claim:

> My mother was a vestal, my father I knew not. . . .
> In a hidden place she brought me forth. She laid
> me in a vessel made of reeds, closed my door with
> pitch, and dropped me into the river, which did
> not drown me. The river carried me to Akki, the
> water carrier. Akki the water carrier lifted me up in
> the kindness of his heart. Akki the water carrier
> raised me as his own son. . . .[25]

This, the oldest of hero legends (c. 2,800 B.C.E.), bears a striking similarity to the Moses story and to the birth of Karna, found in the Hindu epic, *The Mahabharata*. In this account, Pritha, the virgin princess, gave birth to the son of the sun god, Surya. Upon seeing that the child was adorned with golden ear ornaments and with an unbreakable coat of mail, she placed him in a basket of rushes which she set upon the waters of the river Acva. Eventually, the basket reached the Ganges where it was discovered by a charioteer and his wife who raised the child.[26]

There are countless other stories of miraculous births and infancies. Oedipus and Paris were both exposed at birth on account of dire prophecies; Romulus and Remus were raised by a she-wolf; the illegitimate Gilgamesh, tossed at birth from an acropolis where his royal mother was imprisoned, was saved by an eagle; Athena was born from the head of Zeus; the Buddha, born from his mother's side, was immediately able to speak and walk. . . . Just as these stories stretch the bounds of the probable, evoking wonder and laughter—the laughter of amazement and relief—so, too, the drama surrounding Jesus' birth has comic potential. At the same time, it is a quintessentially human story, one filled with cries and pain and blood, with the stuff of humankind.

When my children were in primary school and still had an intuitive sense of the numinous, they would use plush puppets to stage wonderfully dramatic events. One year, their "Christmas Show" was side-splittingly funny. Without any inhibitions, they cast their characters more according to convenience than according to any external resemblance the characters might bear to biblical personages. Jesus, for example, was a tattered yellow chicken; Mary was a pink kitten whose head was almost detached from its shoulders; Joseph was a brown and white dog with a lovesick expression; Gabriel appeared in the form of a red rooster while Herod was a voracious-looking wolf—well-cast, in retrospect.

At the Annunciation scene, Gabriel manifested himself on cue and informed Mary that she was pregnant. "I know that, you silly!" replied Mary. After that auspicious moment, there was no containing the laughter. Inn keepers slammed doors noisily and with expletives; the baby threatened to appear too early and then, following his birth and the immediate arrival of the magi, insisted upon opening the gifts that were supposed to wait for Christmas, causing Mary to box his ears. Unable to correct either Peter or Alexia for their seeming irreverence, I gave up the effort and yielded to laughter. At seven and five years old respectively, they had, perhaps, drawn nearer to the comic essence of the Christmas story than most Christians.

The infancy narratives confront us with the reality that God's ways are not our ways and that apparent folly can be wisdom. The magi, for example, leave the comfort and safety of home to do the ridiculous, that is, to follow a star across the cold and dangerous desert in the hopes that it will lead them to the Divine Child. They are not sure what they will find, nor what they will do once they have reached their goal; nor do they calculate what it will be like to make the return journey. For their part, the shepherds, overcoming their terror at the angelic vision, abandon their sheep to the fields and hurry to find the sign of signs. And what do magi and shepherds find? A child, born in a stable, lying in a manger—the sign of Emmanuel, the sign that God is indeed with us, a sign that will be rejected. Those who are wise by the world's standards—the scheming trickster Herod and his advisors—are the ones who plot and calculate, eager to destroy all that opposes them. They place safety above truth, the status quo above transformation, status and wealth above goodness of heart. And so the Star of Jacob, shining in the glory of straw, is a sign of comic reversal pointing to the madness of the wise and to the wisdom of fools. As Simeon prophesies, the newborn babe "is destined for the fall and for the rising of many in Israel" and the child's own mother will be pierced by grief (Lk 2:34). In the time of sorrow, only those who bend their knees before the manger will share in God's redeeming laughter.

The one story of Jesus' later childhood which has become part of the accepted canon of Christian Scriptures—the story of Jesus among the doctors of the law—is also a story of folly and reversals (Lk 2:41–50). Who is foolish? We might ask ourselves: the parents who search frantically for the child who is not really lost, or the child who is seemingly oblivious to his parents' panic? The parents who, upon finding the child, are not impressed by his conversations with the experts on the law, or the experts who do not seem to have considered that the young prodigy's parents might be looking for him? The mother who embarrasses her pre-adolescent son in front of a group of adult males, or the son who responds to her concerns with a cryptic reference to his divine parent—words reminiscent of Mark: "'Who are my mother and my brothers?' And looking around at those sitting in a circle about him, he said, 'Here are my mother and my brothers. Anyone who does the will of God, that person is my brother and sister and mother'" (Mk 3:3–35).

Later we will see that in Mark's Gospel, the adult Jesus is surrounded by a mesmerized circle of listeners who wonder at the source of his wisdom, just as the elders in Luke's Gospel "were astounded at his intelligence and his replies" (Lk 2:41–50). In both texts, Jesus' relatives fail to understand what he is about, let alone what he is saying. Carroll Stuhlmueller observes that it is "highly improbable that Mary appreciated the divine sonship of her son at this time."[27] Mark, in fact, tells us that when Jesus began his ministry, his family "set out to take charge of him, convinced that he was out of his mind" (Mk 3:21). The Lucan story thus sets the stage for future conflicts with family and establishment: the Wonder Child and the Fool Child are one, and the Fool Child's relatives, dismissing him as a lunatic, are themselves guilty of folly—of the inability to see beyond the surface of things. One can imagine that among the "doctors of the law" there must be those who are quite relieved when the child finally "goes home."

The Good News which we discover in the infancy narratives does not evoke the laughter of mockery or the laughter of the burlesque; rather, as in the passion narratives, it unleashes all the pent-up emotions which have previously driven us to distraction. The Good News that God's dream will prevail in spite of dreadful opposition allows us to laugh in the face of fear, disappointment, anxiety, seemingly insurmountable obstacles, and even death itself. "Comedy," writes Louis Kronenberger in *The Thread of Laughter*, "is not just a happy as opposed to unhappy ending, but a way of surveying life so that happy endings must prevail."[28] We laugh because we know that God's word will be the final word; we laugh because we are neither the victims of tragic fate nor the pawns in some impersonal cosmic game. To approach the comic dimensions of the Gospels with laughter, then, seems an appropriate response to God's actions in the world—and the infancy narratives set the stage for this.

The Embarrassing Baptism

Just as the accounts of Jesus' infancy immerse us in the unexpected, surprising us with reversals and absurd twists, so the very way in which Jesus inaugurated his public ministry was calculated to shock. As in the infancy narratives, there are none of the usual signs of power and privilege at play. Instead, each of the Synoptics records that Jesus' ministry began not with triumphant fanfare but with a striking moment of reversal: the sinless Lamb of God submitted to "a baptism of repentance for the remission of sins" (Lk 3:4). According to Carroll Stuhlmueller, Jesus' baptism by John was an embarrassment to the early church and was gradually edited from the gospel accounts:

> Mk (1:9) clearly states that Jesus was actually baptized by John; Mt (3:13–15) tones it down by saying that Jesus presented himself to be baptized; Lk removes all mention of the Baptist's name and directs attention away from the baptism; Jn gives no account whatsoever of Jesus' baptism.[29]

The baptism of Jesus was problematic for the early church because baptism implied sinfulness and the need for forgiveness. But Jesus—as Holy Fool—did not set himself above the human condition. The one who would be proclaimed as *Kyrios* humbled himself in the waters of repentance as though he, too, were in need of cleansing and public atonement. Paul, underscores this abasement:

> Though he was in the form of God
> he did not deem equality with God
> something to be grasped at.
> Rather, he emptied himself
> and took the form of a slave,
> being born in human likeness. (Phil 2:6–7)

As we will see later, the Holy Fool is one who, taking the cue from the gospel Jesus, is immersed in the human condition, not separate from it; in fact, the feigning of both madness and sinfulness was characteristic of early Fools for

Christ who used such strategies as exercises in humility. At the same time, however, the Holy Fool—as Jesus' Temptation in the Wilderness demonstrates—is capable of being tempted without succumbing to the glamour of evil. In short, the Holy Fool, accepting his or her humanity, lives a life of holiness without laying public claim to superiority or to special privilege.

Rejection in Nazareth

The beginning of the Galilean ministry is also replete with the Holy Fool motif. In Nazareth, Jesus astonished his listeners:

> "Where did the man get this wisdom and these miraculous powers? This is the carpenter's son, surely? Is not his mother the woman called Mary, and his brothers James and Joseph and Simon and Jude? His sisters, too, are they not all here with us? So where did the man get it all?" And they would not accept him. (Mt 13:54–56)

In the Lucan version, as long as his words were polite and gracious, Jesus stood in the favor of his synagogue audience. But like the astute court jester of the medieval world, he knew that the people's tolerance could be shattered as easily as their attention. Responding to their amazement—"This is Joseph's son, surely?"—he reminded them how the prophets were consistently rejected by their own people. He then proceeded to point out that Elijah was not sent to a widow in Israel, but to a Sidonian widow of Zarepath; moreover, he added, the only leper in Israel to be cured by Elisha was the Syrian, Naaman (Lk 4:25–27). It was almost as though he goaded the townsfolk into a negative reaction. Soon, the "home boy made good" was hustled out of town, narrowly escaping being hurled over a cliff. Like many a truth-telling fool, Jesus almost lost his life for speaking that which nobody wanted to hear.

Ironically, in spite of all the signs and wonders recorded in the infancy narratives and in the accounts of his ministry, Jesus' true identity was concealed from his family, friends and neighbors; instead, it was the hordes of demons who trembled at his coming and who were able to name him as the Holy One of God (Mk 1:25). Though Jesus did the "spectacular"—changing water into wine, multiplying loaves and fishes, walking on water, calming storms—it was the demons who howled, "You are the Son of God," begging him to leave them (Lk 4:41). Demons, then, can see more clearly than human beings and may have longer memories than we who try to store things in our hearts. Those closest to him seemed to suffer from amnesia.

Or was it a matter of Jesus being "too much" for those around him? In the delightful story of the Gerasene demoniac (Mk 5:1–20), Jesus can be identified more with the magician archetype than with the fool, but there is humor behind his "magic": perhaps, in confronting the spirit of the irrational, the spirit of mental disturbance, a healer needs a strong sense of comic potential. One can imagine Jesus' imagination being gripped by the horror of the demoniac's predicament. Watching him tear off his clothes, whip up the wind with deranged dance, and set the waves crashing to the beat of mad feet, Jesus heard his howl and responded. Catching sight of swine scratching their fat haunches and snuffling restlessly in the gorse, he knew what must be done. His lips curved slightly at the corners, his eyes twinkled with mischief and, at once, two thousand pigs charged over the cliff, into the lake, while the swineherds fled in terror. . . . And, once again, finding him "too much" for them, the townsfolk urgently implored him "to leave the neighborhood" (Mk 5:17).

Jesus in Bad Company

There is also the question of Jesus' disciples to consider. Here, again, comic reversal is at play. One would expect that a powerful messiah would at least possess common sense, an intuitive grasp of another's worth, if not omniscience. Jesus displayed none of these gifts. Rather than surrounding himself with people of good repute who would enhance his own social standing, he did the opposite; it was as though he went out of his way to look ridiculous. The rough and ready fishermen he called from their nets; the hated tax collector he summoned away from collaboration with Rome; the elitist Nathaniel who, resting under a fig tree, doubted whether any good could come from Nazareth—these were the unlikely people Jesus invited into companionship (Mk 1:16–20; Lk 5:27–28; Jn 1:45–51). Peter the coward, Thomas the doubter, James and John the social climbers, and Judas the betrayer—these very ordinary, flawed human beings, these parasites and simpletons, were the friends to whom he entrusted himself and his message.

By the world's standards Jesus was setting himself up for failure and disgrace. By the world's standards, he was an unmitigated fool. Jesus the Holy Fool surrounded himself with lesser fools—with sinners and prostitutes, as his enemies would observe, with people incapable of understanding what he was all about, let alone what was at the core of the Good News. Yet, for the most part, these sinners and fools had their hearts in the right places—which is why the story ultimately has the proverbial happy ending. Perhaps when all is said and done, only the Holiest of Fools can look beyond imperfection and see what is in another's heart. Perhaps, when all is said and done, only one who is complete in himself can generously reach out to raise the weak and infirm beyond their own pathetic limits.

The very company Jesus kept—that motley crowd of undesirables—became the sacrament of his inclusivity. The sinners with whom he associated became signs of how far the human heart must stretch in acceptance and forgiveness. Those with disabilities and contagious diseases became symbols of how infinitely "touchable" each person is, regardless of society's taboos. By eating with society's outcasts, Jesus overturned the social conventions of table fellowship; by telling parables in which people off the streets—the poor, the lame, the blind , the maimed—are to be invited to the banquet, he caused even greater scandal. The implication was that one could have all "classes, sexes, ranks, and grades all mixed up together."[30]

But Jesus' table fellowship with the marginalized had a deeper message than inclusivity; the meals he shared with the outcasts of society were an expression of both his message and his mission:

> In Judaism, fellowship at table had the special meaning of fellowship in the sight of God . . . every meal is a sign of the coming eschatological meal and the eschatological fellowship with God.[31]

Jesus caused scandal because his table fellowship implied that sinners had a place in God's coming reign. Tax collectors and those who had become "unclean" by breaking religious laws or following disreputable professions frequented the tables at which he ate, giving rise to the question, "Why does your master eat with tax collectors and sinners?" (Mt 9:11). In fact, we learn in Mark 2:16, that "there were many of them among his followers," and we can assume, therefore, that they frequently ate together. No doubt, the "certain women" among his disciples "who had been cured of evil spirits and ailments" also feasted with him; they included "Mary surnamed the Magdalene, from whom seven demons had gone out, Joanna the wife of Herod's steward, Chuza, Susanna, and several others who provided for them out of their own resources" (Lk 8:1–3). Each meal eaten with outcasts was therefore a parody of the eschatological banquet, a mockery of traditional expectations. It was as though the King of Fools had surrounded himself with lesser fools to undermine the very sanctity of all that eating and feasting represented.

Jesus' Folly and Conventional Wisdom

To call Christ "a fool" is not only to assign him a share in the foolishness of God, but also to acknowledge that his sufferings actually originated in this divine foolishness. In other words, if Jesus' attitudes, words, and actions had been in line with the world's wisdom rather than with God's wisdom, he might have come to a very different end. True, his teachings may not have been preserved in the form we know them today, but he might possibly have avoided the humiliation of the cross and the desertion of his followers. Had Jesus aligned himself with conventional wisdom, then the establishment would have embraced him as one of its own and that would have been the end of the story. His teachings, in fact, would simply have reiterated what the people already knew and the church would have become the custodian of accepted beliefs and behavioral norms.

But Jesus' wisdom was not the wisdom of the world. Instead of re-enforcing the status quo, he insisted upon a more penetrating look at law and tradition and, over and over again, he exposed the limitations of a piety based on measurable practices alone. As Marcus Borg points out, "Conventional wisdom is not to be identified with any particular tradition; it is pervasive in all traditions."[32] In both its secular and religious manifestations, conventional wisdom is based on the assumption that certain behaviors merit certain rewards and punishments; by upholding the central values of the establishment, one is guaranteed status, privilege, and security. God, understood as lawgiver and judge, legitimizes conventional wisdom in its religious form, just as the secular powers uphold the values of family, wealth, honor, and purity.[33]

For Jesus, however, the literal observance of rules said little about the disposition of the human heart or about God's heart, for that matter. The path he offered was an invitation to see God as "gracious and womb-like rather than as the source and enforcer of the requirements, boundaries and divisions of conventional wisdom."[34] It was not that he had come to overthrow the Law—in fact, he strongly denied this when he said, "Do not imagine that I have come to abolish the Law or the Prophets. I have come not to abolish them but to complete them" (Mt 5:17–18). Rather, he consistently pointed to love of God and neighbor as the fulfillment of one's religious obligations and as the way of deepening one's relationship with God. As an observant Jew, Jesus knew that these mandates from the Torah, that is, from Deuteronomy 6:4–6 and from Leviticus 19:18, formed the heart of the Law; for many, however, the Law was an end in itself, a means of self-justification, an excuse to avoid ambiguity and uncertainty.

Jesus and Shabbat

Jesus' statements about the Sabbath or *Shabbat* reflect his approach to the Law in general; moreover, as Heschel points out, Shabbat is the "idea that expresses what is most characteristic of Judaism."[35] How Jesus observed Shabbat, then, reflects his attitudes towards Judaism. As is still true of Jewish practice today, the observance of Shabbat created a hallowed time to focus on God and on family. In imitation of God's creative action—or, we might say, in imitation of God's creative restraint following six days of labor—Jews refrained from work on the seventh day. This day became a time set apart from the distractions and cares of daily life. Greeted like a new bride, the day was about a new state of being, about *becoming* a new kind of creation; it was not a day driven by the demands of the external world, but one with a spiritual orientation, a time of rest, and refreshment. To keep Shabbat was both to obey God's commandment and to receive a gift—the gift of oneself as an image of the God who called each individual into a covenant of intimacy: "What is the Sabbath? The presence of eternity, a moment of majesty, the radiance of joy. The soul is enhanced, time is a delight, and inwardness a supreme reward."[36] In observant Jewish homes today, the ritual Friday night welcoming of Shabbat with the lighting of candles and the blessing of light indicates the change of consciousness this sacred time requires; moreover, the custom of savoring fragrant spices at the end of Shabbat is an invitation to allow the fragrance of sacred time to linger with each family, even after sundown on Saturday.

It would be possible to read the Gospels superficially and to assume that Jesus deliberately flaunted the conventions of Shabbat for the sake of sensationalism or to provoke the religious authorities in a foolhardy way. However, in allowing his disciples to pick corn on Shabbat and in healing the afflicted on Shabbat—as for example, the man with the withered hand and the woman who had been bent double for eighteen years, Jesus was not showing disrespect for Shabbat (Lk 6:1–5; 6:6–11; 13:10–13). His words and actions can by no means be equated with medieval mockery of the sacred liturgy or with a clown's debunking of the sacred through obscene words and gestures, or with a scoffer's irreverence. In reality, his seeming disregard for Shabbat points to his deep reverence for God's gift of a time set apart for worship and reintegration; his "folly" was nothing less than an expression of piety.

Through his words and actions, Jesus critiqued a mindset in which the hallowing of time had been reduced to a legal requirement. In Luke 13, in fact, the synagogue official was outraged that the sick and afflicted would have the audacity to present themselves for healing: "There are six days," he said, "when work is to be done. Come and be healed on one of those days and not on the Sabbath" (Lk 13:14–15). Instead of rejoicing that one who had been physically oppressed for so many years had found liberation, instead of joining her in praising God, this official complained about the violation of the Law. He failed to remember an important stipulation about Shabbat—that is, that human necessity always takes precedence over law and that the saving of a human life is more important than strict observance.

Jesus' response was direct:

> "Hypocrites!" he said. "Is there one of you who does not untie his ox or his donkey from the manger on the Sabbath and take it out for watering? And this woman, a daughter of Abraham whom Satan has bound these eighteen years—was it not right to untie her bonds on the Sabbath day?" (Lk 13:15–17)

Clearly, Jesus saw Shabbat as a sign of liberation, as a way of remembering the Exodus experience. To observe Shabbat means to stand before God in freedom, and to be free means to be spiritually unshackled. As the member of a liberated people, it stands to reason that one *could* do good on Shabbat; in fact, that one *should* do it when the occasion arises. To miss this point not only indicated a basic lack of religious imagination, but also a failure of compassion:

> "If any one of you here had only one sheep and it fell down a hole on the Sabbath day, would he not get hold of it and lift it out? Now a person is far more important than a sheep, so it follows that it is permitted to do good on the Sabbath day." Then he said to the man, "stretch out your hand." He stretched it out and his hand was better, as sound as the other one. (Mt 12:11–14)

To say that Jesus "broke the Sabbath," then, or to look at his words and actions as willful folly is a distortion. Because of his intimate relationship with God, he cherished Shabbat as a time of spiritual and physical renewal, as a sign of the Covenant. For him, true observance of Shabbat facilitated entry onto God's holy mountain, into God's house of prayer (Is 56:1–8). More than anyone else, he recognized that when one avoided trampling Shabbat one could find happiness in God and delight in God's presence (Is 58:13–14).

At the same time, there is a certain folly at play here—the folly of self-abandonment and existential risk. While Jesus knew he was not violating Shabbat, even the appearance of violation was enough to incur the wrath of the establishment and the possibility of the death penalty. Jeremiah 17:21 states: "As you value your lives, on no account carry a burden on Shabbat day or bring it through the gates of Jerusalem." Jesus would have been aware of biblical prohibitions against breaking Shabbat, as well as of the precedents for putting to death willful offenders—as for example, the man caught gathering wood on the Sabbath while the people of Israel were in the desert (Num 15:32–36). Stoned to death outside the camp, this unfortunate man became a warning of the dire consequences of not observing Shabbat rest. Jesus, by flirting with meaning and by pointing beyond mere tradition, opened himself up to misinterpretation—and to being condemned as a blasphemer. Acting out of the wisdom of God, he allowed himself to appear a sacrilegious fool.

Jesus and Torah

To view Jesus' attitude towards legalism as a critique of Judaism would be a travesty. It was out of his love for his God and for his tradition that he demonstrated the possibility of a deeper entry into Shabbat—a form of observance which restored dignity and hope to those who were marginalized, thereby honoring God's Holy Name. Similarly, his comments to the religious leaders of his day regarding their hypocrisy and vanity have general application, even if they originated in a Jewish context (Mt 23:1–12). To wear broader phylacteries and longer tassels, to take places of honor at banquets and front seats in synagogues all have their equivalents in other faith traditions, *including* Christianity. His indictment of the scribes and Pharisees in Matthew 23 is an indictment of all who use external observance as a substitute for love; it is a critique of those who scrupulously pay their tithes but neglect the weightier concerns of justice and mercy. Jesus' agenda, then, was to shatter the idol of religious orthopraxy and to demonstrate that there was something of greater importance at stake. Like the court jester, he used shock tactics to make his message clear when words alone would have escaped notice; and, like the court jester, he stood to lose his life for saying what others would consider outrageous—that is, the truth. There was no way in which Jesus intended to debunk the Law. In fact, he spoke about *fulfilling* the Law:

> "Do not imagine that I have come to abolish the Law or the Prophets. I have come not to abolish but to complete them. I tell you solemnly, till heaven and earth disappear, not one dot, not one little stroke, shall disappear from the Law until its purpose is achieved." (Mt 5:17–19)

In spirit, the Law is an avenue to freedom. Its 613 requirements and prohibitions are not so much obligations as signs of the covenant between God and people; when followed with an open mind and open heart, the Law is a path of life, a way of living with integrity in God's presence. Heschel sees

Torah as an antidote to evil, a safeguard against our worst inclinations; a commandment or *mitzvah*, then, is a response to God's will, an act of obedience, "a prayer in the form of a deed."[37] Similarly, Psalm 119 establishes the beauty of the Law, demonstrating that those who cherish God's word find strength, wisdom, consolation and delight:

> 73 Your hands shaped me;
> inspired me to learn your wisdom.
>
> 74 The just see me and rejoice,
> because I hope in your word.
>
> 75 How right your judgments, Lord,
> how wisely you humble me.
>
> 76 Comfort me with your love,
> just as you promised.
>
> 77 Shower my life with tenderness,
> for I delight in your law.
>
> 78 Shame the proud who slander me,
> I ponder your decrees.
>
> 79 Gather your faithful ones
> to acknowledge your rule.
>
> 80 Keep me true to your precepts,
> free of all shame. (Ps 119:73–80)

The sentiments expressed in this psalm have nothing to do with the heavy burdens which Jesus accused the religious establishment of placing upon the people (Mt 3:4–5); on the contrary, Psalm 119 is grounded in genuine gratitude for a way of life which makes every day Shabbat and every Shabbat an experience of dwelling in the Temple which is beyond time and space. When Jesus proclaimed the Good News, he sought to liberate those who had reduced religious life to rote practice, empty words and meaningless legalism. God's reign, he asserted, is more than an eschatological reality but is right here and now for all those who are willing to find it.

Jesus and the Temple

The interplay of divine wisdom with seeming folly is strikingly demonstrated in the scriptural accounts of Jesus' expulsion of merchants and buyers from the Temple.[38] The Temple, like Shabbat, was so sacred in Judaism that even the hint of violation would create scandal. We have seen that Jesus—seeming to lack all prudence—turned upside down the values of his culture. This is especially true of his antics in the Temple, the spiritual center not only of Jerusalem but also of Judaism. His spontaneous response to the buying and selling in the Temple court was guaranteed to enrage Jews everywhere—not only those who witnessed the event, but also those who heard about it. This was comedy at its worst—comedy so dreadful that no one could laugh, in spite of the chaos and ensuing slapstick. We can imagine the tables overturned, the stacks of coins tumbling to the floor, the pigeons squawking in their cages, perhaps breaking free, the people scurrying after money. We can almost see the bewildered expressions and the gritted teeth; we can almost hear the expressions of hatred and rage. . . .

There is a tendency for scholars to view this episode in Jesus' ministry as an "eschatological act in the spirit of Mal 3:1–3," an act which fulfills the promise to the Gentiles in Isaiah 56:7: "For my house will be called a house of prayer for all the peoples."[39] While this interpretation may have validity, especially when seen in the context of the cursing of the fig tree, an indictment of spiritual impoverishment, Jesus' symbolic action in the Temple is also a statement about "right orientation" towards God (Mt 21:18–21; Mk 11:20–22). Business transactions in the court of the Gentiles were traditional and legitimate: here, money changers provided Temple currency and traders sold the animals for sacrificial offerings; these transactions, then, were a necessary part of the daily activity in the Temple. To what was Jesus reacting when he turned over tables and chairs, driving out the buyers and the sellers?

If his attitude to Shabbat is anything to go by, it would seem he was lashing out at a piety which substituted ritual for radical self-giving. Sacrifice of any kind can either express an inner generosity on the part of the one making the offering or it can become a "magical act" which dispenses the offerer from self-investment. When the symbol no longer represents self-giving but becomes a replacement for it, then it is empty of meaning. The covenant at Sinai was based on obedience: " . . . if you obey my voice and hold fast to my covenant, you of all the nations shall be my very own, for all the earth is mine. I will count you a kingdom of priests, a consecrated nation" (Ex 19: 5–6). Obedience, however, goes deeper than outward conformity. Once again, it is a question of the heart. It is not enough to be circumcised in the flesh; what is necessary is to be circumcised at heart, that is, in the place of intellect, feelings, and will, that place which represents one's whole moral nature (Jer 9:24–26). This is why Jesus praised the poverty-stricken widow who donated two small coins to the Temple treasury: because she had given from the little she had to live on, her sacrifice—in contrast to the lavish gifts of the wealthy—was truly a heart-offering made in love, trust, and obedience (Lk 21:1–4).

This brings us back to the cursing of the fig tree. Perhaps Jesus had in mind Jeremiah's vision of the two baskets of figs, one containing excellent figs, the other, inedible ones (Jer 24). The good figs represented the exiles in Babylon: "I will give them a heart to acknowledge that I am God. They shall be my people and I will be their God, for they will return to me with all their heart" (Jer 24:7). As for the bad figs, they symbolized the remnant in Jerusalem, under the leadership of Zedekiah whose hardness of heart had made him impervious to God's word; their fate would be the sword, famine, and plague (Jer 24:10).

The cursing of the fig tree in Matthew and Mark might imply that the spiritual inheritance of Israel would now be available to the Gentiles, but it was also a stark reminder that in matters of spiritual accounting, everyone's "heart" will be measured and weighed, regardless of how liturgically active one may be:

> I hate and despise your feasts,
> I take no pleasure in your solemn festivals.

> When you offer me holocausts,
> I reject your oblations,
> and refuse to look at your sacrifices of fattened cattle.
> Let me have no more of the din of your chanting,
> no more of your strumming on harps.
> But let justice flow like water,
> and integrity like an unfailing stream.
> (Amos 5:21–24)

If Jesus' statements about Shabbat and ritual worship affronted the conventional piety of his day, then his words about the Temple were even more offensive. Though the actual words about the destruction of the Temple recorded by the Evangelists may have originated with the post-resurrection community, after the fall of Jerusalem in 70 C.E., they most likely reflect Jesus' teaching elsewhere. Moreover, Mark cites an accusation against Jesus which surfaced when he stood before the Sanhedrin: "We heard him say, 'I am going to destroy this Temple made by human hands, and in three days build another, not made by human hands'" (Mk 14:58–59); a similar charge is also made in Matthew 26:61–62. False or not, the accusation suggests that Jesus may have publicly spoken about the destruction of the Temple in such a way as to cause scandal.

If Jesus actually did speak of the destruction of the Temple, then a symbolic interpretation seems warranted. Just as he challenged legalism, so, too, he would have cut through the notion of a piety confined to a cultic place. Like the prophets, before him—he stressed the need for a heart-centered response to God, emphasizing a relationship with God that was neither limited by priestly officialdom, nor by a particular location that had been designated as "holy." His conversation with the Samaritan woman in John 4 gives credence to this view. The exchange between the two began with Jesus' simple request for water. The woman, astounded at being addressed by a male Jew, found herself listening to riddles about living water and internal springs. Taking him literally, she begged for living water, only to discover there was more at stake here than she could comprehend. Jesus, like an astute jester, led her from the prosaic (a drink), to the symbolic (living water), to the present-tense prophetic (you have had five husbands), to the future-tense prophetic (the hour is coming. . . .) No doubt, as she struggled to keep up with the conversation, her mind reeled; no doubt she not only wondered about her own sanity but also about Jesus' intellectual capacity. At some point or another, she must have asked herself whether the whole encounter was a mirage brought on by the desert heat.

In response to the woman's assertion that her ancestors had worshipped on Mount Gerazim while the Jews worshipped in Jerusalem, Jesus said:

> "Believe me, woman, the hour is coming
> when you will worship God
> neither on this mountain nor in Jerusalem . . .
> The hour will come—in fact, it is here already—
> when true worshippers will worship God in spirit
> and truth: that is the kind of worshipper God
> wants." (Jn 4:21–23)

No wonder there were shock waves in response to Jesus' words about Temple worship! No wonder many felt threatened and accused him of subverting all they held precious! In speaking of the destruction of the Temple, Jesus was, in fact, declaring that the time of religious monopoly was over. True worship can neither be limited spatially nor cultically. A sacred place cannot take priority over the sanctuary of the individual worshipper; the "house" for which God longs is neither made of cedars nor of marble blocks, but a welcoming human heart. When the psalmist prays to dwell in God's house, this is not to be interpreted as the desire to move into the literal Temple, but to move into that consciousness in which God's presence is tangible (Ps 27). In this way, the individual becomes the locus of the holy, the temple of the Most High; in this way, the physical Temple becomes not only secondary but possibly even an impediment to relationship with God. After all, even holy places can be "deified," just as ritual observance or the Law can become more important than God when there is an unhealthy religiosity at play.

The implications of all this are far-reaching. If God is no longer "contained" within the Temple, then God is fully accessible to all—including Samaritans like the woman at the well. Just as she was able to put down her pitcher—a sign of her dependency upon human efforts—and to move from being enslaved by her past to proclaiming the Good News, so, too, others can be set free (Jn 4:28). In this scheme of things, there are no walls or boundaries to divide people and to create hierarchies of privilege. There are no secret rites known only to a select few upon whom the majority must depend, no mysterious words with which to invoke God's favor, no guardians of orthodoxy to oversee who can enter the Temple and who must be barred from entry. . . . Without a Temple, God is dangerously free. No longer a national icon, God is at liberty to invite all to the divine banquet, regardless of occupation, gender, status, health, ethnic background, or income. Without a Temple, nobody can be designated as clean or unclean, righteous or unrighteous.

On the surface, Jesus' behavior in the Temple could be ascribed to madness or irreverence; as we have seen, however, his sabotaging of the symbols of Temple ritual can be understood as a profound statement of God's availability to all peoples. Again, external actions represented more than they seemed: what looked like random destruction was calculated to make a point. What happened in this episode was not an expression of excess and debauchery, the mere antics of a fool but pedagogy in action. To turn over tables and chairs was to declare that the old ways of religious transaction no longer worked, that it was time for a new way of doing things. To drive out the buyers and the sellers was to demonstrate that God was not for sale in the market place. To scatter the coins and the sacrificial animals was to insist that fulfillment of the law of the heart had nothing to do with the type of currency used nor with the perfection of the sacrificial victim: all that mattered was one's desire to be present to God.

Jesus' words about worshipping in spirit and truth—whether spoken to the Samaritan woman alone or to other people in other contexts—caused outrage precisely because they shattered all notions of religious exclusivity. To suggest that the most sacred place of Judaism, the pride of Jerusalem, would be destroyed—whether symbolically or literally—was to shake every national value. The fate of the Temple, after all, was intricately connected to Jewish history: it was an institution for which national heroes had laid down their lives, a symbol of God's presence in Israel.

The mere suggestion that the Temple might be destroyed undermined the very structures of society. The Jews were understandably proud of their Temple. This is reflected in Mark 13, when a disciple expresses his sense of awe over the size of the stones and the size of the Temple (Mk 13:1). Jesus' response—that not a single stone would remain standing—must have been shocking in the extreme. Attacks on the Temple were attacks on Judaism itself; foreign powers had destroyed or desecrated the Temple at whim, and each time, this reality was accompanied by a period of political and religious oppression for the Jews. Moreover, to make matters worse, on other occasions Jesus also implied that even the most marginalized were deserving of the crumbs of Israel's spiritual legacy—and not just the crumbs, but a portion of the loaf as well, as is symbolized by the healing of the Syro-Phoenician woman's daughter (Mk 6:24–30). Without a Temple, divinity and humanity can intermingle without restraint; God can no longer be an exclusive, tribal God, safely enthroned in the Holy of Holies. . . . Ironically, it was for making exactly the same claims that Stephen was stoned to death (Acts 8:55–60).

Of course, there is nothing wrong with the Temple per se, any more than there is anything "wrong" with the Law or with the practice of observing Shabbat. Over and over again, Jesus denounced those narrow ways of thinking which stifle spiritual aliveness; instead, he proclaimed an alternative way which leads from rigidity to intimacy with God. Like the medieval court jester, he dared to unmask the limitations of the dominant consciousness of his time and to expose hypocrisy, lies, callousness and indifference for what they are. He named what he saw, without fear and without compromise. And—again like the jester—he modeled an alternative consciousness by his very behavior. Ironically—or perhaps, prophetically—the Synoptics tell us that at the moment of Jesus' death, the curtain of the Temple was rent in two.[40] Symbolically, this ripped curtain (most likely, the *katapetasma* which hung before the Holy of Holies) represents the fact that God is now accessible to all.

The Foolishness of Jesus' Teachings

The new order to which Jesus pointed demands a transformation of consciousness, a completely new way of seeing which, in turn, necessitates new ways of thinking, new ways of being. Without such a shift in consciousness, a bystander would consider Jesus' words and actions absurd; it is only by perceiving reality through a different set of lenses that one is able to understand the immense spiritual challenge they present. "Being converted does not consist in pious exercises but rather in a new mode of existing before God," writes Leonardo Boff.[41] To participate in the reign of God, then, means nothing less than undergoing "an interior revolution."

The old structures no longer work; the lies with which we surround ourselves no longer shelter us from the truth. The personae behind which we cower no longer disguise our fears, prejudices, and basic insecurities. The goals in which we invest ourselves no longer provide ultimate meaning. The treasures we have accrued no longer seem safe. Our very futures become uncertain. All is clouded in ambiguity, uncertainty, and unpredictability. How threatening all this is, and yet, as Jesus pointed out, unless we undergo a complete transformation we will not make any progress, spiritually speaking:

> "No one sews a piece of unshrunken cloth on an
> old cloak; if they do, the patch pulls away from it,
> the new from the old, and the tear gets worse. And

> nobody puts new wine into old wineskins; if they
> do, the wine will burst the skins, and the wine is
> lost and the skins, too. No! New wine, fresh skins!"
> (Mk 2:21–22)

When one is willing to change skins and let the wine flow, there is no telling what will happen. Just as the water at the marriage feast of Cana is transformed into the red wine of passion, so the colorlessness of life becomes intoxicating brilliance (Jn 2:1–2). This, as Monika Hellwig points out, may look harmless enough at first, but:

> If it were really carried out, it would cause a chain
> reaction that would shake human history from its
> very foundations, making a new heaven and a
> new earth in which former patterns of privilege
> and power and wealth would make no sense at
> all.[42]

To allow oneself to be transformed is the first step towards renewing the earth. Shifts in individual consciousness lead to shifts in global consciousness. In this way, the fate of the planet is intricately linked to the choices of each person.

The Consciousness of a Child

The quintessential foolishness of Jesus' message of conversion is not hard to identify. The radical change of heart for which he called demands nothing less than abandoning all attempts to control one's life. It is to become a little child in the archetypal sense—that child whom Wordsworth described as "trailing clouds of glory," that child yet unschooled in the ways of the world, that child still innocent enough to remember Eden and what it was like to walk with God.[43] The child is a "naive fool," one who has not yet learned to see as the world sees but, rather, as God sees. Dostoyevsky's Prince Myshkin, the protagonist in *The Idiot*, is a naive fool of this variety. His compassion, his authenticity, his truthfulness, his trusting nature all make him ill-equipped to live in Russian society—or in any society, for that matter; yet Dostoyevsky holds up this character as one who knows the human heart and who is in touch with the heart of God. The Prince is an "adult child" or a "child-like adult" who serves as a paradigm of redeemed human nature, or what it means to live out of the Christ-archetype.[44] No doubt, Jesus would have identified with this delightful character, for when asked who among them was the greatest, Jesus astonished his disciples by drawing a child close to him: "Anyone who welcomes this little child in my name welcomes me; and anyone who welcomes me, welcomes the one who sent me. For the least among you all, that is the one who is great" (Lk 9:46–48).

The status accorded children varies from culture to culture. Here in the West, we have either held that "children should be seen and not heard," completely overlooking the possibility that they may have something of value to contribute, or else we have treated them as "mini-adults," hurrying their growth with designer clothes and adult forms of entertainment, as though their very childishness is problematic. Just as the medieval jester brought gifts of spontaneity, authenticity, and aliveness to the court, so the child in his or her "natural state" can be equally delightful—until these innate qualities are schooled away. Instead of learning from our children, we tend to suppress them. We may see them as cute, we may enjoy indulging them, we may bully them into conforming to our expectations, but we seldom accept them for who they are. Just as the rulers of the court literally reigned in their fools, sometimes chaining them up in an effort to control their antics, so Western society reigns in the youngest and most vulnerable amongst us.

The archetypal child, however, is that child who has not yet been hardened by adult example. In her lack of sophistication, she delights in the world around her, praising God for all creatures great and small; for snakes and birds, wild beasts and tame; for mountains, hills, fruit trees and cedars; for fire and hail, snow and mist, storms and winds. . . . Left to her own perceptions, the child does not dichotomize; for her, all things are good. Incapable of making distinctions between people on the basis of creed, color, gender or status, she accepts all as her equals, seeing sameness rather than otherness. Because she is content, she neither grasps at privilege nor begrudges others their good fortune. Trusting in the goodness of the universe, she does not worry over the future or fret over situations she cannot change; nor does she allow grudges and resentments to color her way of thinking. Free to be herself, she is not ashamed of tears or of showing emotions. Instead, she is herself at all times, completely free from any need to impress others.

This child, then, is a symbol of the new order, a symbol of blessedness. When his disciples tried to block small children from getting close to him, Jesus' response was to say, "'Let the little children come to me, and do not stop them; for it is to such as these that the kingdom of heaven belongs'" (Lk 18:16–17). In fact, unless one becomes like a little child that person will not enter God's reign. In his discourse with Nicodemus, Jesus spoke of the need to be "born again" (Jn 3). Nicodemus, of course, took his words literally and therefore could make no sense of them. What Jesus was referring to, however, was the need to recover those Wordsworthian clouds of glory to which most of us are oblivious once we reach adulthood. To be "born from above" apparently has nothing to do with returning to the womb and everything to do with recovering a way of seeing that is unsullied by egotism, hatred and despair.

This way of seeing is grounded in seeming absurdity. In *The Religions of Man,* Huston Smith presents several examples of the Zen outlook, explaining that it is like "stepping through Alice's looking glass. One finds oneself in a topsy-turvy wonderland in which everything seems quite mad."[45] Smith describes how different masters, when asked to explain the meaning of Zen, resort to such techniques as lifting one finger, or kicking a ball, or slapping the inquirer in the face.[46] He writes, "A novice who makes a respectful allusion to the Buddha is ordered to rinse his mouth out and never utter that dirty word again," and narrates how a monk, seeking instruction from a master, is simply told to wash his breakfast bowl that he might be brought to an understanding of Zen.[47] Smith concludes:

> What goes on here? Is it possible to make any sense out of what at first blush looks like nothing so much as some sort of transolympian horseplay? Can they possibly be serious in this kind of spiritual doubletalk or are they simply pulling our leg? The answer is that though they are never solemn, they are completely serious. . . . Zen is not interested in theories about enlightenment; it wants to plunge its practitioners into enlightenment itself. The shouts, the buffets, the reprimands that figure in Zen training have nothing to do with ill will. They are designed to help the student crash the word barrier; to startle his (sic) mind out of conventional sluggishness into the heightened, more alert perception that will lead to enlightenment.[48]

While—as far as we know—shouts, buffets, and practical jokes were not characteristic of Jesus' pedagogical style, much of his teaching, like Zen, "crashes" our assumptions about life. The folly to which Jesus invites us—the folly of a child—is not the folly of mere slapstick, but the very foolishness of God. It is a foolishness which recommends ambiguity over certainty, innocence over cunning, honesty over deception, humility over pride, simplicity over complexity, living from day to day instead of planning, plotting, and hoarding. In order to help his audience to consider these foolish possibilities, Jesus therefore resorted to outrageous tactics, such as the Cleansing of the Temple.[49]

In many ways, his tactics were thoroughly Jewish. Like many a wise rabbi, he used devices of the unexpected—comic reversal, ironic twists, riddles, and outrageous endings. Speaking of "Jewish salt," Nathan Ausubel explains how wit and irony are products of a history of persecution, "an affirmative and defiant answer to the world's cruelties"; this wit does not merely offer a trenchant commentary on life, but also serves "as a corrective, as a mellowing agent. . . ."[50]

Thus the parables Jesus spun and the ethical standards he presented force us to confront a higher good than self-preservation or than the "upwardly mobile" path. On the surface, many of his teachings were childishly absurd—nonsensical, if you will—but like the Zen master, his wisdom ran deeper than conventional wisdom, and his hidden purpose was to lead his listeners to both enlightenment and compassion.

The Sermon on the Mount

Traditionally, the Sermon on the Mount—and especially the Beatitudes—is regarded as the crown of Jesus' teaching. Just as Moses received the Law on Mount Sinai, so Jesus delivered his law on a hillside, but there are significant differences between the two events; in fact, one could claim that Matthew 5–7 is actually a parody of Exodus 19–34. In the first place, while Moses took the Law from on high down to the people who had been purifying themselves for three days in anticipation of the event, Jesus sat among the people. The drama of Sinai with its flashes of lightning, peals of thunder, and loud trumpet blasts finds its parallel in the teachings of a gentle rabbi who was fully accessible to his followers. Whereas the people in Exodus 19 stood at the foot of Mount Sinai, trembling in terror for their lives as God manifested Godself in fire and smoke, the people surrounding Jesus were amazed at his teaching abilities, for "he taught them as one having authority, and not as their scribes"(Mt 7:28). The Exodus event is an impressive theophany; what happens on the humble hillside is, comparatively speaking, within the realm of the ordinary, though the teachings of Jesus, while not necessarily original, are far from commonplace.

Jesus spoke not from tablets of stone but from the tablet of his heart; what he had to say was clear to those with ears to hear but incomprehensible to those who resisted it. Ausubel, in his chapter on "Holy Men," finds Jesus' emphases to be rabbinic in character: "almost all of the beatitudes in the Sermon on the Mount find their counterparts in the Talmudic literature of that period, almost to the very expressions."[51] In many ways, the Sermon on the Mount could be described as a summary of the whole Torah, an expansion of the Golden Rule. Rabbi Hillel, who lived in Jerusalem in the time of King Herod, is accredited with having been the originator of this Golden Rule: "Do not unto others what you do not wish that others do unto you. That is the whole Torah. Everything else is only commentary."[52] Jesus, then, spoke from within his tradition, pointing to the essence of Torah rather than to external observances. In another selection entitled, "Why Jerusalem was Destroyed," Ausubel writes that certain sages in Israel claimed that the Holy City was laid waste "because her laws were founded upon the strict letter of the Torah and were not interpreted in the way of mercy and kindness."[53] Jesus' teachings could be described as a reinterpretation of Torah according to mercy and kindness.

Because we have "spiritualized" the Beatitudes, we fail to see how radically subversive—how entirely foolish—they must have been to Jesus' audience. The Torah could no longer be regarded as a series of obligations and prohibitions but as a heart-centered response to life; at the same time, Jesus demonstrated that the Decalogue meant more than observing the minimum standards of human decency. He not only presented a set of spiritual values, but a new orientation acceptable only to those willing to regain a child's purity of vision. John L. Mckenzie, in his commentary on Matthew's Gospel in *The Jerome Biblical Commentary*, explains that the paradoxical nature of the Beatitudes institutes a "moral revolution that has not yet reached its fullness"; he points out that the Beatitudes not only repudiate external values of wealth and status, but also "those goods of the person that are achieved and defended by self-assertion and strife."[54]

The Beatitudes turn upside down conventional values and typical strategies for survival; they ask the multitudes to do the seemingly impossible, that is, to live with child-like simplicity and trust. "The norms of the Sermon on the Mount presuppose love, a new human person and one liberated for greater things," writes Boff.[55] "Abandon security," they seem to say. "Put down your defenses and simply be." While

Greek and Jewish wisdom literature based blessings upon success, harmonious family life and faithful friends, Jesus' Beatitudes are different; "They do not derive from common human wisdom but are prophetic sayings, appeals and promises. . . . all values are reversed."[56]

The first beatitude, for example, affirms the "poor in spirit" (Mt 5:3). In a culture which despises poverty, this teaching is particularly difficult, just as it must have been in Jesus' day. As the crowd huddled close, hungry to hear Jesus' words, there must have been those who felt affirmed by what he said, but no doubt there were also those who considered his words to be plain foolish. After all, if the reward of the virtuous was peace and prosperity, why would anyone choose to be "poor in spirit"? Psalm 128 reflects this sense that revering God's path brings material rewards:

> 2 Your table rich from labor—
> how good for you!
>
> 3 Your beloved, a fruitful vine
> in the warmth of your home.
> Like olive shoots,
> children surround your table.
>
> 4 This is your blessing
> when you revere the Lord. (Ps 128:2–4)

Because a natural assumption for many in Jesus' audience would be that riches, health, and a large family were signs of God's favor, the very idea that poverty of any kind might be a blessing was preposterous. Moreover, many of those gathered around him—including his own disciples—were hoping that Jesus would inaugurate a new era of power and privilege in which they would be the beneficiaries. This, the first of the Beatitudes, pops the bubble of material expectation and endorses a world order in which it is the "have nots" who are the blessed while the "haves" are spiritually endangered.

"What is blessed or happy about being poor?" we might ask ourselves. Even our questioning shows the wrong mind set, an inability to perceive anything of significance. The paradox is that when our hands are empty, when we cling to nothing except the presence of God, then we are simultaneously rich and poor—rich in terms of having sold all that we have to find the buried treasure or to purchase the pearl of great price, and poor because we recognize that God and God alone can satisfy the hungers of our hearts. In our poverty, we recognize our immense neediness and are willing to stake everything so as to gain the only wealth that is meaningful. There is no need to hoard property in barns or to bury talents for fear of losing them; there is no point in exhausting ourselves in anxiety over what we are to eat or drink, over where we are to live or what we are to wear. In fact, when seen from the vantage point of the Beatitudes, our puny attempts to safeguard ourselves and our futures are nothing less than ridiculous. Moreover, we are completely deluded if we imagine that our insurance policies, savings accounts, and health plans afford us any real control over the unpredictability of life. In our hubris, we cut sorry figures; puffed up with pride, we flex our muscles against all the forces of disaster, finding ourselves baffled when our plans prove to be inadequate.

When we recognize the stupidity of placing our trust in our own efforts or in powers outside ourselves, then we are more likely to surrender to God's embrace and to recognize God's sovereignty over our lives. Precisely because we are not tied down by possessions or ambitions, we become available to God who is infinitely available to us. In our poverty, then, is our wealth; in our humility is our joy and in our foolishness is our wisdom.

"Happy are the gentle," asserts the second beatitude (Mt 5:4). Once again, our normal strategies for survival are threatened. Most of us have been conditioned to stand up for ourselves and for our rights, to fight, if necessary, to protect our interests, even if it means "playing dirty." We know how to use the law to our advantage, often having a repertoire of alternative strategies to draw on when the law is not necessarily in our favor. But this is not behavior which Jesus endorsed; on the contrary, he advocated the way of peace. Again, by the world's standards, this is a foolish mandate, for those who are gentle of nature seldom get ahead in this world. Typically, they are the ones who are taken advantage of, the ones who would rather abandon their own interests than engage in strife. Unlike the wicked, they do not bare their teeth in rage, wasting their energy in ranting and raving; instead, they put their trust in God alone.

How far the spirit of gentleness is from some of the laws specified in the Book of Exodus! If, for example, men come to blows and cause the death of a pregnant woman, they shall give "life for life, eye for eye, tooth for tooth, hand for hand, foot for foot, burn for burn, wound for wound, stroke for stroke" (Ex 21:24–25). The gentle, of course, are, by definition, blameless and law-abiding. They neither engage in hostilities nor in exacting the full satisfaction of the law. Instead, they prefer mercy and kindness to squeezing advantages out of others. Those surrounding Jesus on the hillside must have found a stark contrast between his teachings and the harsh Mosaic code; many of them, in fact, must have felt confused at the differences.

In the West, gentleness is not a popular characteristic; on the contrary, it is often regarded as a liability, especially on the path to becoming upwardly mobile. It would be difficult, for example, to succeed in law, politics, business, real estate, advertising, or the entertainment industry if one were truly gentle of heart. In such fields, the gentle would be regarded as laughingstocks and failures; popular wisdom holds that it is better to be aggressive and ruthless than to show any vestiges of weakness, especially if one has aspirations to get ahead.

The gentleness which Jesus advocated, however, involves neither subservience nor cowardice; celebrated in our own century as passive resistance, this foolishness entails raw courage. Love of enemies and returning good for evil are Christian mandates, and "neighbor" must be redefined as extending to everyone, without exception. Similarly, walking the extra mile, surrendering one's cloak and turning the other cheek can be interpreted not only as acts of gentleness but also as acts of defiance against the oppressor; each of these responses brings shame upon those who have exacted unreasonable payment, thus reflecting an attitude of inner freedom which oppressive systems cannot crush.

Lefebure explains the moral creativity behind each of these examples, demonstrating how each prods the enemy to "re-think the situation."[57] To turn one's cheek forces "the enemy" to strike the left cheek with an open hand; since one would strike an inferior with the back of the hand, this reversal establishes the "inferior" as equal, thereby shaming the assailant. Similarly, for someone—most likely, a person being sued in court—to give away the extra garment would result in nakedness which was a violation of the Torah (Ex 22:25–27); the one responsible for this nakedness would be held accountable for taking the cloak as a pledge for debts and for causing someone to have no covering as protection against the cold of night. And "going the extra mile would put the oppressor in a difficult position. Roman soldiers were authorized to force subject persons to carry their pack one mile and no further. . . . there were strict and severe penalties for forcing someone to go the extra mile."[58] Ironically, Jesus' strategies of gentleness allow the person who is oppressed to become trickster and to make a fool of the oppressor. Such clowning may bring down a heavier hand, but it also provides a moment of vindication, a moment of experiencing one's inner power.

The third beatitude which promises consolation to those who mourn also appears to be foolish (Mt 5:5). "In what ways can grieving be a blessing?" we ask. "Surely grieving is a liability which gets in the way of productivity and professionalism?" In a world in which worth is measured by usefulness and in which even the natural processes of aging and death are denied, grieving may seem very threatening—especially if one lets down customary defenses and shows vulnerability. "Better to allow the tears to freeze on our faces than to show weakness," we tell ourselves. Typically, our society tells us "life goes on," and if we are "too slow" about pulling ourselves together after encountering major losses, then there are always those who are ready to suggest seda-tion. And yet Jesus—whom we profess to imitate—was not afraid to weep at the death of Lazarus or over the fate of Jerusalem or even over his own approaching death. To weep is to show the capacity to be moved, to have compassion; it demonstrates a willingness to love even when numbing our-selves may seem infinitely more comfortable; it shows that we have hearts of flesh, not stone—hearts which are aligned with the wounded heart of God.

The remaining beatitudes are likewise contradictions of the world's wisdom. To "hunger and thirst for what is right" (Mt 5:6) is to set oneself up for permanent dissatisfaction because what is "right" seldom wins out; conventional wis-dom, on the other hand, would advise "don't get involved because there is always a price to pay." Moreover, conven-tional wisdom would also consider the very experience of hunger and thirst to be foolish; why experience lack when one can stuff oneself with plenty—with intoxicants, posses-sions, TV shows, frenetic activity? . . .

To be merciful (Mt 5:7) means to renounce vengeance and to forgive those who have hurt us, to love enemies and to pray for those who persecute us—even though worldly wis-dom rejoices in paying back enemies in kind, and, sometimes in paying back double, given the opportunity. "Why be fool-ish enough to open oneself to more hurt?" asks the voice of conventional wisdom; "Why forego the satisfaction of seeing one's enemies crushed and disgraced?" Jesus, however, advocated forgiveness as the appropriate response to injury. Instead of brooding over what has been inflicted upon us, instead of allowing our wounds to fester, we are to let go of ill feelings and to risk being foolish enough to love in spite of what has befallen us. Only when we stretch ourselves beyond the limits of earthly wisdom can we be assured of receiving God's mercy ourselves.

To be "pure in heart" (Mt 5:8) suggests we should live authentically, saying what we mean, meaning what we do, without pretense or hypocrisy, without lies or manipulation. The pure of heart see God because they are not afraid to let

God see them in all their intricacies—their most secret thoughts, their deepest longings, their strongest drives. . . . This beatitude is a blessing for all those who are content to be themselves, without apology and without the benefit of public personae; it is a blessing for all who strive to be real and to give God honor and glory simply by being themselves. Between God and self there are no masks and therefore no barriers to a mutual seeing and a mutual delight in the other. In contrast to a merely literal interpretation of the Mosaic code and an emphasis on ritual purity alone, the Beatitudes point to an inner   purity—a purity of whole-hearted allegiance towards God.

"Peacemakers" (Mt 5:9) are happy or blessed because they abhor discord and violence and so seek out resolution, sometimes putting their own lives on line as they strive for better understanding between hostile parties. Those "persecuted in the cause of right" (Mt 5:10) have the courage to challenge unjust structures and to name evil for what it is, regardless of personal cost. And, finally, those who receive ill treatment on account of following Jesus are blessed because they have earned for themselves the same abuse, suffering, and humiliation as their Lord.

The Beatitudes offer a series of reversals which foolishly affirm the beggars and clowns of this world in their blessedness. The experiences Jesus lifted up through his teaching are not those of people who have enjoyed the abundance of life, but of those who have suffered profound losses—loss of property, loss of reputation, loss of loved ones, loss of health, loss of security. . . . They are the experiences of those who, for one reason or another, have lived "on the edge" and, in so doing, have brought upon themselves ridicule, marginalization, ill treatment, and even loss of life itself. Just as Jesus' table companionship affirmed the dignity of society's castoffs, so his hill-top teachings—like those of Moses—established a new community, a community of have-nots. The blessing common to all is that somehow their very experiences can be a source of new life and liberation. What, on the surface, seem to be misfortunes can become opportunities for laughter, while seeming advantages can be obstacles to faith. Bad news does not have to define one's spiritual life; in fact, it can be a source of growth. It is precisely in poverty, in mourning, in hungering and thirsting, in peace-making and in hardship that we are most aware of what it means to be human and that we therefore find the greatest capacity for transformation.

If the event of Sinai is foundational for Judaism, then the Sermon on the Mount is foundational for Christianity. Jesus, the "new Moses," not only ratified all that Sinai represents, but demanded an even stricter adherence to the Covenant—or more accurately, a return to all that the Covenant meant in the first place. If one is to be the salt of the earth and the light of the world, then it is not enough to obey merely the letter of the Law (Mt 5:13–16). The prohibition, "Thou shalt not kill," seems straightforward enough until we realize that breaking this commandment can involve more than the taking of life—it can include breaking another's spirit, destroying someone's reputation, making a fool of another, hardening one's heart against someone. To deal in death is to rob another of life, whether through direct action or through one's attitude towards that person. We are accountable, therefore, for all those ways in which we deprive another of that which is life-giving. Killing can be a slow, cruel process, involving years of abuse, hatred, and mockery.

In the same way, committing adultery is not limited to physical sexual misconduct, but can involve impropriety of words, seductive looks and gestures, lewd fantasies. . . . To commit adultery, then, is a way of treating others as objects designed for one's own pleasure; it is to rob them of their dignity and to exploit them for all they can offer us. Genital expression does not even have to be involved; in fact—though Jesus did not say this—it is possible to commit emotional adultery and intellectual adultery by claiming more than is appropriate in a particular relationship.

Whether he was talking about divorce, about breaking oaths, or about love of neighbor, Jesus' words went beyond literal observance and invited a heart response. Conventional wisdom may say, "Do the bare minimum to stay within the law," but Holy Foolishness—that wisdom incarnate in Jesus—says, "Be foolish enough to respond with the very generosity of God." Jesus saw his teaching as a fulfillment of the Law, as a way of responding to God and to one's neighbor. For him, "right living" entailed going beyond legal requirements and focusing instead, upon God's requirements. There were no black and white rules; rather, right living was "like a work of art, the product of a vision and a wrestling with concrete situations."[59] It involved a profound yielding to God's perspective rather than to human ways of seeing; ultimately, it demanded going beyond one's own will and inclinations and acting as God would act.

For Jesus, as for the prophets before him, the observance of Torah involved nothing less than to have God's law written upon the human heart:

> I shall give you a new heart, and put a new spirit in you; I shall remove the heart of stone from your bodies and give you a heart of flesh instead. I shall put my spirit in you, and make you keep my laws and sincerely respect your observances. . . . You shall be my people and I shall be your God (Ezek 36:26–28).

But to live with a new heart means to live in a state of vulnerability in a world which operates by very different standards. It is one thing to follow the heart when this is endorsed by the structures of society, and it is quite another reality to do so when other "powers" govern.

The Parables

If the Sermon on the Mount represents the *Summa* of Jesus' teachings, then the parables are the tools by which he made his ideas accessible to the crowds. In fact, A.M. Hunter estimates that the parables represent more than a third of Jesus' teaching, and "with the exception of the Lord's Prayer and the Beatitudes, no part of his teaching is better known or loved."[60] Hunter goes on to say, however, that verbal familiarity with Jesus' parables by no means suggests "that we understand them rightly or that we do not often make them teach lessons they were never designed to teach."[61] In fact, because we are so familiar with images of prodigal sons and lost sheep, with good Samaritans and tiny mustard seeds, we imagine we know what they represent.

In Jesus' time, the parable was a common pedagogical tool used by rabbis. Nathan Ausubel states that parable or *mashal* is actually the most distinctly Jewish element in Jewish folklore and that while there are only five parables in the Pentateuch, "they abound with prodigal lavishness in the *Agada* of the Talmud, in the *Midrash,* and in the books of the *Apocrypha* which are the non-canonical, extra Biblical writings."[62] Accordingly, the generous use of the parable by Jesus and the gospel writers "was but a natural consequence of their Jewish intellectual training."[63] Ausubel also explains the reverence with which the rabbis of the Talmud approached this literary form; quoting from the Agada, he writes:

> Do not despise the parable. With a penny candle one may often find a lost gold coin or a costly pearl. By means of a trifling simple parable one may sometimes penetrate into the most profound ideas.[64]

Parables, in rabbinical tradition, were not allegories but "the natural expression of a mind that sees truth in concrete pictures rather than conceives it in abstractions."[65] Whereas allegories tend to illustrate teachings that have general acceptance, "the parable has the character of an argument in that it entices the hearer to a judgment upon the situation depicted."[66] In other words, "the listener must be actively involved in the process of arriving at meaning; and with the parables, meaning can never be taken for granted. At the same time, parables are designed to 'keep congregations from nodding.'"[67]

Just as the Beatitudes called for a new world order, so the parables cut through expectations. "Parables . . . are meant to change us, not reassure us," writes J. D. Crossan; "Parable subverts the world."[68] The alternative wisdom reflected in these stories shocks the listener into reexamining all assumptions about what is just, ethical, wise, and loving. Lured into listening by comfortably familiar images from daily life, members of the audience suddenly realize that there is more at stake than they bargained for: images of who is righteous and who is God-forsaken suddenly shatter; anticipated rewards and punishments lose their validity; notions about who God is and how God operates quickly disintegrate. Instead of responding with laughter or appreciating the literary merit of these stories, listeners are left in a state of discomfort. If they have really heard, then they know that all their former ways of knowing are invalid; that all their previous ways of categorizing and defining are deficient; that God's ways are so beyond their ways that nothing makes sense any more:

> Parables give God room. The parables of Jesus are not historical allegories telling us how God acts; . . . neither are they moral-example stories telling us how to act before God and towards one another. They are stories which shatter the deep structures of our accepted world and thereby render clear and evident to us the relativity of story itself. they remove our defenses and make us vulnerable to God. It is only in such experiences that God can touch us and only in such moments does the kingdom of God arrive.[69]

Parables, then, embody a wisdom so different from conventional ways of thinking that they invite the listener into considering Holy Foolishness as a viable lifestyle.

Jesus the storyteller is trickster par excellence, weaving simple tales that lodge in the throat and stick there until one is ready to view life through new lenses. Hunter regards the true parable as a life-story which "must hold the mirror up to life."[70] This mirror, however, does not capture apparent reality but like a distorting mirror in an amusement park, reflects angles and forms that would otherwise be invisible. In effect, the parables destroy any illusions one might have about being justified before God, or about having spiritual perception of any kind. What seems logical is foolish; what seems lunacy is sane. Crossan refers to Jesus' parables of reversal as "polar reversals": that is, when the north and south poles exchange places, "a world is reversed and overturned and we find ourselves standing firmly on utter uncertainty."[71]

The Parable of the Prodigal Son is a case in point (Lk 15:11–32). Though the drama of this parable focuses on the younger son's wanderings and his eventual return to his father's open arms, it is the older brother who is really the most interesting character. This brother—dutiful, hard working, obedient—represents the dominant conscious- ness. Because he has always obeyed the rules, he assumes he has his father's favor; at the same time, he looks down on the younger brother for having squandered his inheri- tance on dissipated living. Knowing himself to be in the right, he does not waste time watching for his brother's return or lamenting his absence. Unlike his father whose only preoccupation is his absent son's safety, he is quite content to toil in the fields and to carry on with routine as usual. "Life goes on," he says to himself, shrugging his shoulders in indifference.

But indifference soon becomes anger and resentment. Upon hearing sounds of celebration, the elder brother is filled with disbelief. Legally speaking, the younger brother is as good as dead, even if he has returned home, yet the father—immoderate in his joy, foolish in his antics—rein- states him within the family. The ring, the best robe, and the fatted calf suggest that the spendthrift is once again his father's heir; this, of course, implies that the inheritance the older son has banked on as his share will now be reduced. Instead of being rewarded for his loyalty, the elder son may forfeit whatever the younger son receives over and above what he has squandered. To add insult to injury, the lavish celebration reminds this dutiful son that his father has never thrown him a party.

Attitudes of conventional wisdom are clearly at work here. The elder son knows his worth, knows what he deserves, but considers himself a slave (Lk 15:29); he is trapped both by his work patterns and by the way he views himself, he behaves in a servile way—in fact, one wonders whether he ever thought enough of himself or his father to be able to ask for a party or for an early share of his inheritance. He sees his own merit in terms of productivity and believes he can earn his inheritance. The father, on the other hand, demonstrates that his love and acceptance are freely given and have nothing to do with how many hours his sons have worked in the fields. Driven by the need to prove himself and be righteous, this elder son fails to appreciate what his younger brother's return means to their father. Incapable of rejoicing for his father's sake, he sulks and gives vent to anger. It is not enough for him that he has always had his father's company; he needs to see his father's approval counted out in shekels.

This parable offends all sense of propriety. The father—most likely an affluent member of the community with some social standing—not only awaits his worthless son's return, but actually runs to greet him, an action neither in keeping with his age nor with his status. His heart is so moved by the long-awaited homecoming that he allows himself to become a public fool—a spectacle of impropriety. The fact that he embraces his son who has defiled himself with lewd living and consorting with swine shows that he is willing to disregard ritual purity for his son's sake. Common sense does not prevail here: no punishments are meted out, no reproaches are uttered—there is only unconditional love, lavished upon one who deserves nothing and expects nothing. The prodigal son gets to feast while the self-righteous brother absents himself from the party. "How absurd!" says the voice of conventional wisdom; "how offensive!" But Jesus' voice—the voice of alternative wisdom—would say, "This is what the love of God is like—without boundaries, without limits, without requirements. Where God is present, this is how people love each other!"

Such alternative wisdom resounds throughout the parables. The Parable of the Good Samaritan, for example, is Jesus' answer to the question, "Who is my neighbor?" (Lk

10:29–37). In contrast to the priest and Levite who represent the perspective, "don't get involved," the Samaritan symbolizes those who, seeing beyond differences of ethnic background, class, and religion, can therefore embrace "the Other." The Samaritan not only loves his neighbor—in this case, a Jew—but loves him as himself. While the priest and Levite seem to live out of a "play safe" philosophy, the Samaritan extends himself beyond the boundaries of common sense for the sake of "the Other."

The Samaritan has a healthy spirituality grounded in love of God and not merely in outward observance: his willingness to reach out to the unfortunate victim of brutality indicates his ability to see as God sees, that is, with unreserved compassion; he doesn't stop to ask what the Law tells him to do or what common sense dictates, but instead follows his heart. The priest and Levite, on the other hand, are careful to avoid ritual contamination by keeping as far away from their brother Jew as possible. They keep their hands clean, so to speak, but their hearts are impervious to his plight; by observing laws regarding purity, that is, those prohibitions against touching a corpse, they break the higher law of love. Even though they are uncertain whether the traveler is dead or alive, they avoid him all the same, just in case. What image of God, we must wonder, would prompt this distortion of priorities? How do they feel "justified" before their God when they harden their hearts against one in need?

Only those with a secure sense of self have the religious imagination to put compassion before "rules." The Samaritan, unlike the priest and Levite, is able to act decisively because he is accustomed to responding out of charity instead of fear. There is, of course, no textual evidence to support this, but an extraordinary gesture of love does not happen in isolation; rather, it is typical of a person's response to life as a whole. Given the great care and tenderness which the Samaritan extends the injured man, it would seem he is generous by nature. He acts as one who knows himself and who recognizes the common humanity he shares with others.

While the priest and the Levite are merely religious functionaries with all the titles and privileges that accompany
this, the Samaritan is, ironically, driven by the Jewish spirit of
kavanah or inward piety. In this way, he—a Samaritan—fulfills the twin Judaic requirements of loving God and neighbor, while the representatives of the Jewish establishment
observe the letter of law but fail in love.

It is difficult for us to appreciate how shocking this paradox must have been to Jesus' audience. Modern-day parallels
can give us some understanding of the dynamics at work: for
example, if we were to substitute present-day Christian Serb
for the Samaritan and a Bosnian Muslim for the wounded
traveler, we might get close to the original impact; however,
the weight of Law versus *kavanah* and the question of who is
righteous and who is unjustified do not feature in this sce-
nario. There are more than national rivalries at stake in this
parable. Crossan states that "Good" and "Samaritan" are
contradictions in terms which say the unspeakable: ". . . .
when good (clerics) and bad (Samaritan) become, respectively, bad and good, a world is being challenged and we are
faced with polar reversal."[72] The challenge is to suspend all
stereotyping and to enter into the absurdity of the unexpected and the unimaginable.

For Jesus, the wisdom of God goes beyond the predictable outcomes of a codified system of rewards and punishments; in fact, his claims, by the standards of conventional
wisdom, are quite outrageous. The Parable of the Vineyard
Laborers, for example, clearly offends all sense of propriety
(Mt 20:1–16). For the landowner in this story, each of the
laborers is worth the same "fair wage," even though some
have worked from sunrise, through the heat of the day, until
evening, while others have put in barely an hour. If the laborers agreed to their wages, the landowner reasons, then there
is no justification for begrudging others who receive the
same—even if the new hirees have not "earned" their pay.
"Have I no right to do what I like with my own?" reasons the
landowner. "Why be envious because I am generous?" (Mt
20:15–16). It is human instinct, however, to measure, calcu-

late and compare—just as the elder brother does in the Parable of the Prodigal Son. Conventional wisdom has a hard time with generosity precisely because it is freely given: when wages are earned, then workers have some degree of control over what they receive; when the pay scale is arbitrary, they can no longer claim they have earned what they have received. Rather, it has come as a gift.

This, of course, comes as a shock to the audience. All of us like to know what we are going to receive for our efforts whether in terms of our work or our investment in the spiritual world. Though intellectually we may admit that it is impossible to earn God's love, deep within we tend to pride ourselves on our commitment and on our righteousness. The possibility that others who are seemingly less worthy than ourselves will receive the same reward—or more—strikes us as "unfair." It is as though at some basic level we imagine we can actually control God's generosity, winning favor for ourselves while others, through their own inadequacy, are excluded from divine benevolence. Our own efforts at being "righteous" before God, however, fall ridiculously short: with human shortcomings being a given, nothing we can do is likely to impress God.

If we translate this parable into a statement about God's reign, then the implication seems to be that nobody has a monopoly on God's love—no matter how "righteous" that person is. Moreover—as other parables assert—if those in privileged positions fail to live up to their responsibilities, then they may forfeit their rights altogether. When the invited guests make their excuses and fail to show up at the great banquet, then the disenfranchised will be admitted instead: those considered sinners and misfits by the world's standards will take the place of the "righteous" who have erroneously assumed that their place is guaranteed (Lk 14:15–24). Or, as the Parable of the Wicked Tenants suggests, when those entrusted as caretakers resort to violence to safeguard vested interests, then the vineyard will be given to those who respect the owner (Lk 20:9–19). And, as the case of the five foolish bridesmaids demonstrates, those who go through the motions of fulfilling their obligations but lack the necessary inner resources (symbolized by running out of oil) will lose their place at the great wedding feast (Mt 25:1–13).

In God's scheme of things, the disinherited are not the prodigal sons of this world, but the complacent, the violent, the lazy and the self-righteous—those who trample the rights of others and fail to see their own shortcomings. The real fools, it turns out, are those who consider others foolish but have no sense of their own absurdity. A contemporary illustration of this is Mrs. Turpin, the protagonist in Flannery O'Connor's short story, "Revelation." A bigot, a hypocrite, and a religious fanatic, Mrs. Turpin spends her time critiquing the shortcomings of those whom she considers beneath her. Externally cheery and pleasant, she keeps an internal inventory concerning people's bad taste, low class, unfortunate looks, and unpleasant dispositions. Repeatedly she says, "Thank you, Jesus" because she is so relieved that she has all her own virtues and advantages and that she doesn't have the flaws of the people around her. Her bubble of self-satisfaction is pricked, however, when a patient in a doctor's waiting room hurls a book at her head, telling her, "Go back to hell where you came from, you old wart hog."[73] These words find fulfillment in a vision she receives. Seeing a "vast horde of souls . . . rumbling toward heaven," she notes that while she and those like her bring up the rear with "shocked and altered faces," those leading the procession are the "nobodies" she despised:

> There were whole companies of white-trash, clean for the first time in their lives, and bands of black niggers in white robes, and battalions of freaks and lunatics shouting and clapping and leaping like frogs.[74]

This story beautifully demonstrates the premise that the last shall be first and the first shall be last (Mt 20:16). Those who are worthy of receiving the inheritance are those who entrust themselves to God's tender mercy because they know themselves to be lost and broken; the Parable of the Lost Sheep, for example, and the Parable of the Lost Drachma demonstrate that one can only be found if one recognizes that one is lost in the first place (Lk 15:4–7; 15:8–10). If somebody assumes that he or she is secure, imagining that material blessings are a sign of God's endorsement, then, like the rich man in the Parable of the Rich Man and Lazarus, that person will forfeit everything (Lk 16:19–31). Paradoxically, it is the Lazaruses of this world who end up resting in Abraham's bosom because they are poor in spirit.

Jesus' parables cut through all presumption. The reign of God belongs not to the wealthy and the prudent, but to those who hazard everything to receive that which they desire. While the complacent build themselves bigger and better barns to horde their possessions or bury their talents rather than risk losing what they have, the fools of this world receive the inheritance—merchants imprudent enough to sell everything they own to purchase a single pearl of great price or to buy a field that holds a buried treasure.[75] The need for such single-mindedness is reflected in the Parable of the Importunate Friend who pesters his friend so much that the friend finally gets out of bed, opens the door, and gives him the bread that he needs (Lk 11:5–8). It is also reflected in the Parable of the Importunate Widow and the Unscrupulous Judge: the widow is so determined to receive justice that she harasses the judge day and night until he finally grants her rights (Lk 18:1–8). The Parable of the Crafty Steward echoes this theme by presenting the steward's dishonest business tactics as evidence of his ingenuity (Lk 16:1–8). He is to be praised not because he has written off his master's debts, but because he has the foresight to take care of his own future. Jesus' parables teach that God's reign belongs to those who pursue it with passion, energy, and determination.

The Way of Paradox
By definition, a paradox is an apparent contradiction. On the surface, two realities seem to be irreconcilable, but when one probes more deeply, resolution is, in fact, a possibility. Such probing, of course, demands skill. Not everyone is willing to see beyond that which is antithetical; not everyone is willing

to make sense of that which appears nonsensical. The paradox, as a literary form, developed in Jewish tradition via biblical dialectics. Complicated argumentation, riddles, puzzles, and ingenious wordplay emerged from a history of sustained intellectual activity among Jews from the ending of the Babylonian Captivity in the sixth century B.C.E., during the religious reforms of Ezra the Scribe. The obligation to study Scripture ceaselessly led to "a razor-sharpening of wits, to a verbal ease of articulation and to an unusual preoccupation with abstract ideas and speculation"; in later centuries, this study also included the *Mishna*, the *Talmud* and the *Midrash*.[76] Many riddles and folktales were thus passed on from generation to generation; rich in wit and irony, they offered answers to existential questions and insights into the spiritual life. For roughly twenty-five hundred years, rabbis and sages have employed such material for didactic ends, for "by juxtaposing good with evil, light with shadow, grief with laughter, and honesty with sham, it achieves the harmonious unity of opposites that resides in objective truth."[77]

Much of Jesus' teaching—including elements of the parables and the Beatitudes—is paradoxical in nature. Frequently, he pointed to the narrow gate that few will be foolish enough—or wise enough to enter (Mt 7:13). Over and over again, he invited his disciples to consider going beyond the bare minimum of ethical standards, to forget self-preservation and to subject themselves instead to inconvenience and risk. His message is so hard as to appear impossible: it is not enough to refrain from killing or committing adultery, but one must avoid both anger and lustful thoughts; it is not enough to follow the commandments, but one must be ready to renounce one's very self—abandoning home, property, security, relationships and even physical safety, if that is what is called for (Mt 10:37–39). Jesus, conceived of piety as nothing less than the duty of the heart.

How foolish all this must have sounded to his audience! It was as though Jesus were advocating playing the fool as a way to holiness! It was as though he were saying that God was to be found precisely in such folly! It was as though he were suggesting that the more one broke away from cultural norms and expectations, the more scope there was for God's activity! The rich young man turned away, discouraged, when Jesus invited him into a discipleship of poverty (Mt 19:16–22). Nicodemus, a leading Jewish teacher, could not understand what Jesus meant about "being born again" (Jn 3:1–21). The disciples, vying with each other for chief place in God's reign, learned that "the greatest" is as little as a little child (Mt 8:1–4) and that the real leader is the one who serves the rest (Lk 22:24–27). If Jesus' intention were to draw followers to himself by presenting an appealing path, then he failed miserably. In effect, he presented a path on which only fools—not angels—would dare to tread.

This Fool's Path can be described as the Way of Paradox. Just as the paradox as a literary device involves seemingly irreconcilable elements, so this fool's way juxtaposes seemingly irreconcilable values—holiness with stupidity, wisdom with naiveté, common sense with daredevilry, self-preservation with defenselessness. . . . It involves emptying oneself to find fullness, letting go to possess, losing life to find it. . . . It is difficult to describe this path: it is not the path of logic or common sense, or of grasping and understanding, or of having answers and certainty, or of possessing and holding. Rather, it is the way of folly, the way of not knowing, the way of darkness, the way of not having, the way of "no self" which leads, ironically, to the fullest experience of self in oneness with the Trinity. "Play the fool," Jesus seemed to say, "And you will discover what it is to be like God."

When we undertake to follow the Way of Paradox, we do not do so because we hate the world or ourselves, or because we have nothing to give up—neither a self nor possessions—or because we desire spiritual greatness; rather, Jesus presents this "negative way" as the narrow path to true freedom, as an alternative to the burden of materialism, as a direct route to joy. This path is the way of uselessness and stillness, of listening rather than speaking, of trusting rather than controlling, of being rather than doing, of waiting in quiet and humility, without expectation; it is the way of trusting to inner movement before outer movement, of hearing whispers rather than trumpet blasts, of letting God be God. . . .

In reality, this Fool's Path is the path of wisdom: what seem to be poor investments yield a hundredfold, what seem to be irresponsible strategies have happy outcomes, what seem to be acts of self-sabotage lead to self-gain. Contrary to what worldly wisdom tells us, Jesus' paradoxes assure us that all of life can become a place where God can encounter us and speak to us; all of life can be the hallowed ground of the burning bush, the mountain of transfiguration, the moment of the Last Supper, the road to Emmaus. All of life holds the potential for moments of intimacy—if we could only recognize this. Over and over again, he reminds us not to mistake passing happiness for ultimate happiness, or to pursue material goals without spiritual grounding. Instead, his Way of Paradox invites us to the rich banquet of life, even if it means letting go of all that provides security and comfort. It reminds us that as long as our attention is focused on material concerns, as long as our energy is squandered on competition or acquisition, true passion will remain dormant and disordered passions will surface—envy, greed, fear, resentment. . . . Only when we embrace poverty of spirit will we find the fullness of God.

Jesus is unequivocal about what will bring true freedom. His words are hard, challenging, discomforting—and very foolish. There is no logic to his recommendation, for example, that we should leave everything—house, family, and land, ambitions and worries. He instructs us to give alms in secret, to refrain from judging and to trust only in God (Mt 6:1–4; 7:1–5; 6:25–34);. Yes, the gate is narrow but it is the only way: it is the way of the cross, the way to Jerusalem. Jesus, then, calls us to apparent folly—to a life in which nothing ties us down, neither things, people, hopes or fears. He calls us to a life lived on the edge, without security or insurance policies or any guarantees except that this is the path to life, to freedom, to wholeness. . . .

If we are to sum up Jesus' teaching, then, we could turn to the words with which he began his Galilean ministry: "The time of fulfillment is here! The reign of God is at hand! Reform your lives and believe in the good news!" (Mk 1:15). His words announce a new age—the Age of Holy Paradox—in which human destiny can be fulfilled and God's purpose can be accomplished. What is necessary, however, is the complete reorientation of each individual—a conversion so radical that old patterns of thinking, acting and being no longer have validity. What was a certainty must no longer be trusted; what was inconceivable must be passionately hoped for; what was impossible must be dreamed into reality. . . . Just as Moses called forth the Children of Israel from the land of oppression, so Jesus—the new Moses—invited the people of his time—and, indeed, people of all succeeding generations—into an existential freedom. This freedom involves the breaking of all that binds us, whether physically, emotionally, or spiritually, and a new way of seeing that is aligned with God's own vision. Appropriately, Luke puts the words of Isaiah on Jesus' lips to mark the beginning of his ministry:

> "God has sent me to bring the good news to the poor;
> to proclaim liberty to captives
> and to the blind new sight,
> to set the downtrodden free,
> to proclaim the Lord's year of favor." (Lk 4:18)

When Moses confronted Pharaoh about letting Israel go, he repeated what God had instructed him to say: "Let my people go that they may offer me worship in the wilderness" (Ex 7:16). For Jesus, true liberation was also a matter of right relationship with God: the worst taskmasters and slave drivers are those which so rob people of their dignity that they no longer know the Promised Land of themselves, that precious place in which God's heart and their hearts can meet. The paradoxical news he proclaimed was that God is fully accessible in the present moment—a moment to which each of us is invited to respond. Only our bondage can prevent us from seeing this; only our bondage makes us choose death not life.

In *An Interrupted Life,* Etty Hillesum, a Dutch Jew who died at Auschwitz in 1943, models a spirituality in which nothing—not even the fear of death—can disturb her relationship with God. Though deprived of many basic freedoms even before deportation, she maintains a spirit very much in keeping with the inner freedom to which Jesus points. While her neighbors are wise in a worldly sense, preoccupying themselves with burying silver and placing vacuum cleaners into safe keeping, Hillesum is preoccupied only with her relationship with God. Instead of vainly making material provisions for the future or deceiving herself that there is a future awaiting her after the camps, she focuses only on safeguarding that piece of God within herself:

> There are those who want to put their bodies in
> safe keeping but who are nothing more now than
> a shelter for a thousand fears and bitter feelings.
> And they say, "I shan't let them get me into their
> clutches." But they forget that no one is in their
> clutches who is in your arms.[78]

For Hillesum, maintaining consciousness of God's presence is the responsibility of the individual; those around her model a very different consciousness—one which measures security in terms of human effort and material goods. Because her relationship with God is her highest value, Hillesum is foolishly indifferent to matters of loss and survival. The paradox is that foolishness is spiritually liberating. In spite of all the horrors of the deportation, she affirms her belief in God and in life itself; from her transport window, she throws a postcard which is later found by farmers; it says, "We have left the camp singing." Hillesum's final words, her final gesture, are foolish acts of defiance which celebrate God's centrality in her life.

For those of us who find the Path of Paradox difficult to imagine let alone travel, our bondage is so insidious that we fail to notice the shackles tying us down. We fail to see that our preoccupation with providing for basic needs such as food, shelter, and clothing distracts us from acknowledging the Mystery within; we fail to see that the very riches in which we invest ourselves tie us down, preventing us—like the rich young man in Mattew 19:16–22—from hearing God's call; we fail to see that our intellectual sophistication can be a source of hubris, a block to humility; we fail to see that our fears prevent us from speaking the truth and following the path of integrity. . . . Left to our own devices, we are, indeed, like sheep without a shepherd, sinful fools reacting and over-reacting to situations which can be diffused with love. Immobilized by fear and anxiety, we resort to competitiveness, violence, and greed to ensure that we have "our share." Stifled by the desire to control, we reduce our relationship with God to a series of obligations and expected rewards; we imagine we can earn God's love by doing more.

What is called for, asserted Jesus, is a way of life—a paradoxical way—in which we are as free as the birds of the sky, as free as the flowers growing in the fields (Mt 6:25–34). Worrying gets in the way of trust, leaving us with the illusion that we can control the events of our lives. Idolatry—in any form—moves us away from radical dependence upon God and, in effect, dehumanizes us.

The Lukan account of the Temptation in the Wilderness demonstrates this principle at work (Lk 4:13). In many ways, the temptations are farcical, bringing to mind the curious antics and strategies of medieval devils who attempted to lure their victims into selling their souls. The three temptations all offered Jesus the possibility of choosing a different destiny. Instead of grounding himself in his intimate relationship with God and allowing the Spirit of God to lead him, Jesus could have opted for what John Francis Kavanaugh describes as "appropriation, magic and domination."[79] To have chosen mere bread, to have resorted to magical spectacle or to have bowed before the powers of the world would have been ludicrous indeed—unthinkable, given all that Jesus was and lived for. To have made this worldly-wise, spiritually foolish choice would not only have denied the Covenant, but would have provided yet another model of servitude, a form of narcissistic idolatry. Lefebure also sees the issue of proper relationship to God at the center of the temptations; for him, the temptations "recapitulate the temptations that Israel faced in the desert—temptations involving food, power, and the proper object of worship. In each temptation, something finite threatens to usurp the place of God."[80] Jesus' response to demonic seductions, therefore, not only says something about his own value system but also provides a paradigm for "right" human action. Fullness of personhood, it would seem, is intricately connected to one's fidelity to God.

Jesus and Prayer

As a blueprint for spiritual liberation, the Lord's Prayer could be described as a prayer for Holy Fools (Mt 6:7–13). It invites us to stand before God in freedom, no matter how shackled we be. Regardless of the circumstances in which we find ourselves, in spite of our fragility and brokenness, this prayer reminds us that we are made in the image and likeness of God, that we are bearers of God's very breath; it gives us the audacity to know that, no matter what our story has been, God cherishes each of us more dearly than a parent cherishes a favorite child. Boldly, freely, we praise God's Name because such praise is the very reason for our being. As long as we can sing songs of festival—even if in a foreign land—we are no mere aliens but heirs to the reign of God. And as long as we can hope for this reign and work towards its fruition—again, even if hope seems unwarranted and efforts end in frustration—we are asserting our human dignity. Because we are foolish enough to hope, to strive, we can co-create a new world order with God, daring to call an alternative kingdom into being while others might dismiss us as impractical, illogical, naïve, and plain stupid.

By asking for daily bread, we acknowledge that just as the Israelites were dependent upon God for manna during their forty years in the wilderness, so, too, are we dependent upon God for all forms of sustenance during our own wanderings in the wasteland. Such prayer, however, demands that we abandon all claims to self-sufficiency, pride, posturing, and sophistication and instead stand naked before God. Paradoxically, the ability to name such dependence is again a sign of freedom: complete dependency upon God is the only healthy alternative to idolatry and addictive behaviors. Similarly, naming our own need for forgiveness and expressing our willingness to forgive those who have harmed us reflects a freedom from grudges, resentments, self-righteousness, consuming anger, the desire for revenge and even from violent thoughts. This posture of foolishness indicates humility—that is, the ability to see ourselves as people of clay (*humus*), as people who are flawed and whose only claim to being "righteous" is that God loves us absolutely. Finally, when we pray not to be put to the test we are acknowledging our basic human frailty and the fact that, without God's grace, some temptations may be more than we can contend with.

To pray as Jesus prayed is to allow prayer to be a freeing event. Instead of babbling endless needs and petitions, instead of presenting God with dramatic monologues regarding the stresses in our lives, we detach ourselves from personal agendas, allowing ourselves to become the object of God's thoughts.[81] "The focus of prayer is not the self," writes Heschel. It is the "momentary disregard of our personal concerns, the absence of self-centered thoughts, which constitute the art of prayer. Feeling becomes prayer in the moment in which we forget ourselves and become aware of God."[82]

Prayer, then, involves the folly of self-abandonment, a laying aside of the ego so that God can direct "what happens"; in such praying, we discover the meaning of revolutionary holiness. This, of course, only becomes possible when we are foolish enough to trust that God not only knows what is in our hearts, but also knows what is best for us; no amount of begging, cajoling, bribing, or repeating can make God "change God's mind." The Holy Fool knows how to sit in stillness before God, finding freedom in passivity.

When Jesus said, "Ask and it will be given to you; search and you will find; knock and the door will be opened to you," he was speaking about prayer as an act of liberation (Mt 7:7–11). While our individual circumstances interest God, it seems that our desire to be open to the Holy Spirit is of far greater concern (Lk 11:9–13). Rather than banking on specific outcomes, one who invokes the Spirit is open to God's dream for self and for the world. Prayer, then, becomes an occasion for allowing the "will" of God to unfold within the microcosm of oneself; prayer is a way of allowing God room in the small places of our lives. Julian of Norwich writes:

> But when our Lord in his courtesy and grace shows himself to our soul we have what we desire. Then we care no longer about praying for any thing, for our whole strength and aim is set on beholding. This is prayer, high and ineffable, in my eyes. The whole reason why we pray is summed up in the sight and vision of him to whom we pray. Wondering, enjoying, worshipping, fearing . . . . and all with such sweetness and delight that during that time we can only pray in such ways as he leads us.[83]

Jesus and Healing

To pray with the freedom with which Jesus prayed, however, demands freedom in other areas of one's life. To stand before God in freedom is not possible for those locked in servitude—whether self-imposed or external. When trapped by fear or burdened by anxiety, when weighed down with legalities or obsessed with being in control, then one is not free. When one is so conditioned by the world's wisdom that Holy Folly is an impossibility, then there is a barrier between God and self—the barrier of rigidity, of playing safe, of being unwilling to take risks or to trust. To pray with freedom, one must be completely free. This is why Jesus came to bring liberty to captives: by offering freedom to the whole person, Jesus made possible a new way of being in relationship with God.

Whether someone were limited by mistakes of the past (e.g., the Samaritan woman in John 4:1–42) or by the effects of debilitating illness (e.g., the woman with a hemorrhage in Luke 8:40–56), the result was the same: exclusion from the social and religious spheres, fear of judgment, low self-esteem, a sense of hopelessness. . . . Jesus' miracles therefore need to be seen as more than acts of physical healing but as events which symbolize an inner transformation, a coming to freedom. They are acts of liberation whereby the person healed is invited to a new way of being, to a lifestyle which, aligned with the reign of God, conflicts with the values of the establishment. Jesus' healing propels those he encounters onto the Way of Paradox and all its uncertainties.

In typical encounters with those he healed, Jesus would ask, "what do you want of me?" A key ingredient in each healing encounter, then, was a person's desire for wholeness. In Luke's account of the healing of a person with leprosy, for example, the man prostrated himself, imploring Jesus, "'Sir, if you want to, you can cure me'" (Lk 5:12–13). Jesus' spontaneous response, "'Of course I want to!'" had broader implications than removing outward signs of a dreaded disease. Along with all those who found sight or hearing through Jesus' touch, along with all those who were straightened and given use of their limbs, the man could now take his place in the circle of acceptability. No longer an outcast, he—like the countless others Jesus healed—became a sign of God's power at work in the world, a sign that all things are indeed possible for God. His faith—his assertion of radical trust and radical hope—was what facilitated this healing intervention; this reflects the simple truth that when we cooperate with God's healing power, amazing consequences can happen. With a new skin, he must have experienced life differently, never again seeing himself as victim but as one who had felt the very touch of God. What happened to him through Jesus' power must have become a touchstone moment which allowed him to completely reassess his relationship with God.

The story of the woman who had been bent double for eighteen years also offers a paradigm for what takes place when someone is healed of a devastating affliction (Lk 13:10–17). We have few details about her physical condition except she was enfeebled and quite unable to stand straight. Most likely, in spite of having squandered her savings on doctors, this woman had spent much of her life staring at the ground ahead of her. Back contorted like a question mark, limbs twisted from the effort of making do with inadequacy, she knew the weight of years, the scorn of the upright who knew sin when they saw it—hers, her mother's, her grand-mother's, generations of offenses too vile to name.

Used to the crooked trudge over rough terrain, familiar with cruel jibes and taunts, she looked ahead and saw more of the same—more dust, more shame, more despair. And then the unexpected happened, breaking through all that bound her with a few creative words—words which severed the cords of bondage as surely as Lazarus was freed from the linen which bound him when he burst from the tomb (Jn 11:44). Able to stand straight once more, the woman received the gift of health, and , even more importantly, could behold the stars once again—stars which would set her dreaming. Fittingly, her immediate response was to praise God. The work Jesus accomplished in her was an act of liberation by which she could live more fully and give God glory. In effect, this nameless woman, healed on Shabbat to the chagrin of religious leaders, became an icon of God's presence among the poor and dispossessed. Her very wholeness, then, pointed to God's limitless love.

The miracle accounts in the Gospels suggest that Jesus had extraordinary abilities as a healer. Walter Kasper, defend-ing the miracle tradition as part of the earliest strata of the Christian Scriptures, sees Jesus' miracles as teaching in action.[84] While cures, calming of storms, raisings from the dead, and expulsion of demons have their parallels in Rabbinic and Hellenistic miracle stories of the period, and while some of the miracles may have been erroneously ascribed to Jesus, "it does not mean that they have no theo-logical or kerygamatic significance."[85] Emerging from a gen-eral recollection of Jesus as healer, these miracles can be seen as "acts of power," signs of God's initiative.[86] They are also signs of liberation and invitations to full and conscious living.

But while Jesus evidently had healing powers, these were innate rather than learned. Unlike the physicians of his time who had some knowledge of medicine and were skilled in prescribing salves for external maladies, Jesus was completely untrained. He had neither surgical skills nor, as far as we know, any background in diagnosing human ailments or prescribing treatment on the basis of the functioning of the body. As healer, Jesus was the Holy Fool who trusted that God's power alone would be enough for his work to be accomplished; instead of drawing attention to his skills and claiming status, he resorted to what could be described as comical tactics—possibly as a way of highlighting his very ignorance! Take, for example, the case of the man born blind; instead of applying an expensive ointment to the man's eyes, Jesus made mud out of spittle and earth to serve the same purpose—and healing was freely given (Jn 9:1–7). Or take the case of Simon Peter's mother-in-law, who was suffering from a high fever; Jesus' rather unorthodox intervention was to "rebuke" the fever, not to treat the disease (Lk 4:39). The woman with a hemorrhage is another case in point; merely by touching the fringe of his cloak the woman was restored to health (Lk 8:45). Feeling power leaving him, Jesus asked the quintessentially foolish question, "'Who touched me?'" Given the fact that people were milling all around him, even his disciples were struck by the absurdity of the question: "'Master, it's the crowds around you, pushing'" (Lk 8:46).

In some instances, Jesus' methods invited mockery. Upon entering the house of Jairus, he brought ridicule upon himself by insisting to the mourners that the child was "'not dead but asleep'" (Lk 8:53). Luke tells us, "But they laughed at him, knowing she was dead." Undaunted, Jesus took her by the hand and called to her, "'Child, get up'" (Lk 8:49–56). Again, without complicated medicines and treatments, without powerful incantations or ritual gestures, Jesus allowed God's healing power to flow through him. What's more, Jesus also provoked accusations of blasphemy by linking the forgiveness of sins to physical healing. "'Courage, my child, your sins are forgiven,'" are words he used in curing a man who suffered from paralysis. Here, as elsewhere, the response of the scribes was to say, "'This man is blaspheming'" (Mt 9:1–3).

Jesus' ministry focused on raising people from the dust of their lives so that they could experience life as blessing. As Holy Fool, Jesus relied completely on God in his works of liberation; and, as Holy Fool, his purpose was not to draw attention to himself but to bring about God's reign, even if it meant tarnishing his image by associating with those of poor repute. Just as his healing miracles were acts of empowerment, so were his healing encounters with the spiritually afflicted. In each encounter, we see him reaching out to those imprisoned by their own self-definitions and limited ways of thinking, or to those who had taken upon themselves the judgments of society. His well-side conversation with the Samaritan woman, for example, allowed her to see beyond literal water and water jugs and to name her spiritual thirst; going one step further, she was then able to see that God is fully available in the here and now and that true worship is a matter of relationship with God. Touched by the Holy Foolishness of Jesus, she, too, learned to risk everything for the sake of the truth. Putting down her water jug—representing the burden of her past—she hurried back to the town to proclaim all that she had heard to those who were unlikely to take her seriously. Like the man born blind, she overcame her spiritual blindness, becoming a disciple whose testimony amazingly brought others to belief (Jn 4:1–42).

Another powerful example of Jesus' healing encounters is the story of the woman caught in adultery (Jn 8:1–11). Shamed, disheveled, scorned, and brutalized, this woman stood before Jesus, expecting his condemnation. Trembling with fear, she awaited her terrible death—death by stoning. Instead, his terse statement to the crowds pointed to their sinfulness, not hers: "'If there is one of you who has not sinned, let him be the first to throw a stone at her'" (Jn 8:7). As his words scattered the mob, she found herself not only with a reprieve from her death sentence but also with new possibilities before her. Alone with the woman, Jesus looked up—in other words, looked at the woman, thereby asserting her dignity as a person: "'Woman, where are they? Has no one condemned you?' 'No one, Sir,' she replied. 'Neither do I condemn you,' said Jesus, 'go away and don't sin any more'" (Jn 8:10–11). The invitation she received was nothing less than to choose an alternative future for herself, one in which she could reclaim her personhood. Because of Jesus' love for her at that critical moment, she was free to imagine a new way of living, a new way of thinking, a new way of being.

To *want* to be healed can itself be an exercise in foolishness. While we might assume that being spiritually and physically healthy is preferable to being unhealthy, this may not always be the case for everyone. There are those who would rather grip their beggar's cup firmly than seek regular employment; there are those who would rather be set apart by their differences than to fit into society; there are those who would prefer to cling to the role of victim than to become an individuated adult; there are those who would rather depend on others' charity than be responsible for their own lives. There is the notorious case of a man who begs regularly and aggressively on Chicago's commuter trains. Hideously disfigured by a fire, he has refused the freely extended offers of help from plastic surgeons because he makes a good living by capitalizing on his appearance. For him, according to the standards of conventional wisdom, surgery would be a foolish option.

In the episode of the sick man at the Pool of Bethzatha, the Holy Foolishness of Jesus the healer meets the worldly foolishness of one who needs healing at all levels (Jn 5:1–8). John explains how the first person to enter the Sheep Pool after an angel agitated the water was healed of his or her afflictions; he goes on to say:

> One man there had an illness which had lasted thirty-eight years, and when Jesus saw him lying there and knew that he had had this condition for a long time, he said, 'Do you want to be well again?' 'Sir,' replied the sick man, 'I have no one to put me into the pool when the water is disturbed;

and while I am still on the way, someone else get
there before me.' Jesus said, 'Get up, pick up your
sleeping mat and walk.' The man was cured at
once and he picked up his mat and walked away.
(Jn 5:5–9)

The story has much of the ludicrous about it: angels stir-
ring the waters, the mad rush to get into the pool, the invalid's
inability to answer Jesus' question, his carrying of the mat on
which he has lain for thirty-eight years, his failure to thank
Jesus. . . . On the surface, it may seem that a "typical" cure is
recorded in this text, but a close reading reveals there is much
more going on. In the first place, Jesus asked a direct question,
"Do you want to be well again?" (Jn 5:7). As mentioned earlier,
a key ingredient in the healing narratives is that those afflicted
desire healing and are able to name this desire. As a spiritual
director, working extensively with people in need of physical,
emotional, and spiritual healing, I have found that only those
who have the courage to want to be healed can be healed. In
many cases, people cling to their afflictions because they offer
the only reality they know—a way of life, a form of self-definition, an excuse not to take on responsibilities. Sometimes,
when I confront a directee with the question, "Do you want to
be healed?" the answer is either, "No," or "I don't know." In
such cases, I am powerless to help.

The man in John's narrative did not answer Jesus' question; he neither said that he did nor that he did not want to
be cured. Instead, he had two complaints: 1) there was no one
to put him in the pool at the required time; 2) somebody
always got there first. This sounds very much like the
response of one who always saw himself as victim and
blamed the universe for his condition. Perhaps years of waiting at the Sheep Pool, years of disappointment and suffering,
had left him embittered; or perhaps his very attitude to life
had brought about his illness in the first place, leaving him
incapable of even desiring healing. From a symbolic perspective, the pool could represent both the archetype of healing waters and the need to descend into the unconscious:
without immersion in this water, one is unable to experience

spiritual cleansing or psychological integration. Like the Sea of Reeds in Exodus 14, the Sheep's Pool represents the baptismal experience that leads to true liberation—liberation from bondage, from fragmentation, from despair. The man' s inability to enter these waters suggests that his bondage was spiritual, as well as physical; in fact, one could say that his physical limitations mirrored his inner state. At some level, he was terrified of entry into the waters and his own worldly foolishness inhibited him from taking the plunge into Holy Foolishness, that is, into transformation.

Jesus' response, "Get up, pick up your sleeping mat and walk!" lacks his characteristic gentleness; in fact, there is a note of frustration here, a tone of impatience (Jn 5:8). The man's indirect response, together with his failure to ask Jesus for healing, suggests that he could not imagine an alternative future for himself. For him, recovery meant getting into the pool before yet another competitor; he could envision no other options. The fact that Jesus orders him to pick up the mat which had carried him for so many years has powerful connotations; I imagine Jesus saying, "Don't define yourself by your bed any more; instead, get up and carry it—you have the power to move beyond the miserable existence you have created for yourself! For God's sake, choose life!"

Through healing acts and healing encounters, Jesus asserted that there is more to life than the mere beating of time or going through the motions of living— "living and partly living," as T.S. Eliot's women of Canterbury would say.[87] In offering himself as the Bread of Life, Jesus pointed out the limitations of ordinary bread (Jn 6). When we settle for bodily sustenance alone, we ignore the most important dimension of ourselves. When we assume that our greatest needs are material, then we become captives of our needs, wants, and desires. When all our efforts are spent in securing bread for tomorrow, then we miss the holiness of the present moment. True freedom is to be found in eating the bread of liberation, the bread of God's presence. To settle for less is to settle for a life of dust in which all turns to disappointment; to settle for less is to deny the very breath of God within us.

To settle for less is to remain enslaved in "Egypt," that land of oppression. To settle for less is to remain spiritually blind, physically limited, and existentially at risk.

The Price of Holy Folly

Name Calling

Madman . . . Glutton . . . Drunkard . . . Blasphemer . . . Sinner . . . Possessed man . . . Nazarean . . . These unflattering titles show up with as much regularity in the Gospels as the traditional christological titles; together they form a "negative Christology" which reflects not only the hostility of the establishment but also the complete misunderstanding of both Jesus and his mission on the part of those closest to him. Just as the positive christological titles have something to say about the identity of Jesus, so, too, these shockingly negative terms reveal how Jesus was perceived in his own time, and the abuse he took upon himself for the sake of humanity. The Lord who was born into the poverty of the human condition allowed himself to be named as the poorest of the poor—as one on the margins, without a place in society, an object of scorn and derision, a fool, a source of scandal. . . .

Naming is significant. The ways in which we name ourselves and others indicate our own attitudes and characteristic ways of treating self and others. When a person is named in derogatory terms, then he or she can be despised, ridiculed, scapegoated, injured, and even killed—which is, of course, exactly what happened to Jesus. The negative naming of Jesus unleashed intolerance, hatred, mob frenzy, and ultimately, legitimized murder. Moltmann sums this up succinctly: "Jesus was folly to the wise, a scandal to the devout and a disturber of the peace in the eyes of the mighty. That is why he was crucified."[88] In Desiderius Erasmus' satire, *In Praise of Folly,* Dame Folly points to the same reality:

> Christ, in order to relieve the folly of mankind, though himself "the wisdom of the Father," was willing in some manner to be made a fool of when he took upon himself the nature of man and was found in fashion as a man.[89]

In becoming human, then, the Word of God allowed the very holiness of God to be named in sacrilegious terms and to be mocked accordingly.

To His Family, Jesus Was Mad.

Jesus' relatives not only thought he had lost his mind, but also believed he was possessed, for the two terms were synonymous. Was it changes in him following his baptism that led them to this conclusion? After all, it was after his baptism and following John's arrest that Jesus began proclaiming the immediacy of God's reign; we can assume that before then, there was nothing remarkable about his behavior to set him apart from society (Mk 1:14–15). To this day, we define sanity largely as a matter of being able to "fit in" and "adjust to" the standards set by the majority, even if these standards are themselves warped. The "freak" who has greater vision and a higher morality than the majority is still regarded as a "freak" because of his or her maladjustment. And so it was with Jesus.

With a ragged band of followers, he made his way through Galilee, preaching, healing, and casting out demons. While this in itself may have been disturbing to his family— especially in light of John's arrest, no doubt it was Jesus' apparent disregard for convention and for the Law that was most alarming. As early as Mark 2, Jesus was already forgiving sins and claiming a higher law than Shabbat (Mk 2:1–12; 2:23–28). He also kept company with tax collectors and sinners, a violation of all religious and nationalistic values, since tax collectors collaborated with the Romans and sinners were "enemies" of God.

As crowds gathered in amazement and as religious leaders plotted to destroy him, Jesus' own family tried to intervene. Matthew simply tells us that his mother and brothers "were anxious to have a word with him" while Luke states that "his mother and brothers came looking for him" (Mk 12:46; Lk 8:19). Mark is more specific: "When his relatives heard of this, they set out to take charge of him, convinced he was out of his mind" (Mk 3:21). Edward Mally, in his commentary on Mark's Gospel in *The Jerome Biblical Commentary*, writes: "This is equivalently an accusation of demonic possession."[90]

All three Synoptics, however, record Jesus' reaction to his relatives' desire to speak to him in similar terms:

> "Who is my mother? Who are my brothers?" And stretching out his hand towards his disciples, he said, "Here are my mother and my brothers. Anyone who does the will of my Father in heaven is my brother and sister and mother." (Mt 12:48–50)

> "Who are my mother and my brothers?" And looking around at those sitting in a circle about him, he said, "Here are my mother and my brothers. Anyone who does the will of God, that person is my brother and sister and mother." (Mk 3:33–35)

> He was told, "Your mother and brothers are standing outside and want to see you." But he said in answer, "My mother and my brothers are those who hear the word of God and put it into practice." (Lk 8:20–21)

No doubt John's high Christology is the reason the Fourth Gospel makes no record of this event: to have Jesus' own relatives not only misunderstand but attempt to sabotage his ministry hardly adds glory—or credibility—to his person or his message. The fact that all three Synoptics record this unflattering event indicates the reliability of their testimony; together, they suggest that 1) Jesus' activities following his baptism came as a surprise to his family; 2) they were frightened and embarrassed by possible—and probable—outcomes to his words and behavior; 3) they considered him mad and therefore not responsible for what he was doing; 4) their intention was therefore to put an end to his "antics" before he brought disaster upon them all. On the other hand, Jesus' response, quoted above, implies that he believed his family members were neither hearing God's word nor responding to it; if they could hear and respond, then they, too, would have become his disciples.

To His Opponents, Jesus Was a Sinner.

As we have seen, a sinner was somebody who neither feared God nor the Law. Jesus, as Holy Fool, was a respecter of God but no respecter of persons. He associated with whomever he pleased, regardless of their status, completely disregarding all notions of hierarchical seating arrangements. Just as the medieval jester flouted dining room conventions for the sake of levity and to humble the aristocracy, so Jesus ignored societal norms. Because he ate with tax collectors and sinners, that is, with social outcasts who followed disreputable professions or who were known for their infringements of the Law, then Jesus, by implication, was "one of them." The assumption was that if he ate with certain individuals—Levi and Zaccheus, for example—then he shared the same views, followed the same standards and broke the same rules. Moreover, even when he dined in the homes of the respectable rather than with riffraff, unseemly events took place which cast him in a negative light. He was a guest in a Pharisee's house, for example, when the sinful woman in Luke's Gospel washed his feet with her tears, anointed them with costly ointment and dried them with her hair. This lavish gesture of love must have made all those present uncomfortable in the extreme, especially since the woman's reputation was well-known to them (Lk 7:36–50). Moreover, physical contact with a woman of any standing who was not a relative would have been socially taboo.

The question of his table fellowship arises in Matthew 9:10–13, in Mark 2:15–17, and in Luke 5:29–32. Crossan, on commenting on the threat of "open commensality," says that it negated "the very social function of table, namely, to establish a social ranking by what one eats, how one eats, and with whom one eats";[91] his open commensality also subverted ritual law by erasing distinctions between males and females, rich and poor, clean and unclean, Gentiles and Jews.[92] Because, according to his contemporaries, Jesus lacked social discrimination, he was therefore a glutton, a drunkard, and an endorser of sinful behavior. Even his behavior at the Last Supper had shock value: for a public figure to gird himself in a towel and wash the feet of his own disciples was unheard of; it reversed all social expectations, placing a leader in the position of servant and debunking any notions of privilege. This, however, became the standard of service which Jesus expected of his followers—a standard which on all accounts smacked of the ludicrous (Jn 13:1–16).

To the Religious Establishment, Jesus Was a Blasphemer

A blasphemer was one who spoke irreverently about God or who claimed attributes belonging to God alone. In Mark 2:6 and Matthew 9:2, Jesus' words to the man afflicted with paralysis—"'My child, your sins are forgiven'"—caused scandal because the forgiveness of sins belonged to God alone. Similarly, Jesus' claims in the Gospel of John, "'The Father and I are one'" and, "'before Abraham ever was, I am'" almost led to his being stoned (Jn 10:30; 8:58): "We are not stoning you for doing a good work but for blasphemy: you are only a man and you claim to be God" (Jn 10:33). Stoning was a form of capital punishment prescribed by the Torah for blasphemy, idolatry, desecration of Shabbat, human sacrifice, and occultism.[93] One who was stoned, then, was a "fool" in the biblical sense of an apostate, detestable to God, and beyond mercy. When Jesus stood before the Sanhedrin after his arrest, it was ultimately on charges of blasphemy that he was condemned. The high priest's melodramatic gesture of tearing his clothes reflected his belief that Jesus had grievously transgressed the Law:

> And the high priest said to him, "I put you on oath by the living God to tell us if you are the Christ, the Son of God." "The words are your own," answered Jesus. "Moreover, I tell you that from this time onward you will see the Son of Man seated at the right hand of the Power and coming on the clouds of heaven." At this, the high priest

tore his clothes and said, "He has blasphemed. What need of witnesses have we now? There! You have just heard the blasphemy. What is your opinion?" They answered, "He deserves to die." (Mt 26:63–66)

To Many, Jesus Was Possessed

Though the modern medical establishment may have alternative ways of explaining possession, in Jesus' time, to be possessed meant that one was inhabited by evil spirits and forsaken by God. Such a person was afflicted by physical disorders, incapable of good actions and, in fact, a source of great harm. Again, to label the Holy One of God as demonic was the ultimate in absurdity. In the account of Jesus' healing of a possessed man who was blind and deaf the religious leaders concluded: "'The man casts out devils only through Beelzebul, the prince of devils.'"[94] Earlier, they had responded to his healing of a man who was dumb in a similar way: "'It is through the prince of devils that he casts out devils'" (Mt 9:34). And in Mark 3, the charge is even more explicit: "'Beelzebub is in him!'" (Mk 3:22). Jesus quickly pointed out his accusers' lack of logic: "'How can Satan cast out Satan?'" (Mk 3:23). Interestingly enough, it is in this context that he identified the unforgivable sin of blasphemy against the Holy Spirit; it would seem that the refusal to see God's saving action in the world—or rather, to see it and name it as evil—is the ultimate offense against God's Holy Name (Mk 3:28–30).

In Mark's Gospel, demons seem to proliferate: they are present in the demoniac in Capernaum, in the Gerasene demoniac in whom they are "legion," in the daughter of the Syro-Phoenician woman, and in the boy with epilepsy.[95] Mark also tells us that Jesus "cast out many devils, but he would not allow them to speak, because they knew who he was" (Mk 1:34). Ironically, this crew of characters readily named Jesus as "the Holy One of God" while others—including those closest to Jesus—interpreted him and his ministry in negative terms, either because they were slow-witted, stubborn, or spiritually blind. Precisely because he disturbed the status quo, precisely because he called captives into freedom and the blind into spiritual seeing, Jesus became a sign of discord and his very holiness was condemned as folly: "This negative Christology was elaborated by the adversaries of Jesus who were scandalized because of his liberating, profoundly human and noble attitudes."[96]

The Outcome of Holy Folly

The Passion Narratives

If the religious and political establishment regarded Jesus as a fool because of his words and actions, then the grim outcome of this is found in the narratives of his passion and death. We have seen that Jesus preached a "way" that was contrary to the vested interests of his adversaries and to conventional wisdom; given the threat he represented, it is little wonder that he came to a "fool's end." Jesus' death represented the ultimate in humiliation, a "stumbling block to Jews, and an absurdity to Gentiles" (1 Cor 1:23). So shocking was this form of capital punishment that Cicero wrote, "The idea of the cross should never come near the bodies of Roman citizens; it should never pass through their thoughts, eyes, or ears."[97] In fact, it was a form of execution usually reserved for slaves and for those who had forfeited their rights to be treated with human dignity.

One of the earliest depictions of Christ is a *graffito* on the Palatine which represents a crucified figure with a donkey's head; the inscription reads, "Alexamenos worships his god."[98] Far from being a sign of triumph and glory, the cross in the early centuries of Christianity was a sign of scandal:

> In Israelite understanding, someone executed in this way was rejected by his people, cursed among the people of God, by the God of the Law, and excluded from the covenant of life. "Cursed be everyone that hangs on a tree" (Gal 3:13; Deut 21:33).[99]

But the mockery of Christ by the powers of the world began before he was lifted up on the cross as an object of ridicule. Crossan, in *The Historical Jesus*, claims that it is impossible to ascertain the historicity of the "specific details, quoted dialogues, narrative connections, and almost journalistic hour-by-hour accounts of the passion of Jesus"; he proposes that since Jesus' followers fled and since there were no available witnesses, "Jesus' closest followers knew nothing more about the passion than the fact of the crucifixion."[100] What he suggests is that the early Christian community produced a coherent and sequential story from scriptural verses and images and specific prophetic fulfillments, drawn from canonical and noncanonical material alike.

In speaking of those scriptural passages describing the mockery of Christ, Raymond Brown states: "There is no way of knowing whether this happened historically; at most one can discuss the issue of verisimilitude. Is this buffoonery a plausible action?"; the conclusion at which he arrives, however, is that the material is not implausible.[101] Whatever process was at work in shaping the passion narratives, it would seem that there was an early tradition within the postresurrection community that Jesus was humiliated prior to crucifixion. As in the case of the Synoptics citing the concerns of Jesus' relatives concerning his sanity, so a logical supposition here would be that the Gospel writers would not have arbitrarily included material that further shamed Jesus unless they were convinced that it had historical and theological relevance.

Jesus Is Mocked by the Religious Powers
In the passion narratives, Jesus is portrayed as the Suffering Servant and the Man of Sorrows. Caught by a "trick," purchased for thirty shekels, that is, for the price of a slave, betrayed by a kiss, captured by a mob (possibly Temple police) and deserted by his followers, Jesus stood alone before the religious authorities. Paradoxically, the one who embodied holiness itself, the one who staked everything on

fidelity to God and who was himself a sacrament of God's presence, was found guilty of blasphemy. The Synoptics record that it was Jesus' response to the Sanhedrin that provided the ultimate justification for the death sentence. His words—the quoting of two messianic texts, Psalm 110:1 and Daniel 7:13—were basically a declaration that he was the Messiah and the Son of Man: "'Moreover, I tell you that from this time onward you will see the Son of Man seated at the right hand of the Power and coming on the clouds of heaven'" (Mt 26:64–65). While we have nothing in Jewish sources to suggest that a claim of messiahship was regarded as blasphemy, this claim was named as blasphemous and led to the verdict, "'He deserves to die.'"[102]

What follows in Matthew and Mark is physical and verbal abuse towards Jesus. In Matthew 26, the religious leaders themselves engage in hitting and spitting, mocking him with the words, "'Play the prophet, Christ! Who hit you then?'" (Mt 26:28). In Mark, the religious leaders are joined by their servants in hurling abuse and mockery upon him: "Some of them started spitting at him and, blindfolding him, began hitting him with their fists and shouting, 'Play the prophet!' And the attendants rained blows on him" (Mk 14:65). The effect of having the mockery of Christ linked to the charge of blasphemy and assigning responsibility to the religious authorities creates an intolerable situation in which those who should have been the bearers of religious consciousness became torturers and blasphemers themselves. It must be noted here that spitting was not merely a form of abuse but an act of judgment, a cultural expression of outrage against one found guilty of blasphemy.[103] However, while the Gospels provide a particular historical context—that is, a Jewish context—and a particular way of naming Jesus' "adversaries," his opponents are primarily symbolic representatives of conventional wisdom and behavior; Jesus would have received the same treatment in any time and any place—including our own. It is therefore not helpful to stress the "Jewishness" of his antagonists, and, in fact, to do so only leads to anti-Semitism.

Luke, by placing the abuse before Jesus faced the Sanhedrin and by making the guards serve as the perpetrators of mockery, spared Jesus some of the indignity we find in Matthew and Mark (Lk 22:63–65); John's Jesus, brought before Annas and Caiaphas, was not charged with blasphemy at this time, and, instead of being publicly humiliated, was struck in the face once by the guards for answering the high priest (Jn 18:22–23).

In all three Synoptics, it is significant that the abuse of Jesus included the reviling of his prophetic abilities. A prophet is a seer, that is, one who sees; this seeing may involve the ability to predict future events but, more importantly, it has to do with the ability to see as God sees because one shares in what Heschel calls "the heart of divine pathos":[104] "To a person endowed with prophetic sight, everyone else appears blind; to a person whose ear perceives God's voice, everyone else appears deaf."[105] By blindfolding Jesus, by ridiculing his ability to "hear God's voice and feel God's heart," those mocking him were reviling his very core. Symbolically speaking, this mockery represents a vicious attack of "un-seeing" and "un-knowing" upon "inner seeing" and "inner knowing." The one who was light itself was reduced to a state of physical darkness by the forces of darkness.

Jesus Is Mocked by the Secular Powers

Just as Jesus was mocked by the religious powers, so, too, he was made an object of ridicule by the secular powers. The scene before Pilate is surreal. Jesus, found innocent by the governor, was nevertheless condemned to die while Barabbas ("son of the father"), a notorious prisoner whose murderous ways indicated that he was the son of a very different kind of father, was released in honor of the Passover festival. The releasing of Barabbas was a mockery of everything Passover represented; it subverted liberation as a spiritual reality which guarantees the right to worship; it violated the Covenant with its clear mandate that the people should observe certain standards of human decency. Barabbas, in fact, was the polar opposite of Jesus: he was a "fool" in the biblical sense of a godless man, he was the representative of the unrighteous, of the fallen, of the depraved. The crowd, incited by the religious leaders, demanded that Barabbas should be set free and that Jesus should be executed. We could say, therefore, that the power of the mob prevailed and that the might of Rome bent before the whim of its subjects.[106]

While the first mockery focuses on Jesus being considered a false prophet, the second mockery—following his death sentence—focuses upon his being regarded as a false king. In all the passion narratives, Pilate asked Jesus directly, "'Are you the king of the Jews?'" to which Jesus replied, "It is you who say it."[107] In John's Gospel, Jesus explained the meaning of his kingship:

> "Mine is not a kingdom of this world. . . .
> Yes, I am a king. I was born for this, I came into
> the world for this: to bear witness to the truth;
> and all who are on the side of truth
> listen to my voice." (Jn 18:36–38)

Pilate, however, persisted in referring to Jesus as "the king of the Jews"—implying a political kingship—even when he addressed the crowds: "What am I to do with the man you call king of the Jews?" (Mk 15:13)

Because the king motif figures so strongly in this second mockery, it is worth looking at the sequence of events recorded by each of the Evangelists:

> The governors' soldiers took Jesus with them into the Praetorium and collected the whole cohort around him. Then they stripped him and made him wear a scarlet cloak, and having twisted some thorns into a crown they put this on his head and placed a reed in his right hand. To make fun of him they knelt to him saying, "Hail, King of the Jews!" And they spat on him and took the reed and struck him on the head with it. (Mt 27:27–31)

> The soldiers led him away to the inner part of the palace, that is, the Praetorium, and called the

whole cohort together. They dressed him up in purple, twisted some thorns into a crown and put it on him. And they began saluting him, "Hail, king of the Jews!" They struck him on the head with a reed and spat on him; and they went down on their knees to do him homage. (Mk 15:16–20)

Then Herod, together with his guards, treated him with contempt and made fun of him; he put a rich cloak on him and sent him back to Pilate. (Lk 22:11)

Pilate then had Jesus taken away and scourged; and after this, the soldiers twisted some thorns into a crown and put it on his head, and dressed him in a purple robe. They kept coming up to him and saying, "Hail, king of the Jews!" and they slapped him in the face. (Jn 19:1–3)

In each of these accounts, Jesus was decked in the emblems of kingship. Whether he was dressed in a scarlet military cloak, a garment of royal purple, or merely a rich robe, the garment in question was undoubtedly meant to represent royalty; it symbolized the kind of clothing worn by one in command who was worthy of respect, even homage. Ironically, in Jesus' case, the royal cloak concealed utter nakedness and a body freshly torn by scourging; the cruel burlesque involved Roman soldiers pretending to venerate a prisoner who was clearly going to die. As in the case of those mock kings elected to have a brief taste of glory prior to execution, Jesus' predicament was a source of laughter for his torturers: crowned with thorns, holding a reed in his right hand, and hailed like Caesar, he was a parody of a king. The Lamb of God before whom all knees should bend was accorded, in jest, the type of veneration to which the supposedly divine Roman emperors had become accustomed. Mock idolatry, then, was a significant part of Jesus' humiliation; the implication in both Mark and John is that this nonviolent buffoonery was a long drawn out affair which eventually turned to physical abuse.

Possible Sources for the Passion Narratives

There are several possible sources for this scriptural material. In Isaiah's third song of the Suffering Servant, the Servant says:

> "For my part, I made no resistance,
> neither did I run away.
> I offered my back to those who struck me,
> my cheeks to those who tore at my beard;
> I did not cover my face
> against insult and spittle." (Isa 50:5–6)

Clearly, the references to striking, insults, and spittle reflect the abuse Jesus received in both the first and second mockeries; moreover, the passive response of the Servant mirrors Jesus' own silence in the face of accusations, as well as his submission to all that befell him. The description of the Servant in Isaiah's fourth song is also relevant:

> Without beauty, without majesty we saw him,
> no looks to attract our eyes;
> a thing despised and rejected,
> a man of sorrows and familiar with suffering,
> a man to make all people screen their faces;
> he was despised and we took no account of him.
> (Isa 53:2–3)

The "royal" elements of mockery, however, are neither present in these texts nor in Psalms 22 and 69 which also portray the humiliation of the Just One. Raymond Brown lists several historical events which may have helped shape the passion narratives; these include:

1) An incident in Alexandria (38 C.E.) in which Herod Agrippa I was mocked in the person of Karabas, who was mentally disabled. Vested in a rug as a royal robe, crowned with papyrus and holding a reed as a scepter, Karabas, surrounded by mock body guards, was hailed in Aramaic as "Lord" by the crowds.[108]

2) Plutarch's account (*Pompey* 24:7–8) of how pirates mocked a prisoner who insisted upon his rights as a Roman

citizen: "They dressed him up, made fun of him with all honors, and finally made him walk the plank."[109]

3) Games of mockery such as *basilinda*, in which everyone had to obey the orders of the one selected as king.[110]

4) Carnival festivals such as the Sacaean Feast, the Saturnalia and the Kronia, with their elements of "orgiastic buffoonery and a king or master for a time."[111]

In addition, Crossan cites the Epistle of Barnabas as a model of how an allegorical interpretation of the Hebrew Scriptures could have provided the early Christian community with a deeper understanding of the soteriological significance of Jesus' death. Working with Chapter 7 of the epistle, he demonstrates how the "combined motifs of piercing, robing and crowning" were present in the Book of Zechariah and became a layer within the Barnabas text; Zechariah 3:1–5, in particular, originally applied to Joshua, the first high priest after the Babylonian Exile in 538 B.C.E. who is presented as "a type of the destruction/deliverance dyad," could also be applied to Jesus.[112] Crossan explains how the Epistle of Barnabas fuses Joshua and Jesus not just as a biblical basis for the passion but also to link the passion with the Parousia: "The twin states of Joshua/Jesus as first clothed in filthy garments and then regally crowned and robed were correlated with the twin goats from the Day of Atonement."[113] While Crossan's main intention here is to show how the passion narratives may have been woven together from older traditions, the allusions to the scapegoat in his example offer additional imagery which may have influenced the depiction of the mockery of Jesus: just as the scapegoat was spat upon, pierced, crowned with scarlet wool, and then driven into the wilderness, so Jesus—the one who bore the sins of the world—was similarly abused.[114]

Whether historical or not, the first and second mockeries of Christ are not implausible; together, they effectively capsulize the Gentile attitude towards a crucified king and the Jewish abhorrence of a false prophet: "Christ crucified, to the Jews a stumbling block, to the Greeks (Gentiles) foolishness" (1 Cor 1:23):

If we reflect on parallelism, the whole Sanhedrin condemned Jesus to death and some began to mock him as a prophet (Mk 14:64–65); Pilate has condemned Jesus to crucifixion and the whole cohort is called together to mock Jesus as king. The claim that the Gospels excuse the Gentiles but condemn the Jews is scarcely supported by the equally negative portrayal of the two sets of mockers.[115]

Jesus Is Mocked by Spectators

There is a third set of mockeries to consider. Crucified under a sign which read, "This is Jesus, the King of the Jews," Jesus hung between heaven and earth, seemingly abandoned by God, as well as by his friends and followers. While soldiers cast lots for his clothes, the passersby jeered (Mt 27:38). This taunting of the dying Christ is most poignantly presented in Matthew and Mark; both texts present several distinct groups of mockers—casual observers, the religious authorities, and the robbers crucified along with him:

> The passersby jeered at him; they shook their heads and said, "So you would destroy the Temple and rebuild it in three days! Then save yourself! If you are God's son, come down from the cross!" The chief priests with the scribes and elders mocked him in the same way. "He saved others," they said, "he cannot save himself. He is the king of Israel; let him come down from the cross now, and we will believe in him. He puts his trust in God; now let God rescue him if God wants him. For he did say, 'I am the son of God.'" Even the robbers who were crucified with him taunted him in the same way. (Mt 27:39–44)

Luke's Jesus was also abused, but those mocking him made no reference to God having forsaken him; instead, the emphasis is on Jesus' inability to save himself. Moreover, one of the thieves crucified along with him acknowledged his kingship, thereby modifying the virulence of the verbal attacks (Lk 23:35–43). John's Gospel makes no reference to this third mockery.

These final mockeries attack everything Jesus stood for—everything he lived by, everything he taught, everything he modeled in his ministry. While the earlier mockeries were directed at his person and attacked his prophetic gifts and his perceived claims to "kingship," the mockery of the crucified Christ struck at his relationship with God. Just as Jesus was tempted to base his messiahship on power, wonder-working and self-aggrandizement, so, on the cross, he was tempted to "do the spectacular" and save himself (Mt 4:1–11). Even as he hung in agony, then, Jesus was tempted to abandon his trust in God and to trust in his own powers instead. While he had taught his disciples to be willing to take up their crosses and follow him, those mocking him suggested he should exempt himself from his own teachings.

The mockeries tempted Jesus to see himself as one forsaken by God. The words and actions of those baiting him bring to mind the words of the afflicted psalmist:

> 2 God, my God,
> why have you abandoned me—
> far from my cry, my words of pain?
>
> 3 I call by day, you do not answer;
> I call by night, but find no rest. . . .
>
> 7 But I am a worm, hardly human,
> despised by all, mocked by the crowd.
>
> 8 All who see me jeer at me,
> sneer at me, shaking their heads:
>
> 9 You relied on God; let God help you!
> If God loves you, let God save you! (Ps 22:2–9)

Christian tradition has held this psalm to be messianic in nature. The early church used it to illuminate the message of Jesus' death and resurrection and to compose the Gospels. It is helpful, therefore, to look at the psalm in its entirety and not just at isolated lines. Stuhlmueller proposes that Psalm 22 "is not so much a detailed prediction about Jesus as it is a psalm whose fulfillment in Jesus reached even beyond the agony and innocence, the power and influence of the psalmist."[116] While the psalm records both the psalmist's experience of abandonment and the jeers of the mob, read christologically, it "leads us into the suffering heart of Jesus," and into the depths of Jesus' own spirituality.[117] Matthew's Jesus, "obedient even unto death," prays this psalm in his death agony (Phil 2:8; Mt 27:47); what the psalm represents is not so much his experience of God having abandoned him, but his own self-abandonment into God's hands. More than a powerful lament, it is also a prayer of confidence, a request for help, a promise of ritual praise and an affirmation that "God saves." It would seem, then, that even if Jesus felt abandoned, yet he was able to trust, to love and to reverence his God:

> He experienced God as the one who withdraws his very closeness, who is totally other. Jesus experienced the unfathomable mystery of God and his will, but endured this darkness in faith. The extremity of emptiness enabled him to become the vessel of God's fullness. His death became the source of life.[118]

Jesus died as he lived—that is, as a Holy Fool. Like the court jester who punctured the royal consciousness with his wisdom, he overstepped the bounds of safety and so incurred the wrath of the establishment. Turning convention and tradition upside down by his example, he reversed expectations and shattered assumptions about status and privilege. Like the trickster, he trapped his opponents into confronting the limitations of their own thinking, silencing them with the force of his wit and with their own lack of logic. Like the *iurodivii*, he lived in complete simplicity, without any means of self-defense and without any attempts at self-preservation. Just as the court jester could be whipped and sent to bed without supper, or, more ominously, imprisoned and executed at the whim of the ruler, so, too, Jesus came to an ignoble end. And, just as the jester could become a scapegoat, so, too, Jesus was the innocent victim upon whom society could project its unredeemed shadow. But, paradoxically, the one who in death became the "mock king" and sacrificial victim would have the last laugh.

The Last Laugh . . .

The last laugh, of course, is that nothing—not even death on a cross—could suppress Jesus' spirit. He had promised his disciples he would not leave them orphaned and he was true to his word (Jn 14:18). Not only did he break free from the imprisonment of the tomb, not only did he gather the scattered community and restore its hope in the Good News, but he himself became the life of that community—its very heart. And so God does have the last laugh:

> Once in Eden and later on Golgotha, the demons thought they had made the whole plight of man one of never-ending seriousness. The monster death was allowed to close its jaws and then, suddenly, it burst asunder, teeth, jaws and all, with a party-balloon bang.[119]

There is much that is ironic—even humorous—about the Christian story, but we are so used to being "reverent" that we often fail to see the comedy, especially in the narratives of the Passion and Resurrection. This is not to say that we ought to be disrespectful or that we are meant to take God's word lightly; on the contrary, comedy can powerfully affect social and spiritual change—perhaps even more deeply than tragedy. When we confront what is tragic, we are often drawn into our own darkness and hopelessness; though there is such a reality as "cosmic grief" and communal pain, tragedy more often than not numbs us. We find ourselves focusing on images of horror—snapshots of pain like the Stations of the Cross or photos of torture victims from Bosnia, Algeria, Central America, Rwanda. . . . Before such images we can only be silent. We find ourselves recoiling at the inhumanity of the oppressors and at the atrocities they have inflicted upon the oppressed. We journey into the heart of darkness, incapable of uttering anything more than "the horror, the horror . . ." especially when we realize that the very capacity for hatred and violence at which we recoil exists within each of us.

With comedy, on the other hand, there is still the presence of horror but we are able to laugh, sometimes in spite of it, sometimes because of it. Nelvin Voss sees laughter as revelation, as a means of self-discovery, as a form of self-criticism, and as a source of healing.[120] From a Christian perspective, the source of this healing is the conviction that "We are incongruously accepted in spite of our unacceptableness," and that out of this acceptance, God withheld nothing from us—not even God's own self.[121] Laughter, then, could be described as "hope's last weapon . . . our only remaining defense."[122] While, at its worst, laughter can be sadistic or merely artificial, "where it is real, laughter is the voice of faith."[123] "In the presence of disaster and death, we laugh instead of crossing ourselves," writes Harvey Cox. "Or perhaps better stated, our laughter is our way of crossing ourselves."[124]

"Comedy," writes Kronenberger, "is not just a happy as opposed to unhappy ending, but a way of surveying life so that happy endings must prevail."[125] It involves turning the critical lens on oneself, on others, on society, and on situations to expose *what* is in contrast to what is professed to be, thereby purging us of our less noble instincts.[126] But while comedy allows us to see evil for what it is, it helps us to respond from the vantage point of hope: ultimately, it saves us from becoming "victims," no matter what the situation involves, either for ourselves or for others. Comedy guarantees that all will be well, not necessarily in the here and now, but in some future time. The final word, we assure ourselves, is not suffering but a deep-bellied cosmic laugh which will resound through the depths of creation.

Laughter, then, is an appropriate response to the event of Resurrection. "If Christ has not been raised, then our preaching is useless and your believing is useless," writes Paul (1 Cor 15:14). Precisely because Jesus rose from the dead, the Christian story cannot be viewed as a tragedy but as a comedy of "restoration" in which all who suffer death and humiliation are vindicated. Because Christ himself suffered every indignity, every grief, every outrage— and has triumphed— so, too, we will overcome all that afflicts us. Laughter brings relief; betrayal, bitter disappointment, torture and death are not the final realities after all. The worst that could happen has happened and yet all is well and all will be well. Through Jesus' self-offering, we have also been made aware of how intricately and intimately God is immersed in the circumstances of our own lives, suffering *with* us, grieving *for* us, holding nothing back in terms of love, forgiveness, and mercy. . . . Never again do we have to fear being abandoned; never again do we have to dread being alone in our anguish. God is a faithful God, a motherly God, a compassionate God. And so we , too, can find release in holy laughter.

This laughter, this awareness, this vindication—all usher in the new age, the age of the Holy Spirit. Because of what happened in Jesus and through Jesus, the world's stage is set for comic action, that is, for the mending of the broken circle, for the healing of fragmented society. And the agents of this transformation of consciousness are the same followers of Jesus who abandoned him, denied him, lost hope, and hid. By extension, we, in all our frailty and poverty, follow in their footsteps. In this new age, therefore, the reign of God will be ushered in by the spiritually poor and the socially marginalized, and in this, too, there is cause for rejoicing, amazement, and laughter. God, in God's Foolishness, chooses the weak and powerless of this world to accomplish great and wonderful works. God's work, it seems, can be done through the cooperation of anyone upon whom the Holy Spirit chooses to rest.

The Foolishness of the Holy Spirit

The Spirit as Intoxicator

Spirit. . . Holy Spirit. . . God's Spirit hovering over the void of uncreation. . . Spirit. . . Holy Spirit. . . Giver of life to dry bones. . . Giver of dreams to the old, of visions to the young, giver of prophecy. . . Spirit of God descending like a dove on Jesus. . .

Sudden Spirit, powerful Spirit, vociferous Spirit, intoxicating Spirit. . . Spirit of Comfort. . . Spirit of Truth. . . Giver of wisdom and knowledge, of faith and healing, of miracles and tongues and interpretation. . . Paraclete, Befriender, Indweller. . . God's Spirit, hovering still to re-create the face of the earth . . . Spirit of Absurdity. . . Spirit of Foolishness. . . Spirit of Holiness. . .

If Holy Foolishness is part of the divine agenda, then it stands to reason that the Holy Spirit participates in this agenda. If God and Jesus are intrinsically foolish, then the Holy Spirit must likewise be foolish. Until this century, however, theology has largely neglected *pneumatology*, that is, the doctrine of the Spirit, with the result that Christianity has appeared "uninspired and jaded at times." Marie-Henry Keane, O.P., quoting Gregory of Nazianzus' term, *Theos agraptos* (the God about whom nobody writes), explains the consequences of this forgetting of the Spirit:

> We lacked the creative energy which only the Spirit of life could give. Furthermore, we had forgotten how to pray, "Come, Holy Spirit, renew the face of the earth." As individuals and as communities we were often lack-lustre.[127]

Western Christianity has tamed the Spirit into Comforter and Guide, but there is another dimension to the Holy Spirit which more clearly fits our theme: that of *Intoxicator*.[128] By focusing on the behaviors and attitudes of those upon whom the Spirit rests, we will see that her manifestations include rashness, spontaneity, self-abandonment and seeming drunkenness. The Holy Spirit cannot be contained or limited, nor are the effects of the Spirit predictable or controllable. Rather, when the Holy Spirit is active, the irrational prevails. Speaking of God's "dynamism," Elizabeth Johnson writes:

> Spirit, literally meaning a blowing wind, a storm, a stream of air, breath in motion, or something dynamically in movement and impossible to pin down, points to the livingness of God who creates, sustains, and guides all things and cannot be confined. Divine Spirit is not understood to be inde-

pendently personal, as its symbolization in wind,
fire, light and water makes clear, but is the creative
and freeing power of God let loose in the world.[129]

This freeing power—as indicated by the ninth century
hymn, *Veni Creator*—bends what is stiff, warms what is cold
and guides what has gone astray.[130] That which is frozen
melts; that which is fossilized becomes animated; that which
is rigid gains flexibility; that which is held captive breaks
loose. According to the hymn text, this living water, this
flame of love and spiritual anointing, drives away the
"enemy," the source of all harm. Though the nature of the
enemy is not specified, it could be inferred that it represents
all that is antithetical to love, to light, and to divine empowerment. This enemy could be described as the inclination
towards ennui, apathy, lack of commitment, emotional dis-
engagement, repression, egotism, myopia, rigidity, fear, conformity, despair, lifelessness. . . . If the legacy of the Spirit is
life itself, then it is little wonder that Paul VI, echoing the sentiments expressed by John XXIII, declared that "the Church
needs a perpetual Pentecost."[131] The Holy Spirit is what
imparts a quiver of joy, a sense of celebration and festival, a
taste of carnival, an impulse towards Dionysian revelry.

Pentecost and Inspired Speech

If we look at the event of Pentecost, for example, we see that
the presence of the Holy Spirit induces amazingly foolish
behavior. The author of Acts tells us that the disciples, leaving the safety of the upper room, began proclaiming God's
deeds so eloquently that all those gathered heard them in
their own native tongue. Now whether or not the disciples
were speaking "in other tongues" (languages) or "in tongues"
(*glossolalia*), the fact remains that they burst into ecstatic
speech, with no regard as to their safety or as to what others
might think of them. Under the influence of the Holy Spirit,
they preached about the marvels of God, obviously carried
away by their fervor. In their research on glossolalia, behavioral scientists H. Newton Malony and A. Adams Lovekin
explain that many who have studied the phenomenon have

found two settings in which it occurs: in religious cases and in psychopathic cases. Moreover, many researchers have made the two settings synonymous, and "have inferred that those who expressed themselves in this manner were, in fact, abnormal or mentally deranged."[132]

Referring to the more than four hundred books which have been written on the topic of speaking in tongues in the Pentecostalist movement, Yves Congar cautions that it cannot be established *a priori* that present day expressions of glossolalia are identical with what happened at the first Pentecost. "Was it *xenoglossia* (speaking in foreign languages)?" he asks, or was it "an enthusiastic manifestation of exultant praise that witnesses might have taken either as a language which they seemed to recognize or as a drunken delirium?"[133] No doubt there were those in the crowd that Pentecost who wondered about the mental stability of those speaking; Peter, in fact, had to assure the people that the phenomenon they were witnessing had nothing to do with drinking too much new wine—it was, after all, only about 9:00 A.M. Quoting the prophet Joel, he attributed what was happening to God's action:

> "In the days to come—it is the Lord who speaks—
> I will pour out my spirit on humankind.
> Their sons and daughters shall prophesy,
> the young shall see visions,
> the old shall dream dreams.
> Even on my slaves, men and women,
> in those days I will pour out my spirit."
> (Act 2:17–18)

This Spirit, then, is non-discriminating, respecting neither age, nor gender nor social status. All, without exception, can be open to the action of the Spirit; all upon whom the Spirit rests can be moved to passionate articulation that has nothing to do with book learning or other forms of "acquired knowledge." This language may or may not be *glossolalic.* Typically, the language involved—when intelligible—rings with truth and authority, and the speaker experiences himself or herself as a conduit for inspiration, rather than as the author of the utterances in question. Charismatics, for example, speak of "receiving a word" that is meant for the community; it is then incumbent upon them to proclaim what they have heard.

In the Hebrew Scriptures, there are many examples of such inspired speech. Prophetic utterances certainly fall into this category. Jeremiah complained that he was a mere child and could not speak, but God touched his mouth, saying, "There! I am putting my words into your mouth" (Jer 1:9). These words—words of frenzied love, bitter disappointment, and dire warnings—become the characteristic speech of the prophet, making him or her into a laughingstock and fool: "The word of God has meant for me insult, derision, all day long" (Jer 20:8). Likewise, the prophet Ezekiel devoured the sacred scroll, and having eaten his fill of "lamentations, wailings and moanings" was sent to proclaim his imaginative visions and their message of conversion to the House of Israel (Ezel 2:10). The song of three young men—Shadrach, Meshach, and Abednego—in the fiery furnace could also be classified as inspired speech; surrounded by flames rising to a height of "forty-nine cubits," they burst into a song of ecstatic praise, blessing God for having delivered them from their enemies (Dan 3:26–90). Whenever the Spirit inspires, then, women and men speak in unconventional ways that astound all who hear them; "Under the influence of the breath of the Spirit of God, prophets found a wisdom which the ignorant described as 'ravings' (Hos 9:7)."[134]

If we return to the description of Pentecost in Acts 2, we find the Spirit was so intoxicating that about three thousand people, convinced by Peter's proclamation of Jesus' resurrection, were baptized. His passion and clarity of expression left such a powerful impact upon the hearts of his audience that they had no doubts as to the truth of his testimony. There was no trace of the uncouth fisherman who had so recently denied knowing Jesus; instead, Peter shone as a charismatic leader, demonstrating rhetorical skills that were neither learned nor innate. For him, as for the other disciples, the presence of the Holy Spirit brought extraordinary gifts which had no natural explanation. Empowered by this Spirit, members of the fledgling church didn't stop to ask what they should say or to wonder what price they would pay for saying it; instead, they were foolish enough to allow the Spirit to direct them in all things.

The Spirit and the Early Church

Because they were attentive to the inner movement of the Spirit, the first Christians listened to a wisdom very much in opposition to conventional wisdom. Under the inspiration of the Spirit, they were able to move beyond ego concerns and to respond to an invitation which offered a radically different lifestyle; ignoring the wisdom of the world, they embraced what the worldly considered "plain foolishness." Acts 2:42–47 tells us that the early Christian community "lived together and owned everything in common; they sold their goods and possessions and shared out the proceeds among themselves, according to what each one needed." Such communal living contradicted a value system which stressed security, competitiveness, and the importance of property in terms of inheritance rights—especially in a society in which land meant everything. By the world's standards, such communal living was not only counter-cultural but absurdly foolish. It threatened the very fabric of a patriarchal society and called into account the dominant values of the time—and, to add further confusion, it was not undertaken for the sake of some ideological ideal, but in God's Name. Hebraic tradition speaks of the Spirit as *Sophia,* a feminine presence, "a breath of the power of God" (Wis 7:25); one could argue that it was under this feminine inspiration that the primitive church was led to abandon hierarchical social patterns and to experiment with egalitarianism. That same Spirit of Life which brooded over the earth "as if waiting for it to hatch out" would have a motherly concern which encompassed all her children; for Sophia, inequality would be intolerable.[135] Alive with the very Spirit of God, the first Christians acted as fools and drunkards, completely inverting societal expectations.

Fearlessness in the face of worldly powers is another hall-mark of the Holy Spirit's presence. Here we do not mean nat-ural courage or the absence of fear, but a foolhardiness that defies rational explanation—a willingness to speak without tact, without euphemism, without calculation of any kind, with complete disregard for the inevitable consequences in much the same way as the Hebrew prophets and medieval jesters. Even when under interrogation by the temple author-ities, Peter and John showed no signs of intimidation. Surrounded by the rulers, elders, and scribes and "all the members of the high-priestly families," they were not cowed at all, but continued to proclaim God's wonders (Acts 4:5–7). "Filled with the Holy Spirit," Peter fearlessly explained how a man was restored to health through the Name of Jesus—the only Name which offered salvation (Acts 4:10–12). For their part, the religious leaders were "astonished by the assurance shown by Peter and John, considering they were uneducated laymen"; no doubt they were also amazed at their disregard for their personal safety (Acts 4:13).

Clearly, the powers of the world could not control the fol-lowers of Jesus. Though these powers could inflict torture and death, the presence of the Spirit filled the disciples with grace, power, and courage. In fact, the disciples actually identified themselves with God's Spirit: "'We are witnesses to all this, we and the Holy Spirit whom God has given to those who obey God'" (Acts 5:32). Possessed by the Spirit, they became one with the Spirit, losing their finite ego-bound identities in the process. Not only did they work miracles and great signs among the people, but they articulated their beliefs with great clarity, using Scripture to support their position and to show God's saving action in history. Stephen, standing before the Sanhedrin, demonstrated such gifts; filled with the Spirit, he broke into ecstatic speech, giving a powerful account of Jewish history from the time of Abraham to the death of Jesus, reminding his audience of the amazing ways in which God called, guided, and protected the people, forming them into "the chosen ones," against all odds. Though he had been charged with blasphemy—a crime punishable by death—Stephen held nothing back and actually accused his interrogators of resisting   the Holy Spirit; then he intensified the fury of his persecutors by naming their stubbornness. And if this were not provocative enough, upon seeing a vision of Jesus in glory at the right hand of God, he proclaimed what he saw and was stoned to death as a result (Acts 6:8–15; 7).

Throughout the Acts of the Apostles, the Holy Spirit is the driving force behind all decisive events, inaugurating the new era of the Church and its mission. This Spirit—forceful, unpredictable, and transformational—blows where she wills, upsetting the status quo and propelling ordinary people into heroic activities, even at the expense of their lives. This is best exemplified by Saul, persecutor of Christians, who was knocked off his "high horse"—that is, from his platform of ethical superiority—literally to the ground; through his subsequent blindness, he came to recognize his spiritual folly and, following his baptism, became a fearless evangelist. The zeal he had previously used to attack the fledgling church was now directed to preaching the Good News all over the Mediterranean and beyond, while the sheer geographical range of his journeys testifies to something more than common sense.

Paul was well aware of the absurdity of his predicament. A respected member of the Jewish community—one of the elite—he became a "servant" of Christ with no privileges or advantages other than discipleship; instead of being ranked with the kings of the world, with the powerful and the learned, he earned scorn and abuse. Writing to the church in Corinth, he counseled its members to abandon their pride and reconsider the meaning of servanthood in Christ:

> Indeed I wish you were really kings, and we could be kings with you! But it seems to me, God has put us apostles at the end of the parade, with those sentenced to death . . . Here we are, fools for the sake of Christ, while you are the learned ones in Christ; we have no power, but you are influential;

you are celebrities, we are nobodies. To this day, we go without food and drink and clothes; we are beaten and have no homes; we work for our living with our own hands. When we are cursed, we answer with a blessing; when we are hounded, we put up with it; we are insulted and we answer politely. We are treated as the offal of the world, still to this day, the scum of the earth. (1 Cor 4:9–13)

Seized by the Holy Spirit, Paul became the most decisive player in the spread of Christianity, a fact which must have astonished both the Jewish community and those who followed "The Way." Moreover, according to his own testimony, his effectiveness as an evangelizer stemmed from the power of God working through him, even when he was at his weakest (2 Cor 12:1–10). In spite of being subjected to thirty-nine lashes, beaten with sticks, stoned and shipwrecked and imprisoned, in spite of being cold, naked and starving, Paul was content to make his weakness his boast and to "foolishly" declare, "It is when I am weak that I am strong" (2 Cor 12:10). Evidently, the Holy Spirit has a sense of comedy and Paul—a Pharisee and the son of Pharisees—must also have had a few laughs at his own expense. . . .

The Effects of the Spirit
Wherever Christianity has taken root in people's hearts, the presence of the Holy Spirit has driven disciples into a commitment to alternative wisdom or Holy Folly. Even today, those who are not initiated in the mystery of the Spirit find such gifts as praying in tongues and the laying on of hands in healing incomprehensible and absurd. In fact, it is only within the context of faith that the manifestations of the Spirit make any sense at all. How, for example, can one explain what it is to be "slain in the Spirit" to a nonbeliever who has just observed respectable adults falling backwards after having been prayed over? Those without power open themselves to the presence of the Divine, fully expecting that

the impossible *can* happen, should God desire this. Like Jesus, for example, those without medical training allow themselves to be conduits for God's healing power, and others with little formal education speak on God's behalf, whether plainly or "in tongues." Just as artists are seized by a power beyond themselves—the power of inspiration which seemingly possesses them until they produce the "work" entrusted to them—so those seized by the Spirit proclaim through their very being all that they have received. The effects of the Spirit, then, lead to a kind of divine madness— the madness of poet, of prophet, of healer. To become "mad for God's sake," one needs to be wise enough to risk playing the fool.

But while the wisdom of the Spirit can lead us into slapstick and frenzy, it also invites us to look within. The Spirit can have a sobering effect, calling us into the introspection so necessary for "inventory taking" and for dialogue with the divine. Ecstasy and restraint are both foundational for the spiritual life; each needs the other so that balance may be achieved. To be permanently inebriated—even spiritually speaking—would be as counter-productive as to be permanently "sober." The Spirit is not only Intoxicator but also the revelation of the indwelling God; she is that rich inner source which allows us to see God's movement in our lives and to discern new places where God may be calling us. The wisdom of the Spirit is that well of truth in which we see our own reflections without distortion, revealing both our giftedness and our shortcomings and encouraging us to rejoice in all that we are. She is that guide within ourselves which helps us to make life-giving choices and to avoid the path of destruction. She is that rare gift that enables us to offer guidance to others because we have paid attention to our own experiences. Wisdom is that ability to treasure things of the Spirit over material possessions. She gives us a sense of balance, a sense of right order, a sense of proportion; she opens our eyes to deception, teaching us how to be articulate and how to be silent, when to act and when to be still, when to build and when to tear down, how to rule and when to govern. The wisdom of the Spirit reveals to us the treasures of the heart.

But the wisdom of the Spirit is very different from the world's wisdom. Erasmus' Dame Folly explains that Christianity is intrinsically foolish, for it seems to have "a kinship with some spirit of folly, while it has no alliance with wisdom."[136] Briefly summarizing the foolishness mandated by the Gospels, she proceeds to demonstrate that Christians are, in fact, certifiably mad. Possessed by the piety of Christ, those Christians who actually follow his teachings "pour out their wealth, they overlook wrongs, allow themselves to be cheated, make no distinction between friends and enemies, shun pleasure. . . ."[137] Commenting on their tendency to disregard the needs of the body and their disdain for life in general, Dame Folly concludes that Christians have grown "utterly numb to ordinary sensations, quite as if their souls lived elsewhere."[138] What Christians view as happiness, then, is "nothing but a kind of madness and folly."[139]

Dietrich Bonhoeffer articulates the same reality in starker terms:

> Just as Christ is Christ only in virtue of his suffering and rejection, so the disciple is a disciple only in so far as he shares his Lord's suffering and rejection and crucifixion. Discipleship means adhering to the person of Jesus and therefore submission to the law of Christ which is the law of the cross.[140]

In other words, Christian folly is not a moment of madness embarked upon without reflection; rather, it is a way of life in which the disciple embraces folly because that is what the rejected and crucified Christ demands of those who would follow him.

Costly Grace

Bonhoeffer, whose own fidelity to the Gospel and submission to the cross led to imprisonment and death at the hands of the Nazis, distinguishes between "cheap grace" and "costly grace." Cheap grace involves "grace without discipleship, grace without the cross, grace without Jesus Christ, living and incarnate."[141] It represents the world of comfort, habit, security, affluence, and secularization; it waters down the Gospel to a manageable lifestyle and reduces the sacraments to empty rituals devoid of meaning. As such, it is "the deadly enemy of our church."[142] Costly grace, on the other hand, demands nothing less than everything:

> Such grace is costly because it calls us to follow, and it is grace because it calls us to follow Jesus Christ. It is costly because it costs a man his life, and it is grace because it gives a man the only true life. It is costly because it condemns sin, and grace because it justifies the sinner. Above all, it is costly because it cost God the life of His Son: "ye were bought at a price," and what has cost God much cannot be cheap for us.[143]

For Christians, then, "madness and folly" must have a place in the spiritual life; they are charisms of that Spirit which blows where she wills, intoxicating, purifying, and filling all upon whom she descends with energy, wisdom, and grace. In *The Transformation of Man*, Rosemary Haughton examines what really constitutes madness. Assuming that the committed Christian is one who is involved in the needs of "the poor and unhappy," Haughton describes how those who fear for their safety are often threatened by such involvement. Rather than evaluating their own Christian commitment and finding themselves wanting, they prefer to label the dangerous behavior of the unafraid as "mad." Haughton argues that "dangerous" behavior is only a sign of madness if the reason for this behavior warrants it to be so; but "if the reason is the following of Christ. . . . This kind of accusation is a compliment and means that the Church, in some of her members at least, is really carrying out her prophetic mission."[144]

Francis of Assisi is a case in point. In his *Legenda Maior*, Bonaventure presents situation after situation which could lead one to question Francis' sanity: his conviction that there were demons in the pillow he used while he was ill; his insistence that his brother friars should drag him—clad only in his underwear—through the town, rope halter around his neck, because he was a wretched sinner; his obsession with martyrdom; his devotion to poverty; his abuse of his body—humorously named, Brother Ass. . . . But while there is enough documentation here alone to dismiss Francis as mentally unstable, there is more evidence still of his passionate attempt to imitate Christ, to share in his sufferings, and to minister to him through charity to the poor and dispossessed, whatever their station in life. Francis' very "madness," then, is the external manifestation of the presence of the Holy Spirit in his life and of his complete and utter commitment to the crucified Jesus. His folly is a sign of his sanctity.[145]

The same can be said of a modern day saint, Mother Teresa of Calcutta, who left the relative security and comfort of the Loretta Convent to work with the destitute outside the convent walls. Exchanging her habit for a sari, she committed herself to serving those who were dying on the streets. Several years ago, a student of mine worked three weeks at Mother Teresa's side. Moved beyond words by all that she embodied, he could only say that she was the closest he had ever come to the presence of Christ. In her humility, she would prostrate herself before the crucifix, but would also reverence the ground before those whom she served. In her poverty—Spencer estimated that her entire possessions were probably worth no more than $7 or $8—she sold all gifts such as cars, computers, and fax machines, to buy rice for the starving. In her fearlessness, she ventured into hostile areas to minister to the forsaken and abandoned. In her simplicity, she took no credit for her successes but described herself as "a pencil in the hand of God." Without proselytizing, she allowed the presence of Christ to be a source of comfort and hope to the cast-offs of society. Apparently, the very sight of the blue stripe at the hem of a white sari (the habit worn by her Missionaries of Charity) was enough to inspire cries of "Mother! Mother!" from those who had no one else to love them into death. The power of her spirit—and the power of the Holy Spirit within her—was a gift I received through Spencer's account of his amazing journey into the heart of unimaginable poverty and unimaginable love. In the economy of the Holy Spirit, even the telling of the story becomes a source of inspiration and spiritual renewal. The outpouring of love and respect for Mother Teresa following her death in 1997 is indicative of the many hearts she touched during her life. Her "folly," then, in choosing an alternative future for herself provides us with a new understanding of the dignity of the individual and of the immense capacity a single person can have in affecting change.

But there is another consideration to examine here. The Holy Foolishness of Mother Teresa manifested itself in the very absurdity of her mission. To spend one's time, one's energy, on those who are inevitably going to die seems a poor kind of investment. Organizations, such as the Peace Corps and W.H.O. dedicated to working in the Third World, tend to concentrate on measurable outcomes—installing an irrigation system, for example, or reducing the birth rate, or providing AIDS education. Such projects yield results that can benefit whole communities: the labor of a few leads to widespread improvements in the quality of life. In the case of Mother Teresa and the Missionaries of Charity, however, the labors of a few are concentrated on those with only days or hours left to live; the beneficiaries are marginalized individuals who are incapable of passing on the blessings they have received to future generations. The compassion they receive is for themselves alone.

Another contemporary Spirit-filled story is that of Oscar Romero, martyred Archbishop of San Salvador. Appointed as Archbishop in 1977, Romero was regarded as someone who would not "make waves," either for the church or for the ruling political party. The country, at the time, was torn by a vicious war in which those who opposed the government by working for social reform were frequently "eliminated." At first, Romero saw his role as an impartial spiritual leader; his task, as he saw it, was to minister to all parties. Gradually, however, as worshippers were massacred by the National

Guard, as villages were systematically destroyed, and as priests and nuns—including close friends of his—were targeted for assassination, he began to change. Instead of being preoccupied with his own needs, he became a strong, outspoken leader who condemned atrocities, challenged the secular and military authorities, protested U.S. military aid before Congress and even defied the papal nuncio. The following dialogue from Nicholas Patricca's play, *The Fifth Sun*, reflects the values for which he chose to live and die:

> **NUNCIO:** "Oscar, you are letting your passions get the best of you. I like you. I hope to see you in Rome, a cardinal. Fr. Grande was playing politics, the wrong kind of politics."
>
> **ROMERO:** "He was teaching campesinos to read and write."
>
> **NUNCIO:** "He was organizing peasants into labor collectives. That is illegal in El Salvador."
>
> **ROMERO:** "Since Leo III the Church has affirmed the right of workers to form unions."
>
> **NUNCIO:** "He was attacking the institution of private property. Stop playing the ingenue with me! . . . You are letting your mestizo blood cloud your judgment. You are declaring war on this government! You are a politician. And you are not very good at it. I will not support you. Rome will not support you."
>
> **ROMERO:** "You all have your ideas of who I am, of what I am supposed to do, of what I am supposed to say. Where is God in all of this? Does no one consider the simple right and wrong of things?"
>
> **NUNCIO:** "You are either playing the fool or you are a fool!"[146]

Romero was assassinated on March 24th, 1980, while celebrating mass. Following his death, the Spirit which gripped him in life arose in the people, giving them the courage to continue fighting for justice. Romero's story became the story of El Salvador. His personal transformation became a sign of promise for the people, a source of courage. Once again, death and violence were not the final word; once again, God's foolishness prevailed; once again, the Holy Spirit proved to be irrepressible.

Countless other examples of Spirit-filled women and men fill the records of Christianity. As a result of their willingness to be led by the Spirit of God, they—like the prophets and saints of the Hebrew Scriptures—have chosen to live and die by different standards than those endorsed by the world. Their agenda is never personal safety or convenience, but fidelity to God's call; their concern is never "social adjustment" to the norms of the many, but adjustment to God's will for them, however seemingly "foolish." Child-like and trusting, they work against all odds to achieve the goals God has set for them—in spite of limited financial resources, or others' failure to support them, or poor health, or personal tragedy, or even persecution. Filled with God's Spirit—the Spirit of Wisdom—they dare to do the impossible, delighting in the wonderful and amazing ways in which God can use the least likely of people; enthused by this Spirit, they are willing to pay the price tag of "everything" for their obedience and to be driven by divine recklessness rather than by the spirit of timidity.

The Folly of Baptism

From the earliest days, to be Christian by definition meant to be "foolish." In the pre-Constantinian church, the rite of baptism was a dangerous act. Just as the elect were symbolically immersed into the death of Jesus so that they could experience risen life, so, too, they immersed themselves in the possibility of martyrdom. Simply celebrating the rite of election and the enrollment of names was grounds enough for execution; to have one's name inscribed amongst the names of those chosen for initiation was a pledge of fidelity which could very well result in being chosen for death. The story of

St. Genesius—whether legend or history—illustrates the risks. Genesius is reputed to have been one of the players involved in performing a burlesque of Christian baptism before the Emperor Diocletian. In the course of the comedy, Genesius—who had presented himself as a candidate for mock baptism—underwent a religious conversion, embracing Jesus Christ as his Lord. Following his "baptism," and to the amazement of emperor, audience and the dramatic company, he began to proclaim that he was, indeed, a believing Christian. His fate? He was first beaten, then put on the rack, then torn with iron hooks, and burnt with torches before finally being beheaded.[147]

To choose baptism meant to reject the established order and all temporal powers and to submit, instead, to God's rule; it implied a rejection of earthly allegiances—political and familial—embracing a new community based on heavenly citizenship: "This was the existential meaning of baptism as the 'death of the old person' and the birth of the 'new eschatalogical person.'"[148] Only those who were willing to be ultimate fools—that is, fools for Christ's sake—would present themselves as candidates for baptism. The stakes, as we have seen, were high. Under the inspiration of the Holy Spirit, however, courageous men and women simultaneously embraced Jesus and a gruesome death. The litany of those who completely submitted to the waters of death and rebirth—saints such as Apollonia, Basilissa, Cassian, Catherine of Alexandria, Cecilia, Cosmas, Damian, Crispin, Crispinian, Emygidius, Elmo, Florian and Gentian—gives witness to the power of the Holy Spirit in the lives of ordinary men and women.

The practice of baptizing infants with a minimal amount of water has done little to evoke the hazards of embracing Christianity, or the radical dying to self that it requires of each of us. The Rite of Christian Initiation for Adults (RCIA) with its emphasis on personal choice and spiritual formation within the context of the worshipping community invites a more costly commitment—one more in line with that undertaken by the first catechumens. Even so, those whose names were written in the Blood of the Lamb would have difficulty comprehending rites of initiation tamed into social events where the primary symbols are minimalized and all suggestions of real dying are tastefully avoided. And commenting on Catholic practice prior to the liturgical reforms of the Second Vatican Council, William J. Bausch writes: "The Christians of early centuries would be totally baffled and disturbed at the private baptisms on a Sunday afternoon, with no one there, not even the parents."[149] Prior to the reforms, baptism was regarded as a "passport" into heaven for the initiated, as a sign of privilege and a guarantee of "being saved"; it took the whirlwind of the Spirit to remind theologians and laity alike that baptism involves commitment, responsibility and substantial cost.

The Foolishness of the Trinity

Baptism not only represents immersion into Paschal mystery, but also immersion into the life of the Trinity. We have seen that God the Creator's gift of free will was divinely absurd, divinely loving. We have explored the folly of the Incarnation in which God's very Self was made vulnerable. We have examined the ramifications of the Christian path, only to learn that those who would be faithful to the Spirit of Truth, to the Spirit of Jesus, need to follow a different drummer than the rest of the world. The implications of all this would seem to be that Holy Foolishness can be located in the heart of the Trinity.

Recently, when I was a guest at a Unitarian Church, the presiding minister gave a sermon on "the absurd arithmetic of the Trinity." Perhaps he thought he was impressing his audience with his iconoclasm; perhaps his efforts at being witty camouflaged his inability to say anything of theological substance. At any rate, as he joked about the "nonsensical concept of Three in One and One in Three," it was clear to me that in attacking this "absurd arithmetic," in ridiculing the Three-ness of God, he was directly attacking the core of Christianity. In the early church, candidates for baptism were taught creeds not as a test of orthodoxy but as "summaries of faith."[150] The creeds varied in wording according to their place of origin; however, they agreed in content, for all made statements about God the Father, God the Son and God the Holy Spirit. They did not mention the word "Trinity" explicitly, but they told the Christian story—a story with Three Protagonists which reveals something about who God is and what God has done. It is a story filled with absurdity, one which demonstrates how the very Power of God was willing to humble itself and become vulnerable for the sake of wayward humankind; it is only in this respect that Trinitarian arithmetic can be said to be absurd.

And the story tells of a God—God from all eternity—who created the heavens, the earth and the seas and all things that are in them out of nothing but God's creative Word. This God, in accordance with promises spoken through the prophets, sent the Word to become one of us, to be made flesh by the power of the Holy Spirit in the womb of the Virgin Mary; and this Word, the Lord Jesus Christ, preached a new law and a new promise of God's reign among us. He worked miracles and then was crucified, suffering in reality and not just in appearance, dying our common death; then, on the third day, he rose from the dead, later ascending to God's right hand, leaving us the Holy Spirit to guide us, befriend us, and teach us how to live as he taught us.

Absurd as the arithmetic may be, as "foolish" as the actions of the Trinity are by the world's standards, the Trinity cannot be removed from the Christian experience. Our sacred stories are based on God's actions among us as Creator, Savior, and Sanctifier. Our sacred seasons and liturgical observances are also based on the reality of the Trinity. How can we understand Christmas, for example, if we omit Creator and Son? How do we understand the great liturgical cycle stretching from Ash Wednesday to Pentecost if we omit the Holy Spirit? To ignore one of the characters is to change the story; to focus on the person of Jesus only as a "role model" is to observe a form of monotheism that can hardly be called Christian:

> The modern understanding of the Christian faith
> as a practice of living which tries to conform to the
> life of Jesus, in order to carry on his cause, is only
> half the truth, because it only perceives one side of
> what the believer has to give.[151]

Mere imitation of Christ does not make us Christian any more than reading the Koran would make us followers of Islam. There is the question of allegiance of the heart to consider, and whether the Three Persons have a place in this allegiance. But there is more to the Trinity than simply a function for each Person. Unfortunately for the average churchgoer—and, I suspect, for the average minister—the Trinity is an archaic symbol which has little or no contemporary relevance. We celebrate Trinity Sunday, profess belief in the Trinity each time we recite the Nicene Creed, and are vaguely familiar with catechism definitions we learned as children. But most of us have not reflected on what the Trinity means in our own lives. The truth is that while we profess to be Trinitarian, we tend to be "theocentric" in a strictly monotheistic sense in terms of private prayer, and Christocentric only in imitation of Christ, not necessarily in terms of how we relate to him. Are we in relationship with the Trinity or do we simply identify with one Person of the Trinity? Do we pray to a Triune God or is the number "Three" missing from our prayer? Do we participate in the foolishness of the Trinity or do we limit our practice of Holy Foolishness to another paradigm? Moltmann concludes that "Many people view the theological doctrine of the Trinity as a speculation for theological specialists, which has nothing to do with real life."[152]

To reduce the Trinity to a theological definition is to "thingify God," that is, to reduce God to a marketable product which we package according to personal convenience. In the West, we have forgotten the power of words and the sacredness of naming. Unlike the Sufis, we do not have a "working list" of the ninety-nine beautiful names of Allah to enrich our prayer; unlike the Hindus, we do not possess 330 million "gods" to expand our notions of the divine; and, unlike the Jews, we lack the instinctual reverence for the sacred Name which is beyond all names, the Name which is unutterable. The conclusion I draw from all this is that God needs to be liberated from ordinary speech, from theologizing, and from the language of public and private prayer—and the chief means of "liberating God" we Christians have at our disposal is to recover the meaning of the Trinity.

According to Bonaventure's theological framework, the Trinity is dynamic, fluid, productive, supremely good, and supremely loving; of necessity, therefore, there are in the Three Persons "supreme communicability," "supreme consubstantiality," "supreme configurability," "coequality," "coeternity," "mutual intimacy" and "supreme interpenetration."[153] Since "whatever is possessed is given/and given completely," then Holy Foolishness is part of this dynamic, fluid and productive life.[154] If what is true for one Person of the Holy Trinity is equally true for all Three Persons, we can conclude that the Trinity itself is Divinely Foolish. To participate in the holiness of the Trinity is to participate in this Holy Folly.

For Moltmann, the reduction of the Trinity to a "single identical subject," that is, the reduction of Three Persons to three modes of subsistence of the one God, "cannot illuminate salvation history in the fullness of God's open trinitarian relationships of fellowship."[155] At the core of the Trinity is both the capacity for love and the capacity for suffering. Quoting the Patriarch Philareth of Moscow, Moltmann holds that "The Father is crucifying love, the Son is crucified love, and the Holy Spirit is the unvanquishable power of the cross."[156] The Folly of the cross, then, is right at the heart of the Trinity. Moltmann writes: "The pain of the cross determines the inner life of the triune God from eternity to eternity."[157]

Moltmann's theology offers a radical alternative to the modern non-understanding of God as Trinity. His Trinity is more than Aquinas' "moving, causing, necessary, pure and intelligent Being," but a relational God capable of passion and of suffering, who suffers with us, for us, and from us and who has longed for humankind from eternity.[158] According to Moltmann, if God were incapable of suffering, God would be incapable of love, because love for another brings with it the possibility of suffering. Because the Father and the Spirit love the Son who in turn loves them, both Father and Spirit suffer during Jesus' passion; if they could not suffer, then they would be cold, distant heavenly powers—not dynamic, fluid and self-diffusive. Accordingly, Moltmann's very way of naming God as Trinitarian liberates God from centuries of colorless thought and from contemporary indifference. His definitions—like Bonaventure's—set free mystery, ambiguity, paradox and love to be what they already are. His very naming of God, then, helps us to approach God.

A Trinitarian God is relational because God is loving community. In early Greek tradition, this relationship was seen as a dance of love between Father, Son, and Spirit, a dance of intimacy. The fifteenth century Russian iconographer, Andre Rublev, portrayed this dance of love through the forms of three angels—the same angels who visited Abraham and Sarah in their tent near the Oak of Mamre, accepted their hospitality and then predicted the birth of Isaac (Gn 18:1–15). Gazing upon this icon, we come to realize that love is at the heart of this holy circle and that each of us is invited to enter its reality; all that is required is Holy Foolishness—our own capacity for love and our willingness to suffer.

"Three in One and One in Three" may be absurd arithmetic but it is also good theology, powerful theology, radical theology, foolish theology. . . . May the grace of our Lord Jesus Christ, and the love of God, and the communion of the Holy Spirit be with us all. . . .

 *Part Three*

Christian Faith and Folly

Holy Foolishness and Inculturation

Having examined the archetype of the Holy Fool, having explored the Holy Foolishness of God as manifested in all Three Persons of the Trinity, it is now time to draw some concrete conclusions as to the value of looking at Christianity through the lens of Holy Foolishness. What difference does seeing Jesus through the archetype of the Holy Fool make for our faith, for our prayer, for our very relationship with him? When we see Jesus in all his vulnerability, when we observe him "put on" the redeemed aspect of clown, trickster and jester, when we watch him being dismissed as a simpleton or tortured to death as an impious blasphemer, how are we affected in the core of our being? How does Jesus the Holy Fool not only provide challenges for the individual Christian but also for the institutional church?

For Georges Rouault, neither a triumphant Jesus nor a regal Jesus nor a powerful Jesus captured the essence of the Christ who is relevant to the modern world; rather it was the mocked Christ who caught his artistic imagination. The Holy Foolishness of Jesus, then, is a quality which seems to speak to our era.

Every epoch has unique characteristics that set it apart from other historical periods. The industrial age, for example, with its emphasis on production, its movement away from an agrarian economy to an urban, factory-based economy, and its dependence upon the proletariat, could be described as the Age of Prometheus. Prometheus stole fire from the gods, thereby setting humankind on the path of progress while securing his own torment; similarly, the giants of the industrial age unlocked the secrets of mass production, thereby chaining workers to assembly lines and to relentless machinery. Archetypally speaking, Prometheus embodies what is best and worst about a mechanized world—a world marked by order, reason and utilitarianism. He also symbolizes industrialized humanity's consciousness of itself: each person is a cog in the machine of life and each person's dignity is based upon the ability to produce.

Prometheus no longer speaks to our age. The horrors of the totalitarian state, of two world wars and of widespread genocide, together with the constant threat of nuclear annihilation, have given birth to the sense of absurdity which we find reflected in twentieth century existentialist philosophy and literature. Matter proliferates—as in Ionesco's plays— but Godot never comes; instead, like the tramps Vladimir and Estragon, humankind is found with its boots off and its trousers unzipped, waiting, always waiting, for that which never arrives.[1] Simply put, meaning is hard to come by. Prometheus, the noble fire-stealer, heroically defies the gods and suffers accordingly, as a tragic figure; in contrast, Sisyphus—metaphorically "chained" to a stone, rolling it, always rolling it up the mountain, with no end to his labors in sight— personifies the absurdity of the modern human predicament.

The tragi-comic Sisyphus speaks to a world that has lost its fire—the fire of passion, the fire of warmth, the fire of the sacred hearth. Instead, our only fire is the fire of global warming, together with the memory of nuclear firestorming and of the black smoke emanating from Holocaust ovens. In his introduction to *The Theatre of the Absurd*, Martin Esslin describes how Albert Camus diagnosed the human situation through the mythical figure of Sisyphus. In a world of shattered beliefs, modern humanity is in exile, deprived of memories of a lost homeland and lacking the hope that there is a promised land to come; like Sisyphus, modern humanity is divorced from life itself, cut off from transcendental roots and bound to a cycle of absurdity.[2]

But if Sisyphus reflects the existential angst of our time, there is another archetypal figure who is also operative. Dionysus as a figure of the ecstatic represents a reaction to Sisyphus. Those who dare let go of their stones and step off the mountain are free to live out of this archetype in both its positive and negative dimensions. At his worst, Dionysus stands for hedonism—for debauchery, intoxication, revelry, irresponsibility, licentiousness, and wanton cruelty; at his best, he represents spontaneity, aliveness, passion, ecstatic worship, and mystical consciousness. In Euripides' play, *The Bacchae*, it is clear that to deny the Dionysian elements in life is to bring disaster upon oneself and upon the kingdom. Pentheus, King of Thebes, limited by his own rationality, refuses to sanction Dionysian rites or to recognize the god; by repressing his own need for Dionysian experience, Pentheus turns a powerful spiritual force into a force of destruction, thereby securing his own terrible end. Pursued by frenzied Maenad priestesses who are led by his own divinely possessed mother, Pentheus is hunted down like a ritual victim, torn limb from limb and devoured.[3] The price of his rigidity and of his refusal to acknowledge his own animal nature reflects the price modern civilization has paid—and is still paying—for its sterility. As Nietzsche pointed out, when rationality is against instinct, it becomes "a dangerous force that undermines life."[4]

Dionysus is at once a flapper of the 1920s, a flower child of the 1960s, and a pleasure seeker of the 1980s, but he is also one who understands the interrelatedness of spirituality and sexuality, of ecstasy and union with the divine. For him, altered states of consciousness are not mere self-indulgence but ways of being initiated into mystery. Wine, song, dance, and boisterous revelry are not ends in themselves but religious rites through which the drama of life can be expressed, interpreted and transcended. It is no accident that Greek drama was born out of Dionysian rites or that these rites were essentially religious in nature. Both in their wild woodland form and in their later staged manifestations, the rites of Dionysus sparked the religious imagination, offered release for pent-up emotions, and provided worshippers/audience with the opportunity to participate in sacred story. Today, Dionysus continues to speak to us, not from some remote hillside but in the midst of everyday life. Whenever we refuse to define ourselves by our productivity or to settle for what can be described as "statistical living," then Dionysus reigns and both Prometheus and Sisyphus lose their archetypal grip.

Sisyphus generates despair; Dionysus offers the possibility of release. Caught between these archetypal opposites, it would seem that Christians of the present era require a Christ who can push away the stone of meaninglessness while inviting all to drink deeply of the cup of life. It is neither Jesus the Pantocrator nor Jesus the Messiah nor Jesus Triumphant who can best fulfill this role, but Jesus the Holy Fool. Though Nietzsche saw the gospel Jesus as the Anti-Christ, as one—as Kaufmann summarizes—who "stands opposed to this world and this life, and neither takes nor teaches any joys in small pleasures and beauties,"[5] Jesus the Holy Fool laughs at the structures of absurdity and defies all that dehumanizes us.

The Jesus whom Friedrich Nietzsche repudiates is a mere caricature of the Jesus of faith—albeit a caricature which has, unfortunately, been promoted by the churches. As Holy Fool, a very different Jesus holds the Holy Grail before us that we, too, might find the courage to say, "Amen," and to drain it to the dregs. This Jesus is no Sisyphus bound to a cycle of senseless repetition; instead, he breaks open the bread of experience that we may find God in the ordinary events of our lives. As Holy Fool, Jesus asserts that life does hold meaning and that it is not the forces of chaos but God who has the final word. Jesus the Holy Fool invites all who have been shattered, all who are marginalized, all who have ceased to dream, to take their place at the sacred banquet. There, amidst feasting and revelry, the down-and-outs of society discover the laughter of release, the merry dance of love.

Wine flows at the Feast of Cana because Jesus, like the mythical Dionysus, invites us to transform the water of our lives into that which is truly intoxicating—the elixir of the Spirit. This wine fills us with ecstasy, allowing us to taste the inebriating presence of God, even in the heart of the mundane; it fills us with passion, allowing us to love wholeheartedly, to honor our commitments, and to live each moment to the fullest. It gives us the courage to speak truth and to live authentically, while inviting us into the delight of playful spontaneity.

In short, a Christology based on Holy Foolishness moves us away from the absurdity of Sisyphus and from the sterility of modern life into an experience of the ecstatic which could be described as "Dionysian" in the best sense of the term. Such a Christology encourages us to be more intentional about how we invest ourselves in the life of faith. It allows us to understand the difference between conventional wisdom and God's wisdom, between stupidity and heroic risk-taking, between self-centeredness and radical self-giving, between mere eloquence and truth-speaking. In this way, Jesus the Holy Fool invites each of us to become fools for his sake—that is, to consciously choose a path that will be fraught with trials, terrors and absurdity for the sake of God's reign.

Relationship with Jesus the Holy Fool

The core of the Christian life has two distinct components. As "fundamentalist" as this may sound, the first of these is grounded in the reality of a personal relationship with Jesus; the second involves a wholehearted commitment to gospel values for the sake of Jesus. While there are those who would argue that admiration for Jesus or following his example are enough to make one a disciple, it would seem that the Christian life calls for a deeper commitment than mere admiration or imitation. Muslims, for example, as well as some Reform Jews, venerate Jesus as a prophet and yet would recoil at being called "Christian"; similarly, many Buddhists and humanists espouse the same values which Jesus taught and yet they, too, would shy away from any claims to discipleship. For the Christian, then, there is a qualitative difference between "admiration" and "symbiotic relationship," or between "humanistic ideals" and "discipleship." Summarizing the Christian perspective, Thomas à Kempis writes, "Let the life of Jesus Christ, then be our first consideration."[6]

If the life of Christ is indeed our "first consideration," relationship with him is primary. "Christianity without the living Christ is inevitably Christianity without discipleship, and Christianity without discipleship is always Christianity without Christ," wrote Dietrich Bonhoeffer.[7] Hans Küng, in his seminal work, *On Being a Christian,* also stresses that Christ is "ultimately decisive" for Christianity, adding "Christianity exists only where the memory of Jesus Christ is activated in theory and practice."[8] It means love directed not only towards the idea of Jesus, but towards Jesus himself; this, in turn, implies that Jesus can be encountered in the here and now, not merely as the Jesus of history who lived two millennia ago.

But who is this Jesus with whom we seek relationship? Just as there are many Christologies, so, too, there are many Christs and many ways of imitating these Christs. Following Jesus the Holy Fool is a radically different proposition, for example, than following "my buddy Jesus" and practicing a Christianity which can only be described as self-indulgent. Precisely because contemporary Western Christianity has become disconnected from the Holy Foolishness of Christ and from the Dionysian elements of religion, the person of

Jesus has been "tamed" into a marketable construct far removed from the gospel Jesus or from the living Christ who can still be encountered in Third World nations. In contrast to those Central American countries in which even ministering as a catechist can end in becoming a victim of Death Squads, Christian commitment in wealthier, democratic nations is often watered down to the type of self-indulgent spirituality which manifests itself in bumper stickers of the "Honk if you love Jesus" variety. Though, admittedly, other more engaging faces of Christ are still found in the West, the example of "Jesus as buddy" illustrates how the needs of a culture can dictate relationship with the person of Jesus. When the image of Sisyphus dominates the religious imagination, people seek out comfort, certainty, and security, and so turn to a plastic Jesus; at the same time, they cower in dread before the figure of a Dionysian Christ because he is too passionate, too alive, and too challenging to be attractive.

Anastasio Toj, a Catholic catechist who was assassinated in the corn fields of Tabil, Guatemala, in 1982, along with seventeen others (including his teenage son), merely for proclaiming the Gospel, would have a hard time comprehending "My buddy Jesus," as would his widow, Manuela. Fr. Rigoberto Perez, coordinator of the Historic Memory Project in the province of El Quiche—an interdiocesan project for exhuming, identifying and reburying the countless Guatemalan "disappeared" and for assisting survivors in their grieving process—would likewise be nonplussed by such a Jesus.[9] For them, the tortured-murdered-risen Christ, like the dismembered-risen Dionysus, no doubt beckons compellingly from beyond the tomb and from beyond despair.

There are countless Christians from different denominations who are perfectly comfortable labelling Jesus as "friend" and "brother" and yet this appropriation of Jesus as "familiar" often has a hollow ring to it. There can be something too easy, too saccharine, too superficial about this "me and Jesus" spirituality—something too unreflective, too complacent, too self-righteous. "Buddy" language, in fact, suggests un-knowing, not intimacy; sacrilege, not reverence;

apathy, not commitment. The words may be sweet, but they tend to mask an inner life devoid of maturity. They imply a sense of being elect or spiritually privileged whereas the reality is often one of spiritual bankruptcy. Theologian John Shea believes it is possible to have "a real relationship with the concrete, radical person of Jesus of Nazareth," but he, too, expresses caution, for Jesus can be "more grace than we want and more demanding than we can handle."[10]

Relationship with Jesus implies the willingness to meet him wherever he is to be found, even in the heart of Holy Folly. It means allowing oneself to be changed by the encounter, even if it means becoming a Holy Fool oneself; it asks us to respond generously to all the challenges which emerge from this, even if there is a terrible price to pay. As St. Paul would attest, a first encounter with Christ can at times knock us to the ground, make us into laughing-stocks and turn everything we cherish upside down until we yield to his will, allowing our spiritual blindness to be healed (Acts 9:1–19). As in the case of the woman at the well or the woman caught in adultery or the man born blind, such an encounter is utterly life-changing; nothing can ever again be the same, for spiritually speaking, one has indeed been "re-born" (Jn 4; 8:1–11; 9). Like St. Paul, those who have been touched by the presence of the living Christ are invited to put on the Christ, to become the Christ, to breathe the Christ (Col 3:1–4).

A dramatic encounter with Jesus forms the basis of a relationship built on the absurdity of trust, so that when the Beloved is seemingly absent, when the consolations of prayer have disappeared leaving feelings of abandonment in their place, when the vicissitudes of life bring grief and hardship, one does not give up, but continues to love freely—and to be accessible to God, no matter what the cost. Moreover, it is also the basis of a relationship built on the absurdity of hope, for in spite of suffering and chaos, in spite of heartache and loss, one dares to believe that all will be well, in God's time and in God's way. Such loving may make one appear to be a clown, a fool and a simpleton, but it also brings us closer to the waiting heart of God. If we arrive at what Shea names as "an everlasting encounter" with Jesus, then the result is "friendship with Christ, love of God and neighbor, and the continuance of the Christian way of life."[11] This, therefore, is no mere habitual relationship but a relationship characterized by all the immediacy of a first meeting, a first recognition of the Beloved. As such, it is passionate, vital and alive; as such, it makes one willing to risk all for the sake of this relationship.

In contrast, far from being a manifestation of incarnational awareness, "buddy Jesus" spirituality lacks any sense of the numinous. Because it is not based on a decisive encounter with Christ but rather on personal need, such a spirituality fails to extend beyond the finite boundaries of the ego. Instead of responding to Jesus as the very sacrament of God, as the one whose Name is beyond all names, those who subscribe to this type of spirituality often regard Jesus only as comforter and confidant—one with whom we can share the events of daily life without fear of judgment. Such a one-dimensional Jesus becomes an endorser of the status quo, a means of self-justification, even an obstacle to growth; such a Jesus is, in reality, an idol of our own making. In fact, devotees of this Jesus would not only run from the cross, but also from the implications of the parables, the Beatitudes, the paradoxes and even the Lord's Prayer; to them, miracles of healing would offer "the quick fix," rather than an invitation to a radically new vision. Those who tame Christmas into a birthday party for children or who reduce Easter to a celebration of the rites of Spring are following a Jesus who bears little resemblance to the Jesus of the Gospels. In their Christianity, there is no place for Jesus the Clown, or Jesus the Jester or Jesus the Trickster; such a Jesus is too demanding, too disturbing, too ridiculous. And yet this Jesus, vested as "a personification of festivity and fantasy" in an age which has almost lost both, and wearing both grease paint and halo, "is able to touch our jaded modern consciousness as other images of Christ cannot."[12]

It is not that we should refrain from turning to Jesus with our concerns, but we also need to listen to his ongoing call to a new way of seeing—a call which always insists upon our living authentically and courageously, and, at times, with complete disregard for "common sense." Moreover, new vision is often only the prelude to a deeper level of participation in God's "vineyard"; paradoxically, the more we respond to the challenges with which Jesus presents us, the more is expected of us. Always, this involves a movement away from ego-absorption and a movement towards serving the needs of others, even at great inconvenience to ourselves. "Buddy Jesus" piety, on the other hand, typically remains exclusively self-preoccupied. It shies away from self-abandonment to Jesus precisely because he invites us into an experience of love which is beyond our comprehension.

It is appropriate here to return to Bonhoeffer's distinction between "cheap grace" and "costly grace." "Jesus the buddy" does not ask for costly grace; in fact, "Jesus the buddy" is a constant source of consolation, that grace "we bestow upon ourselves."[13] Imitating Jesus the Holy Fool, on the other hand, demands costly grace—that is, the call to radical obedience. This can involve standing up and being counted—that is, allowing oneself to openly critique the powers of this world when such a critique becomes an ethical necessity. At times, one may even be called to critique the church itself when it becomes too "middle class," too aligned with Caesar, or too absorbed in its own institutional machinery to be a prophetic voice in the world.

What Jesus the Holy Fool demands of the disciple is nothing less than the renunciation of security, predictability, and comfort. Bonhoeffer writes:

> The old life is left behind and completely surrendered, The disciple is dragged out of . . . relative security into a life of absolute insecurity (that is, in truth, into the absolute security and fellowship of Jesus), from a life which is observable and calculable (it is, in fact, quite incalculable), into a life where everything is observable and fortuitous (that is, into one which is necessary and calculable), out of the realm of the finite (which is in truth

the infinite) into the realm of infinite possibilities (which is the one liberating reality).[14]

Such discipleship, grounded as it is in the way of paradox, is costly by definition. There is nothing comforting here, if one is looking for reassurance, certainty and predictable outcomes; there is nothing comforting here if one hungers for life in an easy chair. This is discipleship for those who dare to be foolish in the world's eyes. Jesus the Holy Fool invites his followers to stand with the poor, not with the powerful, and to leave behind everything that would get in the way of committed discipleship—relationships, material goods, position in society, comforts we take for granted, respectability.

A "buddy Jesus" spirituality, on the other hand, offers the way of worldly wisdom; it is grounded in the illusion that Jesus came to make us comfortable, to take away our yokes without allowing us to learn from them, to save us from the cross so that we never have to experience what it is to be nailed by pain. Such spirituality also embodies the dominant attitudes of our culture: don't get involved, mind your own business, look after Number One. But true discipleship involves "exclusive attachment" to the person of Jesus, not self-indulgence, self-gratification, or self-adulation.[15] True discipleship means the willingness to be mocked as Jesus was mocked, to endure crucifixion—in whatever form—as he was crucified.

Bonhoeffer, commenting on Luke 9:57–62, reflects on three kinds of disciples who are portrayed in this text, all of whom are tied down by the dictates of worldly wisdom and by their unwillingness to be fools for the sake of Christ. The first says to Jesus, "I will follow you wherever you go" (Luke 9:57) but has no idea what this entails; the words are hollow because the would-be disciple is incapable of meeting the rigorous demands of the journey. Jesus points out, "Foxes have holes and the birds of the air have nests but the Son of Man has nowhere to lay his head" (Luke 9:58). The second would-be disciple places legal obligations (burying a parent) before discipleship, but at the critical moment of being called, "nothing on earth, however sacred," must come between Jesus and the one he has called.[16] And the third—who asks permission to bid farewell to the members of his household—wants to dictate the terms of discipleship. But, as Bonhoeffer stresses, responding to the call involves "the simple alternative of obedience or disobedience."[17] Simply put, to set conditions is to disobey. The true disciple—that is, the one who is open to Holy Folly—responds immediately, leaving behind anything which might come between the self and the call, between the self and Jesus. In his dialogue with the disciple, Thomas à Kempis' Christ says: "You must give all for All and keep back nothing of yourself from me. Know that self-love does you more harm than anything else in the world."[18]

It takes a Holy Fool to understand that the hallmarks of a personal relationship with Jesus are intimacy rather than mere camaraderie, humble discipleship rather than Easy Street. The relationship is not merely that of two "buddies" or "equals"; rather, one leads while the other follows, one teaches while the other learns, one guides while the other seeks, one heals while the other prays for healing. . . . "In buddy Jesus" spirituality it is the finite "I" that does the leading, teaching, guiding and healing while Jesus becomes a slogan, a crusader's flag, a manufacturer's logo, a popular poster. . . . A Holy Fool, however, is drawn into relationship with Jesus not to exploit Christianity for spiritual and material gain, but because Jesus invites each of us to live more fully, more intentionally, more passionately in the context of our own circumstances. In the Good Shepherd discourse, Jesus says, "I have come that you may have life and have it to the full," but to receive this fullness one must first be "empty," spiritually speaking (Jn 10:10). By the world's standards, such emptiness is contemptible folly, for it involves staking all that one is, all that one has, for the sake of God's reign:

> Conforming one's life with Christ, Jung suggested, means living the unique life one has been given as faithfully, as authentically as Jesus lived his life. Lonerghan would probably echo this encouragement by saying that the one who is imitating Christ is growing in human development through

authentic self-transcendence, in obedience to the law of transcendental precepts to be attentive, intelligent, reasonable, responsible, and in love.[19]

Contrary to the expectations of "buddy Jesus" piety, the Christian path is not only about richer living, but about experiencing the richness of God within; it is not only about finding freedom, but about allowing the presence of God to set us free so that our hearts are no longer enslaved by lesser gods; it is not only about following the Gospel but about allowing God to transform us as radically as gold is refined by fire. "You must lead a dying life," writes Kempis.[20] The paradox is that the willingness to pay the price of discipleship leads to finding life in death; the willingness to let go of the false self allows us to participate in the very life of Christ so that his life becomes our very life. This is the wisdom of Holy Foolishness, a wisdom the world cannot comprehend.

Participation in the life of Christ, however, involves more than simply sharing in his life; rather, it means relying on Jesus as the very source of our life. Again, the concept of Holy Foolishness allows us to understand this type of dependency as a spiritual advantage, while more popular Christian piety might advocate "being in control." As the Johannine texts point out, the Christ-source is essential for full, productive discipleship; only by allowing Jesus to be the vine can we, the branches, hope to bear fruit; without him, in fact, we can do nothing: "Anyone who does not remain in me is like a branch that has been thrown away" (Jn 15:6). Separated from Christ, we not only fail to bear fruit but even lose our raison d'etre, that is, to give glory to God; barren and dry, resistive to pruning, we are fit only for the bonfire. As disciples, then, we need to recognize our complete dependence upon Jesus and to draw our life from his life, for "there is only Christ: he is everything and he is in everything" (Col 3:11). We drink from the chalice of his life to be inebriated by his love.

Paradoxically—and it takes Holy Foolishness to recognize this—it is when we are at our weakest that Christ's life-giving presence is most apparent. Incapable of accomplishing anything on our own, completely dependent upon Christ for strength and wisdom, all we can do is allow him to work in us and through us. Troubled by our own varieties of "thorns in the flesh," with St. Paul we can say:

> I shall be very happy to make my weakness my special boast so that the power of Christ may stay over me, and that is why I am quite content in my weaknesses, and with insults, hardships, persecutions, and the agonies I go through for Christ's sake. For it is when I am weak that I am strong. (2 Cor 12:10)

From the perspective of Holy Foolishness, then, relationship with Jesus is more than mere imitation. It involves accepting the lordship of Jesus, surrendering to his love and allowing his very life to become our life. It demands risk-taking, letting go of our attachments and submitting to the dreadful process of transformation; it can lead to being mocked, spat upon and even "crucified." Above all else, it involves believing in his inexhaustible love for us when worldly cynicism might try to convince us that we are quite unlovable. "I saw that he is everything that we know to be good and helpful," writes Julian of Norwich. "In his love he clothes us, enfolds and embraces us; that tender love completely surrounds us, never to leave us."[21]

The Russian Holy Fool

Fools for Christ's Sake

Perhaps it is the Holy Fool of Russian life and literature who best embodies what it means to live a Christian life grounded in God's foolishness. Today, living in a completely secular society, even being an ordinary Christian brands one as "foolish." In other contexts—as for example, in Eastern Christianity—the Holy Fool emerged in a theocratic structure where feigning madness as a form of self-protection allowed him or her to speak with impunity. Here we are no longer in the shadow territory of the reveler, trickster, naive fool, or professional fool; instead we are investigating a highly evolved spiritual state which may, at times, manifest itself as absolute foolishness. This spiritual state is akin to what Jung described as "individuation." In her essay, "The Process of Individuation," Marie-Louise Von Franz explains that this state emerges from "the conscious coming to terms with one's own inner center."[22]

Those committed to the process of individuation will courageously explore their "shadow side," that is, their repressed fears, memories, and desires, bringing to light what was previously hidden. In this way, a new, stronger self is forged from the forgotten fragments of one's identity; the new self is an integrated self fully grounded in awareness—awareness of one's hopes, dreams, attitudes and motives. Gradually, "a wider more mature personality emerges, and by degrees becomes effective and even visible to others."[23] No longer driven by unconscious forces, the individuated self is authentically free, untainted, as it were, by ego needs and other's expectations.

For the Christian, the individuated self is nothing less than the Christ-Self. All that is stripped away allows the real self—the Christ Self—to surface. Petty ambitions, grudges, and wishes fall away; the desire for praise and accolades is extinguished. Instead, one is left with a new compassion, a new willingness to be attentive to God's will, and with an open-handed response to life. One clutches at nothing, while finding everything in one's relationship with God. "Five year plans" no longer have relevance. What is important is the careful discerning of God's call in every aspect of the present moment. Instead of struggling to be in control, the individuated Christian learns to practice surrender. God and God alone is central. By the world's standards, this in itself is folly—a far cry from "my buddy Jesus" spirituality, or from the sterility of Sisyphus or the shadow dimensions of Dionysus.

The Holy Fool is a fully individuated Christian who passionately embraces a life of seeming folly to be a fool for the sake of Christ. While the Western Churches have not shown much sympathy towards Holy Fools, the Holy Orthodox Churches of the East have a long tradition of venerating "fools for Christ" along with martyrs, virgins, and confessors. Not only is folly for Christ's sake an integral part of Orthodox spirituality, but "the fools are among the most beloved saints of the East."[24] In his article, "Holy Foolishness," Jim Forest explains that the men and women who are saints in this tradition (*iurodivii*) often give witness to the Gospel in ways which "fly in the face of what most regard as saintly."[25] In these *iurodivii*, Christ "wears the disguise of madness," for while there is much variety among them, they are in every case "ascetic Christians living well outside the borders of conventional social behavior, including conventional religious behavior."[26]

John Saward traces the history of Russian Holy Fools back to the founders of Christian monasticism in the deserts of Egypt and Syria, explaining that early monasticism exhibited two distinct forms of "holy unwisdom." The first, *Holy Idiocy*, suggests simplicity and ignorance of the world's wisdom: "The term *idiotes* in Greek denotes a private man, with no particular public function or skill. Similarly, the Latin *idiota* means a rustic, one with no science or discipline, an illiterate."[27]

The Holy Idiot was one who was either uneducated but spiritually wise or educated but simple at heart; in either case, the Holy Idiot would be ignorant of the world's wisdom. Among the ranks of such Holy Idiots, were Anthony, Abba Arsenius, and Abba Moses. They did not necessarily behave in foolish ways, but they recognized that the path to God's heart was not through the study of Latin or Greek but through cultivating divine wisdom by prayer, fasting, solitude and other disciplines.

In contrast, the *fool for Christ's sake* was one whom both the world and other Christians deemed as foolish. This foolishness was not only to conceal one's spirituality, but was also a medium for the wisdom of God. Not only did fools for Christ follow the heart of Christian and monastic obedience—that is, to give up self-will—but there were those who by the fourth century saw folly as a definite vocation and a gift of the Holy Spirit.[28] There was Sarapion Sindonites, who lived in abject poverty, clad only in a loincloth; having sold himself to a troupe of Greek actors—whom he converted to Christianity—he wandered from Egypt to Greece and Rome, no doubt leaving a trail of conversions along the way. Then there was Isidora who was considered mad by the other sisters in the convent because of her insistence on living on the crumbs from the table instead of eating regular meals, and Abba Ammonas who simulated madness for the sake of humility. Monastic fools were what Saward would name as "fools twice over," that is, those who were not only counter-cultural for having embraced a life of vowed renunciation but because they appeared foolish even to their sisters and brethren in community.

There were also Holy Fools who played the fool in public, but lived a Christian life in secret. John of Ephesus (c. 507–586 C.E.) records the example of Theophilus and Maria of Antioch "who despised the world and all that is in it and lived a holy life in poverty of spirit, wearing an assumed garb." Dressed as mime-actor and prostitute, they went to the city of Amida "where they used often to perform drolleries and buffooneries . . . making fun of the priests and the people, and having their ears boxed by everyone."[29] At night, however, this comedian and this prostitute kept vigil in prayer, their sanctity completely invisible to the world. No doubt, even their daytime folly served a purpose—that of unmasking religious hypocrisy and self-righteous attitudes. Outwardly, they masked themselves in Dionysian hedonism while living passionate inner lives.

Holy Fools and Russian Piety

There is nothing tame or lukewarm about the Christianity we see espoused by Holy Fools; nor is there anything which suggests the final word about life is its absurdity and meaninglessness. On the contrary, we see a Christianity which is intensely alive, daringly prophetic, and utterly countercultural. The wild and unrestrained spirituality of such fools was possibly carried into Russia via the popular story of Andrew the Holy Fool who captivated the imagination of Byzantine Christianity. Reputed to be the son of a Scythian slave, Andrew had a vision commanding him to live as a Holy Fool; this launched him on a path of simulated madness, complete nakedness and homelessness. Much of the time he pretended to be out of his mind, yet he also showed remarkable gifts for discerning evil. Devoted to the Mother of God, he and a friend (Epiphanius, later Patriarch of Constantinople) had a vision in which Mary stretched her veil over the assembly gathered in the Church of Blachernae in Constantinople, promising to protect her city. By the twelfth century, this event was already recorded in the Pokrov icon, "the Protecting Veil of the Mother of God."[30] John Wortley suggests that since Andrew's vision occurred in 911, the year of the peace treaty between the Byzantine government and Prince Oleg of Kiev, it is likely that his story became part of the renewed "cultural exchange" between the factions and hence made its way to Kiev.[31]

The first Russian Holy Fools seem to have been associated with the Monastery of the Caves near Kiev; they developed a spirituality of monastic poverty, synthesizing the desert spirit of early monasticism with the Studite Rule of Constantinople. Theodosius (d. 1074), who established the Studite Rule, saw Holy Folly as a means of imitating Christ:

> Our Lord Jesus Christ became poor and humbled Himself, offering Himself as an example, so that we should humble ourselves in His name. He suffered insults, was spat upon and beaten, for our salvation; how just it is, then, that we should suffer in order to gain Christ.[32]

Theodosius it is said interceded for ordinary people before princes and judges in pre-Mongolian Russia; he also strongly censured Prince Sviatoslav for persecuting his older brother and for usurping the throne of Kiev. Even upon threat of banishment, he constantly urged Sviatoslav to reconcile with his brother and to return the throne:

> Obviously, the saint did not consider secular and
> political affairs beyond his spiritual competence.
> In striving for justice, he was ready to go into exile
> or death. . . . He believed his duty was to teach
> princes and theirs to listen to his admonitions. But
> he acted towards them not as one having authority
> but as the agent of the meek power of Christ.[33]

Exhibiting a complete disregard for his own safety, Theodosius enforced a strict rule of radical trust in Providence. In this regard, he upheld the principle of not hoarding possessions. Just as God commanded the Israelites not to hoard manna during their desert wanderings (Ex 16:19), so the Abbot of the Kievan monastery insisted that any superfluous food or clothing be burned as "the devil's part." One legend narrates how he threw into the river some loaves of bread a thrifty cellarer had spared for the next day.[34] Whether this story is historically accurate or not, it reflects the community's attempts to live simply and without security. Even a simple gesture such as keeping bread for the next day was viewed as spiritually detrimental.

The great era of Holy Fools in Russia was the sixteenth century. By this time, the *iurodivii* were a national phenomenon, an observable part of daily life and a source of amazement to travelers who were both repelled by their wild behavior and nakedness, and surprised at the license with which they could speak. Basil the Blessed (d.1552), a naked vagabond who scandalized the self-righteous by his compassion for society's outcasts, was the most venerated Holy Fool of his time. One Lent, he presented Ivan the Terrible with a slab of raw beef, though it was a period of rigorous fasting; the point of this seemingly absurd gesture was that since the tsar was murdering his own subjects, there was no point abstaining from meat as this would not save him from hell.[35] Even twenty years after his death, Basil reputedly still managed to make the tsar's life uncomfortable: in one legend, Basil offered him a meal of fresh blood and meat. When the tsar refused to partake of this food, he saw in the sky the souls of all those he had recently butchered in the razing of Novgorod.[36]

The seventeenth century, which brought with it the can-
onization of the last Holy Fool, marked the end of church-
sanctioned Holy Folly. Perhaps the approach of the Age of
Reason accounts for this, or perhaps the growing influence of
Western European thought and customs, especially the fri-
volity and luxury of the French court. From this time, the living reality of the Fool for Christ became a literary motif,
appearing in Pushkin's *Boris Godunov*, in Tolstoy's *Childhood,
Boyhood and Youth*, and Dostoyevsky's *The Idiot*.

In *The Idiot*, for example, the Prince is a child-like idealist
who insists on saying what he thinks to the Russian aristocracy, even though he knows himself to be an object of
ridicule, a fool. In Book 4:7, he blabbers, apologizing for his
excesses; he gets carried away by passion and then wonders
why everyone is laughing at him; he acts like a frightened little boy (after breaking the Chinese vase) and is grateful that
his hosts can forgive him; he lets his audience know exactly
what he is thinking, without any attempt to protect himself
or to present himself in a positive light, referring to himself
as "a boy." In short, he makes a spectacle of himself, becoming feverish in his attempts to communicate. But while the
Prince appears to be a natural fool (as opposed to the artificial fool), he speaks truth, challenging the establishment to
examine their place of privilege and to re-evaluate their attitudes towards the peasants:

> "It's quite true that we are absurd and frivolous,
> that we have bad habits, that we are bored, that we
> don't know how to look at anything or understand
> anything. We are all like that, all of us, you and I
> and everybody! You're not offended because I am
> telling you to your face that you are absurd, are
> you? And if that's so, aren't you promising mate-
> rial? You know, in my opinion it is sometimes quite
> a good thing to be absurd. Indeed, it's much better;
> it makes it so much easier to forgive each other and
> to humble ourselves. One can't start straight with
> perfection! To attain perfection, one must first of
> all be able not to understand many things. For if

we understand things too quickly, we may perhaps fail to understand them well enough. . . .

"You are laughing, Ivan Petrovich? You think that
I was afraid for the others, that I am their advocate,
a democrat, an upholder of equality?" he laughed
hysterically (he kept interrupting his speech every
minute by short, rapturous bursts of laughter). "I
am afraid for you, for all of you and for all of us.
For I am a prince of ancient lineage myself, and I
am sitting among princes. I am saying this to save
you all, so as to prevent our class from vanishing
for nothing into utter darkness, without realizing
anything, abusing everything and losing everything. Why should we vanish and give up our
position to others, when we might remain in the
front rank and be the leaders of men? Let us stay in
the front rank and be leaders. Let us be servants in
order to be leaders."[37]

Madness? Misplaced idealism? Naiveté? However one
might characterize this speech, it is clear that the Prince
espouses gospel values—humility, responsibility, servanthood, gentleness, forgiveness, innocence . . . His values are
not those of status and power, but of self-emptying, self-
negating, self-abandonment—the very foolish standards
modeled by Jesus the Holy Fool. Little wonder, then, that the
party in this scene comes to an abrupt ending, with the guests
dispersing, feeling "a little cross." No doubt the fact that they
can dismiss the Prince as being ill and unhappy prevents
them from being rage-filled. After all, the words of a sick individual—like those of a court jester—do not have to be taken
seriously, even if they strike uncomfortably close to home.

Sonia, the prostitute in Dostoyevsky's *Crime and
Punishment*, is another Holy Fool—not a seemingly "natural
fool" like the Prince, but one who is foolish for the sake of
love and who, like the earliest manifestations of the Holy
Fool, allows her "profession" to mask her true sanctity. Sonia
sells herself so that her T.B. stricken step-mother, Katerina

Ivanovna and her young children, might survive financially. Despised by society, Sonia—little more than a child herself—gives away what she earns without complaint, without resentment, even though it is her father's irresponsible drinking that has landed the family in such straits.

Dostoyevsky clearly respects her self-sacrifice; he delineates Sonia with a gentle pen, showing her strength of character, her child-like innocence, her innate beauty. Through the eyes of the protagonist, Raskolnikov, who murdered Lizaveta, a simple-minded woman with whom Sonia used to read and talk about God, we also gain insight into the author's own compassion for the two women. Raskolnikov, whose very name means "one cut off," regards both his victim and Sonia as "religious maniacs" (or Holy Fools). At the same time, he recognizes that Sonia has preserved her purity of spirit, in spite of all her sufferings; her very goodness becomes a judgment on his own callous sins of violence against Lizaveta and her sister, the pawnbroker—sins which he has rationalized to himself on the basis of his intellectual superiority.[38] Ernest J. Simmons, in his introduction to the Vintage edition of the novel, writes, "Sonia transcends her allegorical significance through the sheer force of the novelist's art. She stands as a kind of living universal symbol of crushed and suffering humanity that bears within itself the underlying seeds of joyous resurrection."[39]

Whether of limited intelligence or brilliant, whether of social ranking or none, the *iurodivii* remind us "of a deeper sanity that is sometimes hidden beneath apparent lunacy: the treasure of a God-centred life."[40] Worldly possessions, family, position, and comfort have no relevance; Holy Fools have no ambitions beyond serving God and fearing God alone. In essence, the self-description of the Pilgrim in the classic, *The Way of the Pilgrim*, could apply to all Holy Fools:

> "By the grace of God, I am a Christian, by my deeds a great sinner, and by my calling, a homeless wanderer of humblest origin, roaming from place to place. My possessions consist of a knapsack

with dry crusts of bread on my back and in my
bosom the Holy Bible. This is all!"[41]

All that is important is the Holy Fool's service to Christ.
For the Pilgrim, this service is the ceaseless recitation of The
Jesus Prayer: "Lord Jesus Christ, have mercy on me." This is
not just prayed with the lips but with the mind and with the
heart, in waking and in sleeping; so intense is this praying
that the Pilgrim walks "in a semi-conscious state without
worries, interests or temptation."[42]

Though associated with Russian life and literature, Holy
Fools are not confined to any particular era or locale; rather,
they appear wherever women and men abandon everything
for the sake of the gospel. I think of two Holy Fools who
belong to a church in Chicago—Brother Bill Tomes and
Brother Jim Fogerty, a community of two in denim patch-
work habits who go to the projects and stand in the line of
fire praying when rival gangs begin fighting. Known to gang
members of varying loyalties, these men minister to the
hardened youth of the city in such dangerous haunts as
Cabrini Green, the Henry Horner Homes, Dearborn Homes
and Rockwell Gardens. Certifiably mad? All we can be certain of is that, through their presence, the presence of Christ
is made manifest. In his article, "Holy Fools: Ushers of the
Next Generation of the Church," Richard Rohr writes:

> It will be "holy fools" who will lead us into a new
> future and the next generation church. The holy
> fool is who the Holy Bible and mythic literature
> have always presented as "the saviour." Holy fools
> are happily, but not naively, innocent of everything
> that the rest of us take as self-evident. It is the last
> stage of the wisdom journey: Jesus in his parables,
> Frances in his patches, and Dorothy Day obedient
> to petty churchmen for paramount reasons.
> Reasonable people will always be able to criticize
> such fools, but they bring to every exile a whole
> new way of imagining —and thereby usher in the
> new age.[43]

If Rohr is accurate in his assessment of Holy Fools, then they not only have wisdom to impart to the church, but they could give rise to a much needed ecclesiology—one in which all believers and the institutional church itself are called to Holy Folly.

Holy Foolishness and the Church Today

Holy Foolishness and Christian Spirituality

If Christian discipleship means more than paying lip service to gospel ideals and enjoying a smug sense of self-righteousness, so, too, following a spiritual path involves more than being "religious" in a conventional sense or merely inheriting a set of religious values. In fact, spirituality does not necessarily mean adhering to a particular tradition or attending church, synagogue, mosque, or temple; on the contrary, one can be a traditional Christian, Jew, Hindu, Muslim, or Buddhist and not be spiritual. For many, the practice of religion can become a substitute for developing a healthy spirituality; instead of looking within for the answers to life's complexities, one looks to the authority of the institution—to its teachings, its traditions, its dogmas, its hierarchical structures and its "conventional wisdom." Ironically, the religious institutions to which we entrust ourselves have too often taken on the behaviors of secular "powers"; they have been more concerned "with certain dogmas . . . than with the practice of love and humility in everyday life."[44]

While, ideally, religious traditions enhance the spiritual path, spirituality itself transcends formal religion. It is a way of living which is intentional rather than accidental. It has nothing to do with habit, and everything to do with being open to the rhythms of life—its mysteries, its gifts, its surprises. Conventional religion often emphasizes orthopraxy and orthodoxy; spirituality, on the other hand, is concerned with that which is most alive about a human being—the intangible, the ineffable, and the invisible and all that lies at the innermost core of self, enduring beyond physical finitude. Traditionally, here in the West we have understood this

to be the "soul," not in the sense of a "thing" but as "a quality or a dimension of experiencing life and ourselves. It has
to do with depth, value relatedness, heart and personal
substance."[45]

All that enriches the soul is therefore the focus of spirituality. How one lives one's life, how one relates to God, where
one invests energy, time and talents are all spiritual questions. The choices one makes about occupation, relationships, worship, diet, exercise, leisure, volunteering, and
other lifestyle issues also have spiritual ramifications.
Everything, it seems, can have a bearing on how one experiences the transcendent and how one advances in the spiritual
ascent. Spirituality, then, encompasses all of life and is that
force which connects us with ultimate meaning.

As we examine the implications of Holy Foolishness for
Christianity, we need to define what Christian spirituality is
not. In its gospel model, it is seldom the religion of the establishment and has little to do with orthodoxy or orthopraxy. It
is not based on authoritarianism, habit, or mere obligation. It
is not characterized by inflexibility, control, lack of choice or
lack of commitment. It is often antithetical to conventional
wisdom and defies any form of reducing life to what John
Francis Kavanaugh describes as "the Commodity Form"—a
frame of perceiving and valuing which reduces people to
"things" and turns our most precious attributes into commodities.[46] It does not seek to manipulate God or to reduce
God to an investment policy. It is not limited by *chronos* nor
by what is "possible" in human terms. Accordingly, neither
Sisyphus nor Prometheus provides an appropriate archetypal representation of the essence of Christian spirituality.

On the contrary, Christian spirituality—as defined by the
Gospels—is passionate, spontaneous, transformational, and
has everything to do with the heart. What is distinctive about
Christian spirituality is what is distinctive about Jesus' pedagogy. As noted earlier, Jesus shattered limited assumptions
and expectations to reveal the reign of God at work in the
most surprising of circumstances and among the least likely
of people. In fact, it is not the learned and the wise who are

spiritually mature but those who are foolish enough to see through the innocent eyes of a child. Willing to embrace ambiguity, uncertainty and mystery, Christian spirituality has as its central concerns relationship with God and the care of the soul.

The Christian life is not something that simply "happens" to one, but a heroic quest to which each of us is called. God—as revealed in and through Jesus Christ—is at the center while the arena of faith is the human condition. Its main focus is to discover God's dream for humankind and to work towards the implementing of this dream. Spending oneself for the sake of the reign of God in the present moment becomes the primary mission of each Christian. It is kairos not chronos which rules. Life is not merely "burnt toast" but an investment of everything one is and everything one has for the furthering of God's will and the glorification of God's Name. Radical surrender, simplicity, purity of vision, trust, and dependency upon God are hallmarks of this journey. Prayer is a freeing event and the only privilege is discipleship itself. In its purest form, Christian spirituality establishes the equality of all the baptized; all are called to be "a chosen race, a royal priesthood, a consecrated nation, a people set apart" (1 Peter 2:9).

It is Holy Foolishness which enlivens Christian spirituality, maintains its authenticity and prevents it from degenerating into sentimentality or "authoritarian religion." In an age when Sisyphus and the shadow side of Dionysus vie for hegemony and when institutions are viewed with mistrust and resentment, Jesus the Holy Fool offers an attractive alternative. Today, the Jesus who merely turns the other cheek in a passive sense or who carries a comatose sheep on his shoulders is not going to inspire a following. Though self-denial, obedience, and surrender have a place in spiritual praxis, when these become the "face" of a tradition rather than facets of it, the tradition itself loses appeal. Young people today seek to contribute their gifts, to follow their consciences, and to chart their own paths; they are not willing to be passive sheep, but expect to be fully responsible for their own choices. It is Jesus the Holy Fool who offers the possibility of experiencing the fullness of life and a Christianity that is a viable alternative to existential angst or hedonism. At his beckoning, "religion" moves away from being merely an inherited component of one's cultural baggage and instead becomes as necessary as the air one breathes—a source of that living water for which the Samaritan woman thirsted so desperately.

When we embrace Holy Foolishness as a dimension of the Christian path, we embrace the change of consciousness which can come from playing the fool. Professional fools are free to be themselves and to disregard the opinions and behaviors of the dominant culture; by imitating the license of the fool, we begin to discover new ways of seeing, of thinking and of being—ways we can barely imagine when we wear the masks of acceptability and respectability. By daring to put on motley, by risking being seen in a fool's belled cap, we give ourselves permission to speak and to do the unthinkable. No longer inhibited by our customary roles, we break through all that would normally constrain us. Through our words, our actions, our choices, we become parables and paradoxes in action, experiencing the utter absurdity of God's call, even as we make public spectacles of ourselves. By living out of the Beatitudes, by meaning what we say when we pray the Lord's Prayer, we discover the amazing depths of God's graciousness, even as others mock our naiveté. As we give away our resources, forgive our enemies and overlook hurts, we begin to align our vision with God's vision, even as we take central place in the circus ring, abandoning ourselves to Dionysian revelry.

This vision has everything to do with assenting to life. "Yes!" is the rallying cry of Holy Fools; it indicates that one is engaged with mystery, choosing life over death, choosing God over mammon. As Mary's "Yes!" indicated, assenting to life can be as dangerous and as foolish as dissenting from injustice. Her "Yes!" not only threatened her relationship with her betrothed, but could have led to her being stoned, the punishment for adultery. Her folly—and her wisdom—

was to trust that God's promises would be fulfilled in her and through her child. "Be it done to me according to your word," is the response we find in Luke 1:38. "What foolishness!" the uninitiated might exclaim. Unable to understand the concept of "surrender," many would balk at the very idea of allowing God free reign in one's life, finding it not only repulsive but also threatening. For most of us, clinging to the illusion of control is our primary spiritual "block"; for most of us, letting go of our wants and desires is too much to ask of ourselves; for most of us, the movement away from mere religious obligation into being fully available to God is more than we can tolerate.

But "Yes!" is key to loving and risking. "Yes!" extends us beyond the limitations of our egos into our true, heroic selves. At some level, saying "Yes!" might be even more heroically foolish than saying "No!" Moral outrage or the urgency of a particular situation can propel us into opposition that we might not ordinarily consider; in contrast, "Yes!" is often a quieter, more hidden response to life involving long term commitment. "Yes!" is often a manifestation of what Paul Tillich names as "spiritual self-affirmation": when we live creatively "in the various spheres of meaning . . . receiving and transforming reality," then we have the courage to be.[47] This is, perhaps, the most profound "Yes!" we can articulate—a "Yes!" to Being itself and to becoming what one desires to become because this is what God desires for us. "Yes!" is the cry of celebration in the midst of horror; it is the cry of triumph in the face of death; it is the cry of ecstasy in the moment of most profound vulnerability. "Yes!" is the negation of all that is death-dealing and soul-destroying; it is the creative word which brings forth life from chaos, from hopelessness, from despair. It is the only answer to the degrading existence of a Prometheus in chains or of a Sisyphus who is affixed to a meaningless stone.

Several models of this "Yes!" come to mind. I think again of Etty Hillesum, the Dutch Jew whose journal reveals a rich inner life both in terms of her relationship with God and of her love for humankind. Before being transported to

Auschwitz, she recorded her desire to be "the thinking heart of a whole concentration camp," the poet who could live life and sing about it:

> "I want to be sent to every one of the camps that lie scattered all over Europe, I want to be at every front, I don't ever want to be what they call 'safe,' I want to be there, I want to fraternize with my so-called enemies, I want to understand what is happening and share my knowledge with as many as I can possibly reach— And, I can, if You will only let me get healthy, oh Lord!"[48]

Hillesum's words are essentially Jewish in that they reflect the basis of Jewish Law—Deuteronomy 6 and Leviticus 19—that is, to love God and neighbor with all that one is; they are also quintessentially "Christian" in that they mirror Jesus' definition of "neighbor" as one who can be enemy as well as friend. In earlier journal entries, Hillesum also shows a concern for God that transcends all forms of conventional piety; her greatest desire is to guard that part of herself in which God resides, to remain conscious of God's presence in the face of terror and torture.[49] Hillesum's "Yes!," then, is the "Yes!" of a Holy Fool who says "Yes!" to God, a "Yes!" to Being, a "Yes!" to love. It is not mere piety but a radical statement of passion in a world stripped of all heart.

The "Yes!" of a Holy Fool is a "Yes!" to love those we are least inclined to love. While in his death agony, Luke's Jesus cries out, "Father, forgive them; they do not know what they are doing" (Lk 22:34). This ability to forgive while suffering the very wrongs others have inflicted is surely a hallmark of Holy Foolishness. Conventional wisdom would urge getting even, if this were possible, or, at the very least, uttering memorable curses. To spend one's last thoughts and last efforts on praying for enemies is nothing short of absurdity—and yet this is precisely what Jesus the Holy Fool urges us to do. Our hearts—if they are filled with the love of Christ—cannot be closed against anyone.

The late Cardinal Joseph Bernardin modeled this love of enemies when he sought reconciliation with Steven Cook, the man dying of AIDS who had falsely accused him of sexual abuse. Realizing that Steven had been a pawn in the hands of those who had wanted to publicly discredit him, Bernardin sought him out to express his forgiveness. The moving account of what happened between the two men was featured in Bernardin's book, *The Gift of Peace:*

> I explained to him that the only reason for requesting the meeting was to bring closure to the traumatic events of last winter by personally letting him know that I harbored no ill feelings toward him. I told him that I wanted to pray with him for his physical and spiritual well-being. Steven replied that he had decided to meet with me so he could apologize for the embarrassment and hurt he had caused. In other words, we both sought reconciliation.[50]

This remarkable ability to extend love to those who have done great injury to us is what makes us most like Jesus the Holy Fool. Just as Jesus excluded no one from his table-fellowship, so we, too, must open ourselves to those in need of our forgiveness. Forgiveness can only be given; it cannot be taken. We can ask for it—as we do when we pray the Lord's Prayer—but we cannot demand it or expect it. It is a free gift—one which we ourselves must be ready to bestow on others, if we are to live as Holy Fools, for the sake of their healing and ours, as well as for the sake of the community. For a reconciling community is a blessed community, while one with unhealed and unacknowledged divisions becomes a community at risk. That which is not forgiven becomes a curse with its own legacy of destruction. Holy Fools know this well.

When the life of faith is lived out of identification with Jesus the Holy Fool, there is no limit to our capacity for courageous self-giving or to our ability to forgive. Boldly, we venture into territories where even angels might fear to tread—places of pain, ambiguity, and darkness which we must traverse if we are to know ourselves fully and grow in compassion for our sisters and brothers. Holy Fools willingly embrace this darkness, even when it threatens to devour them, because they know that it is in this place of seeming abandonment that God can be most active, transforming the *prima materia* of their lives into pure gold—gold that has been refined by fire. By confronting their "shadow"—that is, those repressed memories, dreams, desires and experiences which we all carry with us—Holy Fools learn who they truly are and, in their folly, have the wisdom to invite Jesus the Healer to lay his hands upon them. It is this self-knowledge and this experience of the gift of healing which teaches the deepest levels of forgiveness.

This, of course, entails the willingness to be vulnerable before God, self, and others. Conventional wisdom suggests that we should look our best at all times, that we should not put down our guard, that it is desirable to appear strong and invincible; after all, it is the unprotected who are the victims in this world. Holy Folly, on the other hand, advocates a very different response to life. Holy Fools—child-like fools—are willing to divest themselves of protective masks and to stand in their nakedness before others, completely defenseless just as Jesus stood before those who mocked him during the Passion. Holy Fools—child-like fools—are willing, like the jester, to say what they think and to mean what they say, not twisting truth to serve their own ends. For them, there is no resorting to "prefabricated language," that is, to the language of cliché, hyperbole, and euphemism, nor to the language of manipulation and the direct lie. Holy Fools, like Jesus the Holy Fool, are seekers of Truth who are not afraid to be themselves; they are innocents who live as though Eden were still present among us. And over and over again, they pay the price for being too trusting, too real, too transparent.

In their seeming folly, Holy Fools also recognize the bitter comedy of the Commodity Form of life, the tragic implications of what happens when people are so desperate to get ahead that they allow themselves to become mechanized, to be nothing more than cogs in a wheel. This mode of being represents all that is antithetical to the spiritual life; Kavanaugh writes:

> Persons relate to things as if they were persons;
> they relate to persons—including themselves—as
> if they were things. Having patterned ourselves
> after the image of our commodities, we become
> disenfranchised of our very humanness. Reduced
> to commodities, we lose the intimacy of personal
> touch.[51]

When we dare to see and to think as Holy Fools, we are profoundly aware that everything that is best and most noble about ourselves can be up for sale in the marketplace. If we step back and survey the tragi-comedy, we see how productivity can become both the measure of success and the definition of who we are—even though we were created in God's image and likeness! We note how those who are driven by competitiveness and the inability to live simply hoard possessions, accumulating more and more in order to cram the empty places in themselves. In horror, we observe how the inner life is squeezed dry by greed, ambition, by the fear of failure. "How absurd!" we say to ourselves, even as others point out our own absurdity.

Holy Foolishness, then, provides a critical lens for evaluating what conventional wisdom names as desirable; through this lens we see that what the world deems to be advantageous is deceptively disadvantageous. We learn to recognize that when there's an imbalance, when spiritual grounding is neglected, when one expends energy on the ephemeral, when one mistakes passing happiness for ultimate joy and ignores the soul, then there's a steep price to pay—exhaustion, burnout, restlessness. Happiness seems evasive; one feels cheated, disillusioned. Holy Foolishness helps us to realize that when we pursue the wrong goals, everything falls apart. Goals seem empty, fulfillment is missing, success—interpreted as fame, status and wealth—seems entirely elusive, never to be attained. One can be driven by fears and ambition. One can become a consumer of people as well as commodities. One can become preoccupied with gratification, with possessions, with avoiding aging, with the idea of running out of time. One can become so obsessed with not achieving, with not succeeding, that life becomes nothing more than "burnt toast," not the rich banquet it is meant to be.

Several years ago, I had a significant dream on this subject. I was in a fancy restaurant with my family, waiting to be served. Everybody's food arrived under shining silver warming covers. Filled with anticipation, I watched eagerly as my waiter ceremoniously presented me with my plate, lifting the silver cover to reveal two triangles of burnt toast. I stared in disbelief at my plate, conscious that those around me were already enjoying a gourmet meal. Then I heard a voice which said, "Why spend your money on what is not bread, your wages on what fails to satisfy?" Of course, the text was familiar. My dream, seen in light of Isaiah 55, forced me to examine my priorities, my use of time, my investment of energy, gifts and resources. Three questions surfaced: what did I thirst for? what did I spend myself on? where did I find the wine of passion? Spiritually, I was heading for bankruptcy; spiritually, I was being an unholy fool even though conventional wisdom applauded me for my actions, attitudes and, especially, for my productivity.

It takes Holy Foolishness to recognize that society actually encourages us to spend ourselves, our money, on what is not bread. Bread is life-giving, but we are taught to value what leads to inner darkness—a spiral of spending, competing, and consuming. We are taught to numb ourselves to reality, to live in a fog of lies, to desensitize ourselves, to suspend thought, to be part of the non-thinking crowd. From a very early age, children learn that they look "cutest" in designer clothes and that they are one step up in the world when they wear the "right" gym shoes or carry the "right" brand of toys. Instead of marveling at the wonders of God's universe, they are exposed to forty hours a week or more of television violence and sordid romances. By the time they

begin kindergarten, most children are already firmly possessed by the Commodity Form at its worst. We have all
heard of the "brain drain"—that phenomenon when the
"best and brightest" take off for another company or country;
I believe that our present-day cultural values have created a
"passion drain," a life-style guaranteed to rob us and our
children of all that is life-giving.

Paradoxically—and here again we return to the norms of
Holy Foolishness—it is in emptying ourselves and letting go
that we make room for passion. As long as our attention is
focussed on material concerns, as long as our energy goes
into competition and acquisition, true passion remains dormant and disordered passion—envy, greed, fear, resentment—will surface. One of the paradoxes Jesus taught us is
that only by embracing poverty of spirit do we find the fullness of God. So much of early adulthood is preoccupied with
attaining credentials and getting ahead that we lose sight of
a different way of living—one in which we let go of material
goals and instead try to live out of God's dream for us. I am
not discrediting credentials or career paths—they are necessary—but to live out of God's will, to find happiness in God's
desires, is very different from forging ahead as though we
were in complete control. If God is truly the center and circumference of our lives, then this will make a difference to
the kinds of choices we make and the values we hold. To live
as a Holy Fool allows us to receive our daily bread with
grateful hearts, while entrusting ourselves to God so that we
may avoid the glamor of evil.

And then there is the question of wine, a symbol of the
inner life, the life lived in God. When we are foolish enough
to abandon our lives to God, then, like the devotees of
Dionysus, like the disciples at Pentecost, we can become inebriated with holy joy—the joy of God's Spirit dwelling
within us. In this place of ecstasy, we leave behind all
worldly cares and focus instead on what it means to dwell in
God's house. Though others may consider us mad—a label
Jesus received before us—we find ourselves delighting in
what it means to be most ourselves, most real, most con-

scious, most in touch with the divine dimension of self. Here, we are comfortable being rather than doing, for we don't have to prove ourselves; we already know that we are loved and accepted, regardless of what we do or don't achieve. Here, we surrender to God's initiative, readily abandoning everything to the movement of God within. Here, we stop all the struggling, all the wasted energy, all the pushing to succeed; instead, we learn to rest in God's embrace. Here, recognizing superficialities for what they are, we willingly invest ourselves in ultimate meaning. Jesus the Holy Fool holds out to us the chalice of his Passion that we may leave behind all that is prosaic, all that is anti-life.

This place—if, indeed it can be called a place—is far removed from the halls of conventional wisdom and from their obsession with *chronos*, that dimension of time we measure by the clock. It is not limited by our experience of time as seconds, minutes, hours, days, weeks, months, or years, nor by our understanding of time as linear and historical; nor does it fall into categories of past, present, or future. No, the spiritual life has a time of its own. There it is possible to encounter Timelessness itself—what T.S. Eliot calls "The point of intersection of the timeless/ With time."[52] In this experience of kairos, precisely because we are willing to put on the folly of innocence, all time becomes sacred and the experience of Eden is once more a possibility. Figuratively speaking, the primordial sacred ladders, sacred chains, and sacred poles are re-instated once more, so that humankind and the divine can mingle freely. Dichotomies break down, as do the divisions which so distort our relationships with those who might seem different from ourselves. Clasping hands with one another, oblivious to all that society says should separate us, we are free to join the holy dance of love and to lose ourselves in merry-making.

Holy Foolishness and Worship

A distinctive feature of Christian spirituality is that it is communal. Jesus gathered people from the highways and byways to take their place at God's all-inclusive banquet; he did not intend them to pick at a tasteless "TV dinner" in isolation. In the Christian context, to dance alone, to feast alone are impossibilities; when the disciples asked Jesus to teach them how to pray, the first words he taught them were, "Our Father," not "My Father." Using the metaphor of the "marriage feast" in his parables and demonstrating the lavishness of God's love in his choice of table companions, his concern for the hungry crowds, and his offering of himself as the Bread of Life, Jesus made it clear that his followers were to celebrate the reign of God together, as a community. Just as the devotees of Dionysus broke into communal ecstatic song and dance in the woodlands, later enacting the sacred mysteries in a theatrical context, so the followers of Jesus are to share the bread and wine of his presence and to find their identity in the sharing. In contrast, a feature of the existential angst represented by Sisyphus is isolation, a reality which goes against the spirit of communal religion.

A spirituality grounded in the Holy Foolishness of Christ has definite liturgical implications. Now, beyond the words attributed to Jesus at the Last Supper, "Do this in memory of me," Scripture provides no clear liturgical guidelines. We know that the early Christian community gathered in one place to celebrate the Lord's Supper and that the celebration took place in the context of an actual meal; we also know that these celebrations were characterized by what Cullman translates as "exuberant joy":[53]

> In the Book of Acts (2.42 and 46; 20.7), instruction, preaching, prayer and the breaking of bread are mentioned, and mentioned in such a way as clearly to show that these elements were, from the beginning, the foundation of all the worship life of the Christian community.[54]

But while Jesus may not have left his disciples the specifics as to how they were to gather in his Name, we can arrive at some conclusions at to what would be in keeping with the spirit of Holy Foolishness. Throughout this work, we have established that Holy Foolishness is a response to life which is playful, joyful, outrageous at times, authentic, inclusive, prophetic, countercultural, naive, uninhibited, transformational, spontaneous, passionate and daring. A liturgy that is inspired by the Holy Foolishness of Christ would possess these characteristics and would be far removed from ritual which is only pro forma.

Sadly, it is my experience both in the United States and in Europe that instead of arising from basic human needs, Catholic liturgy all too often leaves the assembly angered, alienated, bored, or indifferent. It is not so much the form of the liturgy which is problematic but, rather, the way in which the liturgy is conducted. In parishes where liturgy is not a high priority, the pace is rushed, with little or no attention to silence; the prayers and responses of both presider and people are rote; symbols and gestures are minimized ; the proclamation of the Word is passionless; the preaching is irrelevant; the sacraments are dispensed with assembly-line efficiency. Or, in those rare churches which pride themselves on the quality of their liturgies, the liturgical experience can be reduced to mere performance, with the church becoming a showcase to demonstrate liturgical principles. In such places, the preaching and singing may be flawless, the environment may capture the essence of the liturgical season to perfection, and yet, as an experience of the people, the liturgy may be utterly sterile, a production without heart. At the end, people leave, having performed their "Sunday obligation" but without having experienced the transformational presence of God and without having celebrated the significant moments of passage in their own lives. Instead of leaving renewed and empowered, they can strike one more task off their calendars.

When liturgy fails to move the heart, when ritual boredom sets in, it is often because the rituals have come to reflect the dominant culture; the sterility of Sisyphus deflates the experience, and the rituals are "thingified," reduced to commodities. Two possibilities are at play:

> Either the rituals, in their form, content and manner
> of performance, have lost touch with the actualities
> of people's lives and are thus simply arcane; or

else the people have lost the ability to apprehend
their very need of ritual, do not see what rituals are
good for, and thus do not find them even potentially valuable.[55]

Whatever the case, it seems that too many Catholic liturgies have too little Holy Foolishness about them. Jesus the
Holy Fool could not have intended that his disciples would
memorialize him in ways which were devoid of passion,
humor, and life; nor could he have imagined that the festive
banquet of God's presence would be regulated by complex
rubrics separating what is "liturgically correct" from what is
"liturgically inappropriate." Nor would he have tolerated
the notion that children should be excluded from the assembly to avoid distracting their elders. As Holy Fool, Jesus
would see liturgy as "the work of the people"—messy and
imperfect but authentic; he would not see it as a "product" or
a commodity to be judged by abstract principles. For him,
"good" liturgy would be whatever touches the hearts of
those involved and brings them closer to their God. Like
Dionysus, Jesus offers freely flowing wine, the water that
quenches all thirst, but today many churches have corseted
the power of ritual with "liturgical rigidities."[56]

As a weaver of stories filled with surprising twists and
shocking endings, Jesus the Holy Fool would not approve
the manipulation of the Word to reflect the values of the *status quo*; in fact, he would be shocked by "the unholy alliance
between liturgical order and a social order that has set its face
against the significant change that justice and peace
require."[57] At the same time, Jesus, the inventor of parables
and paradoxes, would be nonplussed by preaching that
focuses only on exegesis and theological abstractions. As one
who captivated the crowds with his teaching, Jesus the Holy
Fool would question preaching that is a "head trip" filled
with impressive citations instead of the presence of God;
likewise, he would object to mere sentimentalism without
challenge or substance, or, worse still, to a weekly account of
golf outings or movie reviews. As one who understood the
complexities of "showbiz," he would be amazed at how the

Word is trivialized, robbed of its bite even as it is being proclaimed.

As Holy Fool, Jesus not only understood the power of words and the Word, but also of gesture. Because he understood people's need for ritual expression, he was not afraid of touching others or of letting them touch him. Earlier, we saw that instead of attempting to pass himself off as a professional healer, he relied upon unusual strategies such as the use of a mixture of spittle and dust as an ointment for blind eyes (Jn 9:6–7). In fact, in nearly all the narratives of healing, Jesus used words and touch to bring about cures, to forgive sins and even to raise the dead; at the same time, these physical acts were expressions of the power of the God whose Name he invoked in prayer. From this we can conclude that Jesus did not divorce body from spirit and that he did not expect his disciples to do so, either. Jesters and clowns understand the importance of earth, as did Jesus. Accordingly, we might expect that liturgy grounded in Holy Foolishness would involve "embodied ritual." Unfortunately, too many worshippers leave their bodies at the church door; uncomfortable with movement or gesture, they sit stiffly in their pews, eyes fixed on the altar or on the presider who, more likely than not, is as uncomfortable with physicality as they are. As jester and clown, Jesus would be disappointed by the lifelessness of those gathered in his memory; he would nor be impressed by rows of people wearing invisible straightjackets as they repeatedly stand, sit, kneel, stand, sit, kneel, stand, sit, kneel. . . .

Just as Jesus overturned the vendors' tables in the Temple Court, scattering buyers, sellers, and sacrificial animals, today, Jesus the Holy Fool might be inclined to disturb the peace in more than one or two churches. Undoubtedly, in his zeal for God's Name and for God's House, he would be outraged by lukewarm prayer and inattentiveness to the holy; perhaps he would interrupt the liturgy to warn the people that unless they enter fully into the sacred story and sacred rituals they are in danger of losing their very souls. "To ritualize," writes Driver, "is to make oneself present. It is to find a way of strongly presenting oneself, and by doing so to invoke the presence of that god, or person, or force whom it is necessary to confront."[58] How "present" are we to the sacred action? Is an encounter with the divine really possible when we are so inattentive to the holy moment? No doubt, like the *Constitution on the Sacred Liturgy*, Jesus would insist on "full, conscious, and active participation."[59] However, this would entail more than joining in the responses, communal prayer and singing but would mean praying with complete self-abandon—the abandon of a Holy Fool. Wearing one's "Sunday Best" is no guarantee that one is ready to take the risk of being authentically present to God.

As Holy Fool, Jesus would want the liturgy to be a vehicle for the Good News. A stark environment and solemn mood might be appropriate for Good Friday, but a glimpse of the resurrection is necessary for any celebration of the Paschal Mystery. The cross and resurrection together are a statement about the meaning of Jesus' life, but our liturgies too often emphasize only the cross; even the worshipping environment tends to give prominence to the sufferings of Jesus, whether through a large cross in the sanctuary, or through a multiplicity of crosses throughout the church. So how do we depict Good News? How do we develop our awareness of resurrection? Jesus, like the professional jester, would encourage us to see beyond the darkness and to "lighten up." Liturgical action may be solemn but it does not have to be somber; it has the sacred as its focus but this does not mean that some levity is inappropriate. Just as the cross moves us to tears, so the event of resurrection should be laughter-producing. After all, death has lost its sting, even if, at times, we fail to believe this.

A Christology based on Holy Foolishness challenges all those who plan, preside at, and participate in the liturgy to examine how life-giving—or sterile—a worship experience really is. It leads us away from habitual worship so that each liturgical experience can become a new creation, a new opportunity for connecting with God and with each other. It begs us to enter holy mystery with the fullness of who we are, so that we cease to be passive spectators and instead become participants in the events we remember as a community. It asks us to evaluate what we are doing well and what we could be doing better—and perhaps to consider what we should not be doing at all. It invites us to make each gathering an authentic celebration of God's presence in our midst—one in which we dare to laugh, to sing, to clap, to cry out, and even to dance, if we are so moved.

The chorus in *The Bacchae* describe the holy merriment with which they follow Dionysus:

> From far-off lands of Asia,
> From Tmolus the holy mountain,
> We run with the god of laughter;
> Labour is joy and weariness is sweet,
> And our song resounds to Bacchus! . . .
>
> On, on! Run, dance, delirious, possessed!
> Dionysus comes to his own;
> Bring from the Phrygian hills to the broad
> streets of Hellas
> The god, child of a god,
> Spirit of revel and rapture, Dionysus![60]

Does not Jesus the Holy Fool invite us to run with him? Does not Jesus the Holy Fool give us the gift of his own spirit that we, too, might be possessed with divine ecstasy? Does not Jesus the Holy Fool take our burdens upon himself that we, too, might be filled with holy sweetness, the nectar of his presence? Sadly, our liturgies have little of passion about them; too often, all that possesses us are concerns about capital campaigns, the amount of the weekly collection, and who is—or is not—in "good standing." And this, I believe, gives Jesus the Holy Fool cause to weep. . . .

Holy Foolishness and Justice
To live a life of Christian Holy Foolishness has global ramifications. While worldly fools live for themselves and for their own narrow range of interests, Holy Fools recognize that the

choices they make have an impact on the whole community of life; in fact, the liturgy we celebrate together is for the sake of the world and not only for the sake of the church, whether local or global. And what we do in memory of Jesus we do not only for our own transformation, but to advance God's plan for all creation. This does not mean that we should be about the business of converting members of other faith communities to Christianity; rather, when our lives reflect gospel values, then we become the presence of Christ in a world very much in need of peace, justice, love, and healing. Just as Jesus reached out beyond the Jewish community to the Samaritan woman, the Roman centurion and the Syro-Phoenician woman, so we need to reach beyond the boundaries of our own spheres of involvement; just as Paul, Barnabas, and other members of the early Christian community embarked on hazardous journeys to preach the Good News to the Gentiles, so we need to be concerned about our brothers and sisters in faraway lands.

The Global Ethic, the visionary document which emerged from The Parliament of the World's Religions in 1993, begins with the declaration, "The world is in agony. The agony is so pervasive and urgent that we are compelled to name its manifestations so that the depth of this pain may be made clear."[61] This agony affects all living things—people, animals, the environment—and can be linked to an ethically foolish way of life. Arising from exploitation, the abuse of power, lies, and economic greed, it reduces people to commodities.

Unholy fools neither care about future generations, the state of the planet or other life forms because they are completely possessed by their own ego-driven agendas. Holy Fools, on the other hand, recognize the interdependence of all living things. Because they understand that every choice has ramifications beyond the present moment, they are willing to forego immediate gratification and convenience for the sake of a higher good, even if others are amused by their zeal. While conventional wisdom advocates taking care of Number One, that is, oneself, Holy Fools understand that humankind will be able to save the planet from destruction only by observing the Golden Rule. Unless people embrace the seeming folly of treating others the way they themselves would like to be treated, and forego seeking "an eye for an eye," there is no hope for any of us. What is needed is a complete transformation of consciousness, and this, in turn, has to begin with the individual, for "Earth cannot be changed for the better unless the consciousness of individuals is changed first."[62] Without spiritual renewal, without a change in inner orientation, there will be no solution to the environmental, economic, political and social problems of earth.[63]

In his ground-breaking work, *Christ of the 21st Century*, Ewert Cousins evaluates what a shift in consciousness might mean as we begin a new millennium. Defining "global consciousness" as the convergence of disparate cultures and religions in such a way as to retain and even intensify diversity in the midst of unity, Cousins speaks of the need for each person to be aware of "belonging primarily to the entire globe—not merely to an ethnic group, tribe or nation, but directly to the whole."[64] This, in itself, demands Holy Foolishness, for conventional wisdom tends to be "local" rather than global and to consider anything "beyond the pale" as either a threat or irrelevant. From this limited perspective, expending energy and taking risks for the sake of broader communities is pure lunacy—unless there are economic interests at stake!

Observing how the forces of secularization are stripping cultures of their religious heritage, Cousins explains how during the period of history Karl Jaspers names as the First Axial Period (800–200 B.C.E.), consciousness shifted from being primal—that is, "cosmic, collective, tribal, mythic and ritualistic"—to being individual, self-reflective, rational, analytic, ethical and spirit-based.[65] Now, as we move into the Second Axial Period (Cousin's own term), what is necessary is a retrieval of the lost collective and cosmic values of pre-Axial consciousness. "We must re-capture the unity of tribal consciousness by seeing humanity as a single tribe," writes Cousins; "And we must see this single tribe related organically to the total cosmos."[66] Here again, a Christian spirituality that is grounded in Holy Foolishness can pave the way for this new focus. Letting go of old prejudicial attitudes and behaviors is no easy task, but shifts in group consciousness can come when individuals are willing to play the fool so that others can realize their own destructive folly.

One such prejudicial attitude, for example, which was certainly prevalent prior to Vatican II, was the notion that only Catholics were on board "the one true ark of salvation." It took Holy Foolishness on the part of a few daring Catholic theologians to promote a different perspective—one which, in fact, shaped *Nostra Aetate* (1965), the church's declaration on non-Christian religions:

> Humanity forms but one community. This is so because all stem from one stock which God created to people the entire earth, and because all share a common destiny, namely God. . . . The Catholic Church rejects nothing of what is true and holy in these religions. It has a high regard for the manner of life and conduct, the precepts and doctrines which, although differing in many ways from its own teaching, nevertheless often reflect a ray of that truth which enlightens all men and women. . . . The church, therefore, urges its sons and daughters to enter with prudence and charity into discussion and collaboration with members of other religions. Let Christians, while witnessing to their own faith and way of life, acknowledge, preserve and encourage the spiritual and moral truths found among non-Christians, together with their social life and culture.[67]

Because of their willingness to risk censure and ridicule, the theologians who drafted this declaration opened the doors of possibility in terms of interreligious appreciation and cooperation. No longer would it be possible to use one's Catholicism as an excuse for spiritual and cultural isolation, or to justify spiritual elitism. The declaration does not settle for mere tolerance or tokenism, but advocates active dialogue and collaboration. For many, this must have seemed like a radical departure from previous encounters with the world's faith traditions and from a theology of exclusivity. No doubt, the church's "about face" involved "costly grace" on the part of those who affected the change; no doubt there were times when they found themselves on the fringes of orthodoxy, hence of acceptability; no doubt they were, at times, labeled as fools, possibly as heretics.

Just as Jesus made choices which subverted the values and traditions of his day, so we are called to do likewise within the contexts of our own lives. Not that values and traditions are harmful *per se,* but when they become ends in themselves, when conformity is valued more than authenticity, and when "law" conflicts with compassion or justice, then Holy Foolishness calls us to align our perspective with that of Jesus. But what is this perspective? we might ask ourselves, sharply aware of the differences between Jesus' world and our own. Observing Shabbat and maintaining ritual purity are issues unlikely to confront most of us. How, then, does Holy Foolishness challenge us in our own era?

The Holy Fool—like the court jester—subverts law and tradition not merely to evoke laughter but to point to a higher value. Jesus, for example, consistently pointed to the ethic of love, showing how its demands transcend legalism. To live out the Holy Foolishness of Christ means to be conversant with the legal structures of our own day—whether familial, ecclesial, societal, or global—and to know when being subversive is not only a choice but an imperative. Commenting on unjust laws in a pamphlet on passive resistance, Mohandas K. Gandhi stated that to follow such laws is to go against the spirit of religion and to accept slavery:

> We are sunk so low that we fancy it is our duty and
> our religion to do what the law lays down. If man
> will only realize that it is unmanly to obey laws
> that are unjust, no man's tyranny will enslave him.
> This is the key to self-rule or home rule.[68]

Without authentic "self-rule," we cannot be advocates for ourselves, let alone the planet. Holy Fools, while seemingly advocates of chaos, are quite familiar with the concept of self-rule. This, of course, is more than a political term but also involves allowing the "self" to be ruled by a higher wisdom than Caesar's; for Holy Fools, it is not willful self-indulgence which rules but the willingness to serve God's agenda for all creation.

Too often, those who call themselves "Christian" fail to see options for themselves in terms of confronting injustice, thereby becoming morally enslaved. Because following the rules is a guarantee of safety, many prefer to do what is required of them while remaining ignorant about those situations in which fellow employees, parishioners, family members, or citizens are mistreated. How different the world would be if each of us listened to the call of Holy Foolishness and dared risk everything for the sake of justice! How transformed each of us would become if we opened ourselves up to the Holy Fool in our lives! Sadly, many "good Christians" refuse to respond to the call of Holy Foolishness because they prefer "cheap grace" to "costly grace." Instead of naming evil and actively resisting it as Jesus would have done, they prefer nonaction, noninvolvement, and zero-culpability.

But just as there is a price to pay for following the "call," so, too, there is a price for ignoring it. Each time we say "No!" to where life is inviting us, we dry up like the "raisin in the sun" in Langston Hughes' poem, *Harlem;* the life within evaporates and we are left desiccated, stripped of self-respect, bereft of comfort.[69] In our worldly-wise attempts to stay "safe" and remain respectable, we lose a little piece of ourselves; foolishly, we think we are gaining the world but, in reality, we are losing everything that sanctifies life. Worse still, each refusal to respond means that we are less likely to hear the "call" the next time. Heroism does not consist of isolated actions which dazzle our autobiographies every now and again; rather, it is a consistent way of life built on daily choices, some of which are more noticeable than others.

Mistaken notions of loyalty, codependent behavior, and fear of using one's own power have no place in Holy Foolishness. To be a Holy Fool—a Christ-like fool—means to be capable of outrage, of righteous anger, of bold action, of defiance; it means having the courage to place justice before security, to put on the mantle of the raving prophet, and to stand in solidarity with the oppressed. Jesus the Holy Fool stands before us, inviting us to right action, into seeming lunacy, no matter what the price. While conventional wisdom advocates locking up such fools, or, worse still, "doing them in," Jesus the Holy Fool beckons us with a wave of the mock scepter in his hand and with a nod of his thorn-crowned head. Sadly, too many of us are afraid of becoming public freaks, the butt of merciless critics. We are afraid of breaking the laws of complicity, uncritical collegiality and silence, for to do so means that we will be pilloried by the cruel mob. It is always easier to remain a loyal part of a dysfunctional group than to stand alone, in protest.

Our inability to become fools for the sake of Christ means that we become very different kinds of fools—fools who, lacking integrity and courage, obey conventional wisdom rather than God's wisdom. And just because there are countless fools who lack moral fiber doesn't make those who join their ranks any less despicably foolish. The failure to speak out and the failure to act can become deadly matters. The complicity in dysfunction can become complicity in death. For example, Christian apathy and even active assent during the Holocaust or *Shoah* are realities which every Christian must acknowledge. Though the late Cardinal Bernardin considered the *Shoah* to be as profoundly anti-Christian as it was anti-Jewish, he stated in his address at Hebrew University, March 1995:

> In the church today, we must not minimize the extent of Christian collaboration with Hitler and his associates. It remains a profound moral challenge that we must continue to confront for our own integrity as a religious community.[70]

Hitler's "final solution"—that is, his plan to exterminate all Jews—was implemented on a massive scale because there were too few women and men who were willing to put on the motley of the jester and speak the truth. Too few dared put on the nakedness of an Andrew the Holy Fool or of a Basil; too few dared strip themselves of security and safety for the sake of crying out against Hitler's genocidal strategies. When faced with terror, many resorted to the basic survival tactic of "discretionary silence"; another strategy, practiced then as now, was keeping a low profile in the hope of escaping notice. To assume that most Europeans did not know what was going on would be naive indeed; it is far more likely that people chose to be worldly fools, that they "turned a blind eye," preferring not to be involved than to ask questions about the stench of burning flesh coming from the death camps or why their neighbors had been herded into cattle cars without provisions for the journey.

But if there is any lesson to be learned from the *Shoah,* it is that "no one group can successfully preserve its own well-being while ignoring blatant assaults against the dignity of others. Sooner or later, the bystanders become the victims as well."[71] Martin Niemoller, a pastor in a German Confessing Church, spent seven years in a concentration camp; he wrote:

> First they came for the Jews
> and I did not speak out—
> because I was not a Jew.
> Then they came for the socialists
> and I did not speak out—
> because I was not a socialist.
> Then they came for the trade unionists
> and I did not speak out—
> because I was not a trade unionist.
> Then they came for me—
> and there was no one left
> to speak out for me.[72]

Not everyone who fails to speak out against oppression will necessarily suffer the same fate as the oppressed; however, without a doubt, everyone who fails to speak falls victim to moral disintegration and spiritual atrophy. Each missed opportunity to promote peace and justice in the outer world brings about inward decline.

In the face of such horrors as the world has seen this century, what is needed is neither complicity, nor silence, nor apathy but what Elie Wiesel has termed "a kind of moral madness." This moral madness is the madness of Holy Foolishness, a willingness to take seriously the social evils which threaten the planet and to say, "No more!" Rabbi Byron Sherwin of the Spertus College of Judaica in Chicago defines this madness as follows: "'Madness means: not to be seduced by appearance and social convention; to love where there is only indifference and hate; to try to live humanely in an inhumane world; to believe in humankind in spite of what we have done.'"[73]

When we fail to be Holy Fools, then, we allow ourselves to be seduced by the powers of the world, selling our souls for the sake of security, just as the foolish Faust sold his soul for the sake of knowledge. Ironically, just as Faust's seeming knowledge turned out to be abysmal ignorance, so our seeming security is, in fact, a complete illusion. Soul-less and lost, we not only lose the capacity to love and to hope, but we ourselves become part of the system of oppression and mediators of evil. In effect, we become possessed by that which we hate and fear the most. What we have to acknowledge is that systemic evil can only happen when individuals allow themselves to be coerced into participation. Each time we refuse to draw on the power within, that power which enables us to say "No!," then, in effect, we give away our power until we are literally power-less in a negative sense—filled with the power of moral darkness and of the absence of love.

Holy Foolishness, on the other hand, involves claiming the power given us by virtue of being human. Just as Jesus befriended the woman caught in adultery, scattering her accusers, and compelling them to drop their stones by the sheer force of his own integrity, so Holy Fools know the strength of relying on their inner resources (Jn 8:1–11). Just as Jesus in the passion narratives maintained his dignity in the face of the might of Rome (represented by Pilate) and in the face of the might of the state (represented by Herod and the religious elders), so Holy Fools throughout history have defied external power. Once, in a conversation with my niece, Michelle, then about four years old, I expressed concern that she and her elder brother engaged in violent fights. In response, she said she had need of some weapons—preferably a gun or two. I suggested that she learn to use her "inner power" to deflate potentially difficult situations. Michelle thought carefully about this for a few minutes; eventually, she informed me that while inner power was desirable, having some outer power (the weapons) would make her doubly effective.

Puny David hurling his sling at the mighty Goliath serves as a wonderful metaphor for the effective use of "inner power" or what we have come to term "passive resistance." Wearing neither helmet nor breastplate, carrying neither sword nor shield, the boy David stood before the Philistine and, protected only by the Name of God, felled him with one smooth stone (1 Sam 17:32–54). Was it the stone that killed Goliath, we might ask, or was it the boy's conviction of his God's support and his fearlessness in the face of great danger? Surely "inner power" was at work here? When young shepherds defy great warriors and when unarmed pro-democracy students block the path of military tanks as happened in Beijing's Tiananmen Square in 1989, then something out of the ordinary is happening. The weak and the unprotected put on the armor of righteousness—of Holy Foolishness—and stand their ground against the powers of the world. The puny clowns of history shake their fists at the Death Machine of the universe, and giants and tanks stop in their tracks, emasculated. "When I refuse to do a thing that is repugnant to my conscience, I use soul-force," wrote Gandhi.[74] To use soul-force, one must dare engage in seemingly futile battle, while refusing to believe that it is futile. So ridiculous was the sight of the youthful David that Goliath was filled with scorn (1 Sam 17:42); ironically, it was the giant (armed with shield-bearer, sword, spear and javelin) who fell flat on his face, losing his head to the cutting edge of his own sword. Cast in circus language, the mighty ring-master slipped on the banana peel, while the smallest of acrobats turned somersaults around him.

Whether we name it as "inner power," "soul force," or "passive resistance," Holy Foolishness is at play. For Gandhi, passive resistance as a means of securing justice involved observing perfect chastity, adopting poverty, following truth and cultivating fearlessness.[75] What he advocated, then, was complete abandonment of ego drives, a "death" of the self. From this it can be seen that passive resistance is more than risk-taking but a way of life based on what is ludicrous in the world's eyes. Jesus, like Gandhi, also advocated peaceful strategies in response to violence. Just as at the time of his arrest he instructed Peter, "Put your sword back, for all who draw the sword will die by the sword," so he calls each of us to renounce violence (Mt 26:53). For Christians, the answer to injustice is to put on the armor of Christ. Just as David armed himself with God's Name, so we must arm ourselves with the presence of Jesus, calling upon his power as we confront forces stronger than ourselves. Just as David cut an absurd figure, so we may look ridiculous as we confront injustice with little more than crossed fingers and a fervent prayer as armor. From a Christian perspective, Holy Foolishness is not something to be indulged in every now and again but a way of life which has the risen Christ as its very source. To follow this way, we must—as Gandhi urged—be disciplined. I would add, we must also be committed to prayer, or rather, to a life that *is* prayer.

Holy Fools of the Christian variety can only fight for justice because Jesus has modeled what it means to be both holy and foolish. From his words and actions, we learn that it is possible to confront evil without resorting to evil ourselves. From his willingness to accept humiliation, we learn that the laying down of our wills, of our drives, of our ambitions, is the surest way to puncture the apparatus of Death. Paradoxically, the only way to work for justice is to put oneself at the mercy of all that is unjust. To engage in appropriate Holy Folly on any given occasion means that one has a prayerful understanding of what one is doing and why. Relationship with Jesus the Holy Fool provides a lens through which to view reality—a prophetic lens, one might say. By immersing oneself in the Gospel, by praying to know the mind of Christ, would-be Holy Fools open themselves to divine directives. Then, having discerned where God is calling them, the pray-ers are now ready to activate their Holy Foolishness. Prayer shifts from being essentially the practice of obedient listening to becoming a source of courage, comfort and wisdom; true Holy Fools cannot function without it.

Holy Foolishness is not for the spiritually soft. Often, as demonstrated by the life of Jesus, it involves the sacrifice of the self, and one can only face such sacrifice if one has practiced detachment in other areas of one's life. During World War II, for example, there were those who defied the genocidal policies of the Nazis at considerable risks to themselves. The Holy Folly of Aage and Gerda Bertelsen is a case in point. The Bertelsens headed the Lyngby group, a rescue operation in Denmark which saved 1,200 Jews from the death camps. Not only was their opposition to the Nazis foolish, but their rescue tactics bordered on the insane: they smuggled the refugees by night, right past a flotilla of German warships, before depositing them safely on Sweden's shores.[76] Similar Holy Foolishness was displayed by the people of Assisi, home of St. Francis; the city not only became a haven for Jewish refugees but also printed the false documents which ultimately helped save eighty percent of Italy's Jews.[77] All over Europe, women and men of courage absorbed Jews into their families, provided escape routes, or assisted in hiding Jews until the threat was over. Instead of saying, "What can one person do against the might of Hitler?" these people were bold enough to believe that their efforts could make a difference. Armed only with conviction and quick-thinking, these clowns of the Resistance saved countless lives while risking their own. When asked if they had been aware of the hazards, they would no doubt have responded in much the same way as the French priest, Charles Devaux: "Of course I knew it, but this knowledge could not stop me from doing what I considered to be my duty as a Christian and as a human being."[78]

Holy Foolishness, while essentially Christian, is not exclusively Christian; in other words, while all Christians are called to Holy Folly, not every Holy Fool is necessarily a Christian. Saying "No!" to the forces of violence and oppression is the responsibility of all people everywhere. The death-dealing situations threatening our planet are diverse: racism, sexism, homophobia, anti-Semitism, classism, economic exploitation, discrimination against minorities, the decimation of the rain forests, the pollution of natural resources, the annihilation of species of animals, the proliferation of weapons, the naming of the "Other" as "enemy." All these situations cry out for a response—not just for words, not just for objections, but for all those specific actions which, like David's sling against Goliath, will make a difference.

It takes a Holy Fool, however, to believe in the impossible and to risk inviting others into the same divine madness; it takes a Holy Fool to understand that saying "No!" has value, even if no one else hears the "No!" and even if one loses one's life in the process of uttering it. Once uttered, that "No!" to injustice has left its mark on the universe, whether or not it is recorded for posterity; once uttered, that "No!" becomes part of the heritage of the human race as it haltingly struggles towards perfection. And for Christians, the crucified Jesus provides the ultimate paradigm of Holy Foolishness; his "No!" is the creative word which brings forth life, defying the forces of death and destruction. His brokenness is the guarantee that even when we are most shattered, suffering can be redemptive, both for ourselves and for all created life.

Holy Foolishness and a New Ecclesiology

Just as Holy Foolishness invites Christians into a deeper and more challenging commitment to the gospel, so it invites the church to examine its own understanding of itself and of its relationship to the world. In every age, ecclesiology has been shaped by different images. In the first centuries, for example, the church was seen as "a boat at sea, tossed by the waves and often creaking in all its joints, but always with its helm pointing towards the one goal—the safe port."[79] This image did not suggest a "solid rock" in the face of danger, but a frail vessel that would struggle against the storm, comforted by the presence of Christ.[80] Such a church was aware of its vulnerability and complete dependence upon God; it was a humble church, a prayerful church—a ship of Holy Fools, if you will. This ship clung to the Gospel for security, preaching its message of salvation while immersed in the storms of life. It was a witness to the fact that while there would be tempests, it would prevail against all odds as Christ had promised; it was a sign of the reign of God made manifest among us.

In an unsafe world, such a paradigm has a great deal of appeal. The church as a storm-rocked boat suggests that the Christian spiritual path is not to be worked out in the confines of an ivory tower or behind massive monastery walls, but right in the heart of suffering and uncertainty. As ship, the church does not claim privilege or exemption from difficulties, but allows itself to be immersed in the human predicament, just as Jesus was. At the same time—in spite of all the odds—this ship is not swallowed by the waves. Like Noah's ark, it is a sign of hope that all will be well, in God's time and in God's way. This, in fact, is the sense of church that is articulated in *Gaudium et Spes,* for it "travels the same journey as all of humanity and shares the same earthly lot with the world."[81]

The ship, however, is only one among many images of church. While various Christian denominations have had their own operative models of church, in the Roman Catholic tradition, the post-Reformation church was the Church Triumphant, the church of the 1940s–1950s was the Mystical Body of Christ, the Conciliar church was the Pilgrim Church, and post-Conciliar images include the church as the People of God and Servant Church. Avery Dulles explains that images carry within themselves transformational capabilities. He writes, "To some extent they are self-fulfilling; they make the Church become what they suggest the Church is."[82] The image of Holy Fool, then, might well be a fitting paradigm of church and might offer the opportunity for ongoing renewal. Certainly, in an age in which Sisyphus and the shadow side of Dionysus reign, a Holy Fool church offers a corrective to the meaninglessness and hedonism which threaten the human race. It is, in fact, a sign of an *aggiornamento,* a "bringing up to date." This, as Edward Schillebeeckx points out, is more than a matter of external adaptation:

> Our task of bringing the church up to date goes much deeper than this. The good news must be heard, now, in our times, as the original Christian message and as none other. It must also be practised as the original Christian message. Otherwise it will no longer be possible to assimilate it in our lives.[83]

A working image of church grounded in biblical sources and resonating with the experience of the faithful has the power to move the institution into new territory, spiritually, liturgically, and theologically. Even so, the usefulness of the image can be determined only after the institution has lived out the consequences to which the image points.[84] We should not assume that one particular image or model of church is definitive; on the contrary, "we must recognize that our own favorite paradigms, however excellent, do not solve all questions."[85] At the same time, however, just as familiarity with a range of christological titles can lead us to a rich encounter with Jesus, so, too, a range of models of church can infuse new life into the institution. When the church fails to reevaluate its images of itself, the result is stagnation, exclusivity, complacency, rigidity, authoritarianism, and spiritual bankruptcy. Similarly, a focus on any single model—however appropriate it might be—will "lead to distortions."[86]

"The contemporary crisis of faith is . . . in very large part a crisis of images," writes Dulles; the old, worn images need to be supplemented with images "that speak more directly to our contemporaries."[87] According to Dulles, certain models may have redeeming features, but over time, their less beneficial characteristics have gained ascendancy. The model of church as institution, for example, may provide a strong corporate identity but it also encourages passivity and blind obedience on the part of the laity; similarly, while "People of God" legitimizes the concept of "salvation history," fostering a sense of unique calling, it also promotes spiritual exclusivity and a monopoly on grace.[88] The church as Holy Fool would be a church that is vibrantly alive, all-inclusive and appropriately humble.

Later in the same work, Dulles summarizes what he considers to be the signs of disease in contemporary Catholicism:

> Too much turned in upon itself, the Church has become increasingly concerned with its own internal affairs and correspondingly more estranged from modern civilization, to the point where communication between the Church and the World has become very difficult. This has brought about in the Church a loss of numbers, a loss of vitality and a loss of influence. The language and structures of the Church have not kept pace with the development of human culture in general.[89]

Harsh as this assessment may seem, I find it supported by the mass exodus of youth from their traditions of origin, particularly from Catholicism. In my work as a Chicago-based university minister and as a professor of Religious Studies, I see more young people estranged from the church—referring specifically to the Roman Catholic Church—than who actively belong to it; when I ask the reasons for this alienation, students consistently cite 1) institutional hypocrisy, 2) lack of justice, 3) pedophilia, 4) failure to adapt to the diverse cultural needs of its members, 5) dearth of imagination, and 6) authoritarianism.

This student list corresponds to complaints I have heard in the United States from all age groups over the last decade and more. In many cases, the students provided personal anecdotes of precipitating events which caused them to "walk" either into atheism, or another Christian denomination or Zen Buddhism or, as is becoming increasingly common, into the practice of Wicca or White Witchcraft. The stories were variations on the same theme: family members denied burial because of suicide or failing to contribute financially to the local church; parents denied the Eucharist because they were divorced (sometimes when they had remained single); homilies which were theologically unsound, trite, judgmental, irrelevant, threatening, or manipulative; discrimination on the basis of race or nationality; discomfort in churches which were entirely homogenous; alienation caued by the use of androcentric language; infant relatives denied baptism because of non-practicing parents; traumatic experiences with the Sacrament of Reconciliation; hearing no more than pious platitudes when wrestling with grief, anger, or despair. . . . There were instances, of course, which might have been less alienating had the students possessed a more sophisticated background in canon law or theology; pastorally speaking, however, some representative of the church had missed a "teachable moment" or had failed to communicate empathy and goodwill. Evidently, for many youth today—and for their seniors—the church has ceased to be a viable option for spiritual growth.

Typically, there are always students in my classes who claim to have been "raised Catholic," but who want no further association with their Catholic roots. Many display anger towards the church, clearly believing that Catholicism and the intellectual life are mutually exclusive. For them, to be Catholic is a liability and an embarrassment. They have asked me to account for how I, "an intelligent feminist," can possibly remain in a church which oppresses women; they remind me of the church's not-so-admirable record in terms of human rights. Again, many students lack the critical capacity to make allowances for the mores and attitudes of a particular era, but while one may excuse away the Crusades or the treatment of a Bruno or Galileo as being "time bound," it is harder to make a case for more recent failures:

> Instead of encouraging and supporting those developments which have brought increased freedom and human betterment, the Christian Churches have often found themselves allied with colonialism and autocratic governments, supporting outmoded social and political structures, viewing the advance of scientific knowledge with suspicion and even fear.[90]

Schillebeeckx, in *Church: The Human Story of God*, explains that unless the church is constantly engaged in renewal, it moves away from its roots as a liberation movement, and becomes, instead:

> A power structure that oppresses men and women, diminishes them and makes them suffer. Therefore, the Church itself, head and members, constantly remains under the gospel criticism deriving from the Kingdom of God as a Kingdom of freedom, non-violence and defenceless vulnerability.[91]

Clearly, many young people today experience the church as being out of tune with its gospel mandate and regard it as an institution of repression. Failing to look at the church wholistically and to see that it has more to offer than their own particular situation of alienation, students typically form their judgments exclusively on the basis of their personal experience; and personal experience tells them they have been betrayed. In describing the perceptions of young Catholics today, Robert Ludwig explains how they tend to believe that it is the divisive issues of the church that lie at the heart of Catholicism. Largely illiterate in terms of the church's sacramental life or its rich history of teachings on social justice, the young perceive the church as "unjust and immoral."[92]

While many are perfectly content with their experience of Catholicism and would be shocked by the critique offered above, it is a grave mistake to assume that the voices of Generation X are the voices of an insignificant minority. The future of the church—as of any institution—depends upon the loyalty of future generations. Unless we can offer today's youth a compelling model of church, they will want no part of Roman Catholicism's future. At a time when the institutional church seems to have lost its "salt" and its leavening power, the model of church as Holy Fool could offer a key to revival. By demonstrating what it means to place integrity before safety, the church, like the medieval jester, would invite today's youth to examine their own values. By manifesting passion instead of repressing it, the church would invite its members to join in the merry dance of love and justice. "Only by assuming a playful attitude toward our religious tradition can we possibly make any sense of it," writes Harvey Cox.[93]

By taking itself less seriously, the church would have more to say about "who belongs" than about who should remain outside the fold. Moreover, to a generation which largely finds Sunday liturgy "boring," the church as Holy Fool would seek to offer liturgical experiences which engage hearts and imaginations. "Kids get bored with going to Mass," said a seventeen-year-old participant in the biennial National Catholic Youth Conference. "It is supposed to be a celebration, but if it is, it's one of the worst parties I've ever been to. Nobody gets up to have fun. We need to have more celebrating."[94] Clearly, a large dose of Holy Foolishness is in order.

As Holy Fool, the church would need to redefine itself. Though the pre-Vatican II image of the church as a solely hierarchical pyramid has been offset in the Conciliar documents by the "People of God," the reality is that the church as a pyramid of power still dominates. Much decision making still happens in Rome, with little or no consultation of the laity. The appointment of bishops and cardinals, for example, is a "Vatican affair," influenced by religio-political agendas; pastoral concerns, it seems, are secondary to ensuring the continuation of worldviews in line with Rome's. Dissenting viewpoints—such as those of Hans Küng, Matthew Fox, Leonardo Boff, Charles Curran, Carmel McEnroy, and others—are simply not tolerated, especially on topics concerning the ordination of women, inclusive language, liberation theology, and sexual morality. And even when the expertise of lay specialists is solicited—as for example, by Pope Paul VI prior to his drafting of the encyclical, *Humanae Vitae*—their findings and recommendations have been ignored.

If the church were to live out the paradigm of Holy Fool, the pyramid of power would have to be dismantled. Holy Fools, after all, are not used to accolades and status; on the contrary, they always point beyond themselves to the humble Christ. Crowned with thorns and wrapped in robes of mockery, this Christ stands at the bottom of the pyramid, along with all his disenfranchised brothers and sisters. Jesus the Holy Fool renounced worldly power so that he could stand in solidarity with the powerless of this world; accordingly, it would be difficult to imagine how a hierarchical church could be consistent with all that he represents. This is not to say that there would no longer be appropriate distinctions within the church itself. The first chapter of *Lumen Gentium* describes the church as a mystery characterized by a "diversity of members and functions, establishing the importance of the apostolic succession."[95] The same document, however, while distinguishing between ordained priesthood and the priesthood of the laity, also asserts:

> All the laity, then, have the exalted duty of working for the ever greater extension of the divine plan of salvation to all people of every time and every place. Every opportunity should therefore be given to them to share zealously in the salvific work of the church according to their ability and the needs of the times.[96]

Sadly, clerical monopoly did not end with Vatican II. Though much of the mystique and privilege that once drew young men to the priesthood is a thing of the past, and though few still view ordination as a means of social betterment, ordination still represents authority and power—both of which can be abused. Precisely because some of those vested in spiritual power use it as a source of ego-gratification, they are unwilling to empower laity who by calling, education, and spiritual maturity are ready and able to share in ministerial functions, whether at the local level or higher.

Worldly fools cling to power as a means of self-definition. Delighting in all that separates them from "lesser mortals," they use their power over others for their personal satisfaction and aggrandizement. Instead of imitating the humble Christ who modeled selfless service, such worldly fools fail to translate what they have grasped intellectually into praxis. When worldly fools receive Holy Orders, they not only distort the function of the priesthood, but also alienate those in their care from the church itself and sometimes, even from God. They fail to recognize what Harvey Cox defines as the church's task in the secular city: that is, "to be the diakonos of the city, the servant who bends . . . to struggle for its wholeness and health."[97] Uncomfortable with the idea of riding an ass into Jerusalem, they expect a gilded horse-drawn chariot.

Holy Fools, on the other hand, have no need of titles, status or emblems of privilege. By definition, they are selfless and willing to embrace absurdity for the sake of God's reign. Just as Jesus the Holy Fool was willing to gird himself with a towel and bend before his disciples, so Holy Fools of the ordained variety are willing to empower others to do what they themselves might be able to do better. "Excelling" or being in the limelight is not their agenda; nor is the church a "career path" up the pyramid. Rather, they delegate that power and authority they have for the sake of God's reign, for the empowerment of God's people, and for the glory of God's Name. Moreover, they know how to use their power to effect change, to transform unjust structures and to challenge death-dealing attitudes. For them, "all the faithful enjoy a true equality with regard to the dignity and the activity which they share in the building up of the body of Christ."[98] They understand that it is not the ring master who draws crowds to the circus, but all the clowns, acrobats, and animal trainers who fill the ring; accordingly, they are willing to step back so that others may be more visible. At the same time, they are sharply aware that pyramids only exist when they are supported by the broken backs of those crushed by their weight.

Ken Feit was a Holy Fool with a new understanding of priesthood. He left the seminary because he could not reconcile institutional priesthood with his unique call to be a "priest fool." But while "Ken the Fool" was clown, poet, story teller, puppeteer, mime, musician, and jester, "he was no fool," writes Joseph Martin: "While he was not a priest, he performed priestly functions," gathering people, leading celebrations, defying ennui, boredom, apathy, and all forms of living death.[99] He quotes Feit's words regarding his vocation:

> When the calling of the fool came to me in a conscious way . . . there was a certain reluctance. I wished to remain on my journey towards priesthood. Somehow I had no choice, though. It seemed to me that the full paradox of the fool was something that had embraced me, and now I had to embrace it. I called myself after that 'a priestly fool' and left the formal calling of the institutional priesthood and stayed where fools belong—on the edge of the institution, on the periphery, the desert, the mountain top, the wilderness, the garbage can. That's where fools seem to end up.[100]

For Feit, the Fool is an agent of spirituality, the source of true wisdom.[101] Following in the ancient tradition of jongleurs, galliards, and jesters, the fool's function is to be "a discerner of wonder, mystery, and paradox . . . a proclaimer of truth (verbally and nonverbally) . . . a servant and healer of the poor." In addition, in spite of living on the periphery, the fool gathers the community and "resymbolizes, reritualizes and remythologizes for the tribe."[102] Through clowning, the fool also mirrors the frailty and absurdity of the people, facilitating the laughter which leads to healing and forgiveness:

> Thus the clown serves as a general confessor to the people, first by taking on their sins . . . and then by absolving them through laughter. It is the mystery of crucifixion and resurrection reenacted.[103]

As Holy Fool, the church would establish very different criteria for ordination than those which presently exist; it would completely overhaul priestly formation. In recent years, the church in the United States has tended to attract and ordain rigid men with little life experience or Fool in them but with a strong dedication to the institutional church and to all that it represents. They may exhibit strong loyalty to Rome and to the traditions and teachings of the Roman Catholic Church, but they are often incapable of critical thinking, are unwilling to listen to opposing viewpoints and demonstrate an insensitivity to the alienation of many church members. Such servants of the church may have learned "the rules," but have often missed the harder lessons involved in personal transformation. Unlike Ken Feit, they fail to understand that the mystery of priesthood lies in the passionate celebration of life and death and in the willingness to confront unjust structures with playful disorder. Unwavering in their convictions, priests of this variety espouse conventional wisdom and are not inclined to step into the arena of Holy Folly—that is, into the arena of vulnerability, ambiguity, uncertainty, creativity, truth-speaking and risk-taking. They might become strong parish administrators or exemplary bishops but they fail to demonstrate what it is to struggle with gospel values, to be filled with passion and compassion or to be actively engaged in their own conversion process. These worldly-wise priests are functionaries, not shamans or clowns; they fail to inspire their flocks but instead shepherd them into conformity. Comfortable in a world of "black and white," they are unwilling to caper in the territory of "gray" for fear that becoming ludicrous, they will be defrocked.

The seminary system—as it seems to exist in many parts of the world—still tends to offer a life of privilege for those preparing for service. Instead of being immersed in the human condition, many seminarians are set apart in a way that makes them ill-equipped to develop healthy interpersonal skills, especially with women, or to deal with real life issues. Because many seminary professors are celibate ordained men or, more rarely, celibate women religious, candidates for priesthood receive a worldview that is ivory tower, insular, and far-removed from the day-to-day struggles of ordinary people. Moreover, because the curriculum is heavily academic, they are seldom exposed to the kinds of experiential courses that might assist them in their own formation. Consequently, the spiritual life is reduced to book-learning, and those destined to be the religious leaders of tomorrow remain spiritually impoverished. As Holy Fool, the church would take seriously Vatican II's instruction on priesthood as found in *Presbyterorum Ordinis*. While this document establishes that by vocation and ordination, priests are in some way set apart within the people of God, this is to assure that they are "completely consecrated to the task for which God chooses them." Were they to be aloof from their flock's life and circumstances, "they would be powerless to serve people."[104]

"Rome is a good city in which to become aware of the need for clowns," writes Henri Nouwen.[105] If one were to interpret Rome as a symbol of the church, much of what Nouwen says can be applied to the institutional priesthood as it stands today. Extending his circus imagery, Nouwen speaks of the temptation to join the lion tamers and the trapeze artists, in other words, those who attract attention by the color and drama of their work. But, he continues, there is something of greater significance than the spectacular and the sensational; namely, the clowns who appear between the scenes:

> The clowns show us by their "useless" behavior, not simply that many of our preoccupations, worries, tensions and anxieties need a smile, but more importantly that we, too, have white on our faces and that we, too, are called to clown a little.[106]

To me, the pressing issue regarding priesthood today is not so much a matter of who should—or should not—be ordained, but the need for ministers who are not afraid to demonstrate either their own absurdity or the struggles they share with those they serve. Priestly formation and ordination need to be reconsidered in light of the mandate to be fools for the sake of Christ; unless this is given priority, those who wear the collar are unlikely to have the skills necessary to lead the church into the next millennium, regardless of gender.

If Holy Mother Church could be Holy Fool, there would be less of a focus on orthodoxy and orthopraxy and more on inclusivity. Holy Fools are flexible by definition; rigidity, harshness, excessive punishment, lack of charity are foreign to them. They prefer to suffer censure and abuse than to leave others out in the cold; they would rather bend than marginalize those who hold different beliefs or "break the rules." As Holy Fool, the church would no longer be obsessed with which members are "in good standing" or which ones should be denied the Eucharist or barred from teaching in Catholic institutions; instead, there would be a compassionate attempt to invite the alienated home because they need to be there and because the church needs their presence. The Good Shepherd who was foolish enough to leave the ninety-nine "good" sheep to go in search of the one lost sheep would wonder why the very souls who need the most care are the ones being crushed by the full burden of the Law. As Holy Fool, the church would cease to be an exclusive club but would dare to become a haven for those who have, for one reason or another, fallen from grace, from happiness, from belonging. As prodigal parent, a church that is Holy in its Foolishness would extend itself in generosity as fully and unrestrainedly as the father of the prodigal son extended himself in love. Such a church would indeed be absurd, but it would also be close to God's heart.

The inclusivity of such a church would also be manifested in openness to diverse cultures. Just as territorial colonialism imposed a European face on the continents of the world, so spiritual colonialism of the Roman Catholic variety has made Roman law, language, and liturgical expression normative for the global church. As Holy Fool, the church would question whether such Romanization is just and whether it is in the best interests of a particular people or of the church as a whole. With increasing decentralization and respect for its non-Roman members, "the Catholic Church in various regions will be able to enter more vitally into the life of different peoples and to relate itself more positively to the traditions of other Christian denominations."[107] Thus in areas of the world in which wheat flour and grape wine may be hard to obtain, local equivalents would become liturgically appropriate for the celebration of the Eucharist; or in cultures with strong rites-of-passage traditions, these rites could be incorporated into the sacramental life of the local church. Honoring what "is already there" is a far cry from imposing rules from above.

While credal unity is desirable, to "Romanize" the religious experience of other peoples smacks of spiritual arrogance. It is worldly folly, for example, to ignore the rich theological and pastoral contributions of Third World churches. Summarizing angry reactions to the Synod for America, held in Rome in 1997, Giulio Girardi, an Italian theologian with many years of pastoral experience in Latin America, decried the Rome-centered ecclesiology imposed upon the synod:

> The intention is that the American synod is to be Roman, that it is to be a synod about America but not from America. This all adds up to a more general politico-theological project: that the American church is to be Roman.[108]

As Holy Fool, the church would be humble enough to dismantle the apparatus of prejudice and to allow the Holy Spirit to blow freely in every culture and among every people. Presently, according to Girardi, the church's conceptual starting point is the institutional church, not the people. As Holy Fool, the church would need to open its ears to the cries of those who live beyond the pale of the Vatican. As Holy Fool, the church would hear the voices of the poor and indigenous; it would no longer promote the religio-political agenda of the wealthy and powerful. In an article published in *Christus*, Brazilian theologian Jose Oscar Beozzo writes:

Why not allow the cry of the poor, the shout of the excluded, of the indigenous peoples, of the African-Americans, of the landless peasants, of the unemployed, of the women, of the old people, of the young, and of so many silent voices—why not let them be heard? Is it possible that we should not pay attention to this weeping? Is it possible that the voice of none of the churches of the continent is judged appropriate to express the sufferings and anguish, the hopes and desires of these peoples of the continent?[109]

In 1997 I gave a series of presentations in the Chicago area on the subject of Holy Foolishness: one was at my own parish, St. James Church; another two were addressed to deacons and their wives during a symposium sponsored by the archdiocese; and two more were directed towards members of lay spirituality groups. At the end of each session, having defined Holy Foolishness and having demonstrated its relevance to Christology, I asked participants to consider how the church would "look" if it were to live out of the paradigm of Holy Fool. They answered that the church would not act as God but as God's servant in the world. As such, it would be a haven for Christians who live lives of Holy Folly, a place of support on the spiritual path. It would challenge its members to risk Holy Foolery if they have not already done so. The focus would be "truth, justice, and the spiritual way"; "pomp, ceremony, materialism, and rote practices would decline."

As Holy Fool, the church would move away from rule-based spirituality, rigidity of judgment, and collusion with earthly powers. The faithful would be encouraged to obey God's Law above all else and to follow their consciences, even if this means going against humanly established law. "Perhaps," wrote one participant, "many of our arguments over black and white issues would disappear or at least recede in their importance or diminish the time they tend to occupy in the institutional church's thinking." Another person felt that if the church could go beyond the letter of the law, the life of its members would be enriched.

Love and authentic freedom would be practiced regularly, and not held up simply as ideals to be strived for. More in touch with the people, bishops would willingly undertake the dismantling of the pyramid of power. The disenfranchised—especially the divorced and gays—would be welcomed back along with other "hurting people." Just as Jesus was foolish enough to forgive, the church would not only forgive but learn to ask forgiveness. One person wrote, "Lots of walls would be broken down between fellow believers—and ultimately God's quest would be realized." Another person suggested that a Holy Fool church "would take seriously the meaning of the Body of Christ"; the institutional church "would no longer be so institutionalized—it would become stronger, and be a distinctive voice in our midst, but not without persecution."

Finally, if the church really embraced Holy Folly, it might exert a wider influence: "We might really become that mustard seed, planted and thriving—what a wonderful way to go into the new millennium!" Just as Holy Fools exude aliveness, so the church would be filled with energy, enthusiasm, and passion. As one participant put it: "We—the People of God—would be a greater witness of joy. We would be alive—welcoming. And our numbers would increase, for who is not drawn to happiness?"

Conclusion

In Federico Fellini's film, *La Strada*.[1] Gelsomina is a natural fool who is "sold" by her mother to the brutish Zampano to be a sidekick in his travelling road show. Having somehow been responsible for the death of Gelsomina's sister, Zampano shows no indication of treating his new assistant with any tenderness. He trains Gelsomina as a cruel animal trainer might teach a dog, not sparing the switch; he expects her to be sexually available while he preys on any other woman around. In spite of the physical and verbal abuse which comes her way, Gelsomina takes childish delight in the life of show business; surprisingly, we see her develop real affection for her "owner," despite his violence and unethical behavior.

But Gelsomina also loves Nazzareno, an angel of a fool—a tight rope artist who plays ethereal music and knows how to tease Zampano into a jealous rage. When Zampano is arrested for trying to stab Nazzareno, Gelsomina has the opportunity to escape with her friend; however, because Nazzareno suggests that Zampano may actually love her, she decides to stay with him, for his sake rather than her own. This decision, based as it is on her own generosity of spirit, is nothing less than Holy Foolishness. Not surprisingly, there is costly grace involved. Zampano kills Nazzareno in a fit of violent rage; Gelsomina, unable to face this reality, goes mad. After Zampano hides his crime, her continual lament is, "The fool is hurt!" This, of course, refers both to her deceased friend and to herself. Unable to work any more, she constantly plays a poignant refrain on her trumpet which she learned from Nazzareno.

Zampano demonstrates new consideration for his now useless assistant. We see him tending to her needs; eventually, however, the task becomes too much for him and he abandons her. Some five years later, he hears a woman singing the melody which Gelsomina used to play on her trumpet; eagerly, he asks where she learned the music, only to find that it was from a woman, now dead, who having lost her senses, spent her time weeping and playing her trumpet. Overcome, Zampano staggers to the seashore where, resisting the impulse to drown himself, he throws himself on the sand and weeps. . . .

What, one might ask, does this film have to do with Holy Foolishness? In the first place, it presents a world very much in need of redemption. The cruel and violent Zampano embodies the shadow side of humanity; he is not only himself—bestial, heartless, and unconscious—but he also represents every oppressive individual, institution and regime. He is the destroyer of life and of dreams. He is one of the godless, those who have drifted far from the law and from justice, respecting neither God nor humans. His rituals—the breaking of chest-binding chains—are a parody of true liberation: while he resorts to his own brute strength to snap the chains which bind him, he is imprisoned by invisible chains that render him incapable of loving. His heart is made of the same iron in which he chooses to encase himself.

Gelsomina, on the other hand, is a defenseless fool whose childlike simplicity offers a refreshing contrast to Zampano's cutthroat ways. Her natural expression is that of a clown's, with her eyes and mouth clearly expressing joy and sorrow, depending on the situation. She is in touch with her feelings; he doesn't recognize the existence of feelings at all. While Zampano is not above stealing from a community of nuns who sheltered them for the night, Gelsomina takes joy in little things like planting tomato seeds or making a new friend. Like the court fool, she is not afraid to speak out against his evil ways; nor is she afraid to weep when he violates her sense of right and wrong. Just as Jesus the Holy Fool took upon himself the sins of the world, so Gelsomina bears the weight of Zampano's sins, at the cost of her faculties. And just as Jesus redeemed the world by embracing the cross, so Gelsomina is the agent in Zampano's own redemption: his tears reveal that his iron heart has become a heart of flesh. . . .

Gelsomina exemplifies what can happen to spirituality, ritual, and justice when Holy Foolishness prevails. In her purity, she models what it is to become "The Christ" in terms of the cost and consequences involved. In her sufferings, she demonstrates that the foolish act of pouring out one's life for the sake of another can be redemptive. Zampano learns to love the fool because the fool has taught him how to love; while he has constricted his heart with iron chains, she sets him free by loving him unconditionally. A church holy in its foolishness would learn to do likewise.

The church and its members have much to learn from the Holy Fool. Notwithstanding all the affliction they bring upon themselves by virtue of who they are, Holy Fools insist upon being hopeful and joyful. Though at times they may weep—and weep copiously—they also have an extraordinary capacity for laughter. Resilient as the circus clown, witty as the trickster, outrageous as the court jester, and uncompromising as the Holy Fools of Russian Orthodoxy, Holy Fools imitate the foolishness of Christ precisely because they know that he has already lost and gained everything for them. The last laugh has already resounded through the universe; death has already lost its sting. What is necessary, then, is for each of us who dares to be Holy Fool to live with the sound of that laugh ringing in our hearts that we, too, may laugh with unrestrained joy. And, I believe, it is through this laughter that we most delight God. . . .

Notes

Introduction

Jesus, Lord and Fool

1. Cf. Oscar Cullman, *The Christology of the New Testament* (Philadelphia: Westminster Press, 1963), 237.

2. Cf. Ibid., 126.

3. Ibid., 164.

4. Ibid., 68.

5. Ibid., 161.

The Christ of Many Faces

6. Robert S. Schreiter, *Faces of Jesus in Africa* (New York: Orbis Books, 1991), 5–10.

7. R. S. Sugirtharajah, *Asian Faces of Jesus* (New York: Orbis Books, 1993), viii.

8. Ibid., 3.

9. Cf. Ibid., 4.

10. Pierre Courthion, *Georges Rouault* (New York: Harry N. Abrams, Inc., 1984), 100.

11. Ibid., 103.

12. Ibid., 86.

Approaching Jesus

13. Leopold Sabourin, *The Names and Titles of Jesus* (New York: Macmillan Co., 1967), 315–317.

14. John Saward, *Perfect Fools* (Oxford: Oxford University Press, 1980), ix.

Part One: Jesus and Human Folly

Psychological Archetypes

1. C. G. Jung, "The Concept of the Collective Unconscious," in *The Portable Jung,* edited by J. Campbell (New York: Penguin, 1971), 60.

2. Robert Johnson, *Inner Work* (New York: Harper & Row, 1986), 27.

3. Jolande Jacobi, *The Psychology of C. G. Jung* (New Haven: Yale University Press, 1973), 42.

4. Cf. Carol Pearson, *Awakening the Heroes Within* (New York: HarperCollins, 1991), 15–17.

5. Cf. Ibid., 19.

6. Ibid., 50.

7. C. G. Jung, "Approaching the Unconscious," in *Man and His Symbols,* edited by C. G. Jung (New York: Dell Publishers, 1964), 87.

8. Jolande Jacobi, *The Psychology of C. G. Jung* (New Haven: Yale University Press, 1973), 127.

9. Ibid., 129.

10. Wayne Rollins, *Jung and the Bible* (Atlanta: John Knox Press, 1983), 90.

11. Farid Ud-Din Attar, *The Conference of the Birds* (Harmondsworth: Penguin, 1986), 30–32.

12. Ibid., 219.

13. Ibid., 16.

14. Marie-Louise von Franz, "The Process of Individuation," in *Man and His Symbols,* edited by C. G. Jung, (New York: Dell Publishers, 1964), 169.

15. Edward Edinger, *Ego and Archetype* (New York: Penguin, 1972), 96.

16. Cf. Dante Alighieri, *Il Purgatorio,* edited by Dorothy Sayers (London: Penguin, 1955).

17. John of the Cross, *The Collected Works* (Washington: ICS Publications, 1979), 97.

18. Huston Smith, *The Religions of Man* (New York: Harper & Row, 1986), 156.

19. Helen Luke, *From Dark Wood to White Rose* (New York: Parabola Books, 1989), xv.

20. John of the Cross, *The Collected Works* (Washington: ICS Publications, 1979), 122.

21. Ibid., 335.

22. Alois Haas, "Schools of Late Medieval Mysticism," in *Christian Spirituality. High Middle Ages and Reformation*, edited by Jill Rait (New York: Crossroad, 1988), 150.

23. Cf. Dante Aligheri, *Il Purgatorio* (London: Penguin, 1955), 75.

24. Evelyn Underhill, *Essentials of Mysticism* (New York: Dutton, 1960), 246.

25. T. S. Eliot, *The Complete Poems and Plays* (New York: Harcourt, Brace & World, 1971), 145.

26. Edward Edinger, *Ego and Archetype* (New York: Penguin, 1972), 135.

Plain Fool versus Holy Fool

27. Carroll Stuhlmueller, "The Gospel According to Luke," in *The Jerome Biblical Commentary*, edited by R. Brown, J. Fitzmyer, R. Murphy (Englewood Cliffs: Prentice-Hall, 1968), 154.

28. Dietrich Bonhoeffer, *Letters and Papers from Prison* (New York: Macmillan, 1967), 30.

29. William Shakespeare, *The Complete Works* (New York: Harcourt, Brace and World, 1968), 1161.

30. Dietrich Bonhoeffer, *Letters and Papers from Prison* (New York: Macmillan, 1967), 31.

The Fool as Archetype

31. Robert Johnson, *Inner Work* (New York: Harper & Row, 1986), 27.

32. Richard Boston, *An Anatomy of Laughter* (London: Collins, 1974), 93.

33. Ibid.

34. Paul Radin, *The Trickster: A Study in American Indian Mythology* (New York: Schocken Books, 1972), xxiii.

35. Ibid., 29.

36. Ibid., 209.

The Fool as Professional

37. Cf. James Frazer, *The Golden Bough* (New York: Collier Books, 1922), 675–679.

38. Raymond Brown, *The Death of the Messiah* (New York: Doubleday, 1994), 876.

39. Ibid., 877.

40. Cf. William Willeford, *The Fool and His Sceptre* (Evanston: Northwestern University Press, 1969), 154.

41. Ibid., 57.

42. Ibid.

43. Plautus, "The Prisoners," in *The Pot of Gold and Other Plays* (Harmondsworth: Penguin, 1955), 60.

44. Cf. Enid Welsford, *The Fool: His Social and Literary History* (Gloucester: Peter Smith, 1966), 7.

45. Cf. John Towsen, *Clowns* (New York: Hawthorne Books, Inc., 1976), 25.

46. Enid Welsford, *The Fool and His Scepter* (Gloucester: Peter Smith, 1969), 119.

47. Ibid., 18.

48. Paul Radin, *The Trickster: A Study in American Indian Mythology* (New York: Schocken Books, 1972), 196.

49. Ibid., 197.

50. Cf. Ibid.

51. Cf. John Towsen, *Clowns* (New York: Hawthorne Books, Inc., 1976), 8.

The Fool as Scapegoat and Sage

52. Enid Welsford, *The Fool: His Social and Literary History* (Gloucester: Peter Smith, 1966), 73.

53. William Shakespeare, *The Complete Works* (New York: Harcourt, Brace and World, 1968), 1161.

54. Ibid., 1148.

55. Edward Hays, *Holy Fools and Mad Hatters* (Leavenworth: Forest of Peace Books, 1993), 25.

56. Ibid.

57. William Willeford, *The Fool and His Sceptre* (Evanston: Northwestern University Press, 1969), 48.

58. Carol Pearson, *Awakening the Heroes Within* (New York: HarperCollins, 1991), 221–222.

59. Ibid.

The Fool as Spiritual Quester

60. Robert Johnson, *He: Understanding Masculine Psychology* (New York: Harper & Row, 1989), 78.

61. *The Wickerman,* produced by Peter Snell, 1961.

62. Edward Hays, *Holy Fools and Mad Hatters* (Leavenworth: Forest of Peace Books, 1993), 24.

63. Ibid.

64. Ibid.

65. Ibid., 25.

Biblical Precursors of the Holy Fool

66. John Saward, *Perfect Fools* (Oxford: Oxford University Press, 1980), 1.

67. Francis Landy, "Humour as a Tool for Biblical Exegesis," in *On Humour and the Comic in the Bible,* edited by A. Brenner and R. Yehuda (Sheffield: Almond Press, 1990), 100.

Part Two: Jesus and Divine Folly

The Foolishness of God in Creation and Election

1. Thomas Aquinas, *Of God and His Creatures* (Westminster: The Carroll Press, 1950), 22.

2. Ibid., 3.

3. Ibid., 13.

4. Brian Davies, *The Thought of Thomas Aquinas* (Oxford: Oxford University Press, 1992), 67.

5. Cf. Exodus 3:14; Exodus 3:3; Exodus 13:21; 1 Samuel 3:4; 1 Kings 19:12; 2 Chronicles 5:11; Isaiah 27:2; Nahum1:2; Hosea 11:3; The Song of Songs.

6. Augustine, *Confessions* (Harmondsworth: Penguin, 1961), 33.

7. Ibid., 28.

8. Cf. Brian Davies, *The Thought of Thomas Aquinas* (Oxford: Oxford University Press, 1992), 256–257.

9. Abraham Heschel, *The Prophets* (New York: Harper & Row, 1962), 26.

10. Cf. Ibid.

11. Ibid., 22.

12. Cf. Ibid., 56.

13. Ibid.

14. Dennis McCarthy, "Hosea," in *The Jerome Biblical Commentary*, edited by R. Brown, J. Fitzmyer and R. Murphy (Englewood Cliffs: Prentice-Hall, 1968), 254.

15. Ibid.

16. Abraham Heschel, *The Prophets* (New York: Harper & Row, 1962), 57.

17. Jurgen Moltmann, *The Crucified God* (Minneapolis: Fortress Press, 1993), 276.

18. Lars Thunberg, "The Human Person as Image of God," in *Christianity: Origins to the Twelfth Century,* edited by B. McGinn, J. Meyendorff and J. Leclercq (New York: Crossroad, 1987), 308.

19. Francis Varillon, *The Humility and Suffering of God* (New York: Alba House, 1983), 43.

20. Leo Lefebure, *The Buddha and the Christ: Explorations in Buddhist and Christian Dialogue* (New York: Orbis Books, 1993), 52.

21. Jurgen Moltmann, *The Crucified God* (Minneapolis: Fortress Press, 1993), 24.

The Foolishness of Jesus' Actions

22. Cf. Raymond Brown, *The Birth of the Messiah* (New York: Doubleday, 1977), 25.

23. Ibid.

24. Elizabeth-Anne Vanek, "Apophatic," in *Extraordinary Time* (Canton: Life Enrichment Publishers, 1988), 25.

25. Otto Rank, *The Myth of the Birth of the Hero* (New York: Vintage Books, 1964), 15.

26. Cf. Ibid., 18.

27. Carroll Stuhlmueller, "The Gospel According to Luke," in *The Jerome Biblical Commentary,* edited by R. Brown, J. Fitzmyer and R. Murphy (Englewood Cliffs: Prentice-Hall, 1968), 126.

28. Louis Kronenberger, *The Thread of Laughter* (New York: Alfred A. Knopf, Inc., 1952), 3.

29. Carroll Stuhlmueller, "The Gospel According to Luke," in *The Jerome Biblical Commentary*, edited by R. Brown, J. Fitzmyer and R. Murphy (Englewood Cliffs: Prentice-Hall, 1968), 128.

30. John D. Crossan, *The Historical Jesus* (New York: HarperSanFrancisco 1991), 262.

31. Walter Kasper, *Jesus the Christ* (New York: Paulist Press, 1976), 101.

32. Marcus Borg, *Meeting Jesus Again for the First Time: The Historical Jesus and the Heart of Contemporary Faith* (New York: HarperCollins, 1994), 79.

33. Cf. Ibid., 81.

34. Ibid., 85.

35. Abraham Heschel, *God in Search of Man* (New York: Octagon Books, 1972), 417.

36. Ibid.

37. Ibid., 411.

38. Cf. Matthew 21:12–16; Mark 11:15–19; Luke 19:45–46; John 2:13–22.

39. Edward Mally, "The Gospel According to Mark," in *The Jerome Biblical Commentary*, edited by R. Brown, J.Fitzmyer and R. Murphy (Englewood Cliffs: Prentice-Hall, 1968), 47.

40. Cf. Luke 23:45; Mark 15:37–38; Matthew 27:51.

The Foolishness of Jesus' Teachings

41. Leonardo Boff, *Jesus Christ Liberator: A Critical Christology for Our Time* (New York: Orbis Books, 1978), 64.

42. Monika Hellwig, *Jesus, the Compassion of God: New Perspectives on the Tradition of Christianity* (Delaware: Michael Glazier, 1983), 90.

43. Cf. William Wordsworth, "Ode on Intimations of Immortality from Recollection of Early Childhood," in *The Golden Treasury*, edited by F. Palgrave (London: Oxford University Press, 1963), 309–314.

44. Cf. Fyodor Dostoevsky, *The Idiot* (Harmondsworth: Penguin, 1955).

45. Huston Smith, *The Religions of Man* (New York: Harper & Row, 1986), 189.

46. Ibid., 189–190.

47. Ibid., 190.

48. Ibid., 190–194.

49. Cf. Luke 19:45–48; Mark 11:15–19; Matthew 21:12–13.

50. N. Ausubel, ed., *A Treasury of Jewish Folklore* (New York: Crown Publishers, 1948), xx.

51. Ibid., 105.

52. Ibid., 106.

53. Ibid., 55.

54. John McKenzie, "The Gospel According to Matthew," in *The Jerome Biblical Commentary*, edited by R. Brown, J. Fitzmyer and R. Murphy (Englewood Cliffs: Prentice-Hall, 1968), 70.

55. Leonardo Boff, *Jesus Christ Liberator: A Critical Christology for Our Time* (New York: Orbis Books, 1978), 71.

56. Walter Kasper, *Jesus the Christ* (New York: Paulist Press, 1976), 84.

57. Leo Lefebure, *The Buddha and the Christ: Explorations in Buddhist and Christian Dialogue* (New York: Orbis Books, 1993), 42.

58. Ibid.

59. Abraham Heschel, *God in Search of Man* (New York: Octagon Books, 1972), 296.

60. A. M. Hunter, *Interpreting the Parables* (London: SCM Press, 1960), 7.

61. Ibid.

62. N. Ausubel, ed., *A Treasury of Jewish Folklore* (New York: Crown Publishers, 1948), 56.

63. Ibid.

64. Ibid.

65. C. H. Dodd, *The Parables of the Kingdom* (New York: Charles Scribner's Sons, 1961), 5.

66. Ibid., 11.

67. N. Ausubel, ed., *A Treasury of Jewish Folklore* (New York: Crown Publishers, 1948), 56.

68. John D. Crossan, *The Dark Interval* (Sonoma: Polebridge Press, 1988), 39, 42.

69. Ibid., 99.

70. A. M. Hunter, *Interpreting the Parables* (London: SCM Press, 1960), 10.

71. John D. Crossan, *In Parables: The Challenge of the Historical Jesus* (San Francisco: Harper & Row, 1973), 55.

72. Ibid., 58.

73. Flannery O'Connor, *The Complete Stories* (New York: The Noonday Press, 1971), 500.

74. Ibid., 508.

75. Cf. Luke 12:13–21; Luke 19:11–27; Matthew 13:44–46.

76. N. Ausubel, ed., *A Treasury of Jewish Folklore* (New York: Crown Publishers, 1948), xix.

77. Ibid., xviii.

78. Etty Hillesum, *An Interrupted Life* (New York: Pantheon Books, 1981), 151.

79. John Kavanaugh, *Following Christ in a Consumer Society* (New York: Orbis Books, 1981), 71.

80. Leo Lefebure, *The Buddha and the Christ: Explorations in Buddhist and Christian Dialogue* (New York: Orbis Books, 1993), 34.

81. Abraham Heschel, *Man's Quest for God* (New York: Charles Scribner's Sons, 1954), 10.

82. Ibid., 15.

83. Julian of Norwich, *Revelations of Divine Love* (Harmondsworth: Penguin, 1966), 129.

84. Cf. Walter Kasper, *Jesus the Christ* (New York: Paulist Press, 1976), 89.

85. Ibid., 90.

86. Cf. Ibid., 91–98.

87. T. S. Eliot, *The Complete Poems and Plays* (New York: Harcourt, Brace and World, 1971), 180.

The Price of Holy Folly

88. Jurgen Moltmann, *The Crucified God* (Minneapolis: Fortress Press, 1993), 24.

89. Desiderius Erasmus, *The Praise of Folly* (Princeton: Princeton University Press, 1941), 116.

90. Edward Mally, "The Gospel According to Mark," in *The Jerome Biblical Commentary,* edited by R. Brown, J. Fitzmyer and R. Murphy (Englewood Cliffs: Prentice-Hall, 1968), 29.

91. John D. Crossan, *The Historical Jesus: The Life of a Mediterranean Jewish Peasant* (New York: HarperSanFrancisco, 1991), 262.

92. Ibid., 263.

93. Cf. Leviticus 24:16; Deuteronomy 13:6–10; Numbers 15:32–36; Leviticus 20:2; Leviticus 20:27.

94. Matthew 12:24; Mark 3:22; Luke 11:14–16.

95. Cf. Mark 1:21–28; Mark 5:1–20; Mark 7:24–30; Mark 9:14–29.

96. Leonardo Boff, *Jesus Christ Liberator: A Critical Christology for Our Time* (New York: Orbis Books, 1978), 144.

The Outcome of Holy Folly

97. Walter Kasper, *Jesus the Christ* (New York: Paulist Press, 1976), 113.

98. Jurgen Moltmann, *The Crucified God* (Minneapolis: Fortress Press, 1993), 33.

99. Ibid., 33–34.

100. John D. Crossan, *The Historical Jesus. The Life of a Mediterranean Jewish Peasant* (New York: HarperSanFrancisco, 1991), 375.

101. Raymond Brown, *The Death of the Messiah* (New York: Doubleday, 1994), 874.

102. John McKenzie, "The Gospel According to Matthew," in *The Jerome Biblical Commentary,* edited by R. Brown, J. Fitzmyer and R. Murphy (Englewood Cliffs: Prentice-Hall, 1968), 110.

103. Raymond Brown, *The Death of the Messiah* (New York: Doubleday, 1994), 574.

104. Abraham Heschel, *The Prophets* (New York: Harper & Row, 1962), 26.

105. Ibid., 16.

106. Cf. Mark 15:15; Matthew 27:34; Luke 22:23; John 19:12–16.

107. Matthew 27:11; Mark 15:2; Luke 22:3; John 18:34.

108. Raymond Brown, *The Death of the Messiah* (New York: Doubleday, 1944), 874.

109. Ibid., 875.

110. Cf. Ibid.

111. Ibid., 877.

112. John D. Crossan, *The Historical Jesus: The Life of a Mediterranean Jewish Peasant* (New York: HarperSanFrancisco, 1991), 378.

113. Ibid., 379.

114. Cf. Ibid., 376–383.

115. Raymond Brown, *The Death of the Messiah* (New York: Doubleday, 1994), 877.

116. Carroll Stuhlmueller, *Psalms 1* (Collegeville: The Liturgical Press, 1983), 151.

117. Cf. Ibid.

118. Walter Kasper, *Jesus the Christ* (New York: Paulist Press, 1976), 118.

119. Nelvin Voss, *For God's Sake Laugh!* (Atlanta: John Knox Press, 1967), 40.

120. Cf. Ibid., 68–69.

121. Ibid., 69.

122. Harvey Cox, *A Feast of Fools* (New York: Harper & Row, 1969), 157.

123. Ibid., 155.

124. Ibid., 157.

125. Louis Kronenberger, *The Thread of Laughter* (New York: Alfred A. Knopf, 1952), 3.

126. Cf. Ibid., 5.

The Foolishness of the Holy Spirit

127. Marie-Henry Keane, "The Spirit of Life," in *Doing Theology in Context: South African Perspectives,* edited by J. de Gruchy and C. Villa Vicencio (New York: Orbis Books, 1995), 69.

128. Ibid., 72.

129. Elizabeth Johnson, *She Who Is: The Mystery of God in Feminist Theological Discourse* (New York: Crossroad, 1992), 83.

130. Cf. Yves Congar, *I Believe in the Holy Spirit, I* (New York: Crossroad Publishing Co., 1983), 109.

131. Ibid., II, 151.

132. H. Newton Malony, A. Adams Lovekin, *Glossolalia: Behavioural Science Perspectives on Speaking in Tongues* (New York: Oxford University Press, 1984), 3.

133. Yves Congar, *I Believe in the Holy Spirit, II* (New York: Crossroad Publishing Co., 1983), 173.

134. Marie-Henry Keane, "The Spirit of Life," in *Doing Theology in Context: South African Perspectives*, edited by J. de Gruchy and C. Villa-Vicencio (New York: Orbis Books, 1995), 75.

135. Ibid., 71.

136. Desiderius Erasmus, *The Praise of Folly* (Princeton: Princeton University Press, 1941), 118.

137. Ibid.

138. Ibid.

139. Ibid., 119.

140. Dietrich Bonhoeffer, *The Cost of Discipleship* (New York: Macmillan, 1937), 77.

141. Ibid., 26.

142. Ibid., 35.

143. Ibid., 37.

144. Rosemary Haughton, *The Transformation of Man* (Springfield: Templegate, 1967), 265.

145. Cf. Bonaventure, *The Soul's Journey into God: The Tree of Life: The Life of St. Francis* (New York: Paulist Press, 1978).

146. Nicholas Patricca, *The Fifth Sun* (Woodstock: Dramatic Publishing Co., 1984), 34–35.

147. Michael Walsh, *Butler's Lives of Patron Saints* (San Francisco: Harper & Row, 1987), 190–191.

148. John Zizioulas, "The Early Christian Community," in *Christian Spirituality: Origins to the Twelfth Century*, edited by B. McGinn, J. Meyendorff and J. Leclerq (New York: Crossroad, 1987), 29.

149. William Bausch, *A New Look at the Sacraments* (Mystic: Twenty-Third Publications, 1988), 61.

The Foolishness of the Trinity

150. Cf. Frances Young, *The Making of the Creeds* (London: SCM Press, 1991), 3.

151. Jurgen Moltmann, *The Trinity and the Kingdom* (Minneapolis: Fortress Press, 1993), 7.

152. Ibid., 1.

153. Bonaventure, *The Soul's Journey into God: The Tree of Life: The Life of St. Francis* (New York: Paulist Press, 1978), 104.

154. Ibid., 105.

155. Jurgen Moltmann, *The Trinity and the Kingdom* (Minneapolis: Fortress Press, 1993), 157.

156. Ibid., 83.

157. Ibid., 161.

158. Cf. Ibid., 4–12.

Part Three: Christian Faith and Folly

Holy Foolishness and Inculturation

1. Cf. Samuel Beckett, *Waiting for Godot* (London: Faber and Faber, 1971).

2. Cf. Martin Esslin, *The Theatre of the Absurd* (Harmondsworth: Penguin, 1968), 23.

3. Cf. Euripides, *The Bacchae and Other Plays* (Harmondsworth: Penguin, 1972), 191–244.

4. Friedrich Nietzsche, *On the Genealogy of Morals and Ecce Homo* (New York: Vintage Books, 1967), 271.

5. Ibid., 207.

Relationship with Jesus the Holy Fool

6. Thomas à Kempis, *The Imitation of Christ* (Harmondsworth: Penguin, 1952), 27.

7. Dietrich Bonhoeffer, *The Cost of Discipleship* (New York: Macmillan, 1937), 50.

8. Hans Küng, *On Being a Christian* (New York: Doubleday & Co., 1984), 126.

9. Cf. Paul Jeffrey, "Guatemalan Catholics Find the Path to a New Future, Confront Sins of the Past," in *The National Catholic Reporter* (13 February 1998), 3.

10. John Shea, *The Spirit Master* (Chicago: The Thomas More Press, 1987), 20.

11. Ibid., 31.

12. Harvey Cox, *A Feast of Fools* (New York: Harper & Row, 1969), 139.

13. Dietrich Bonhoeffer, *The Cost of Discipleship* (New York: Macmillan Co., 1937), 36.

14. Ibid., 49.

15. Ibid.

16. Ibid., 51.

17. Ibid., 69.

18. Thomas à Kempis, *The Imitation of Christ* (Harmondsworth: Penguin, 1952), 130.

19. John Welch, *When Gods Die: An Introduction to John of the Cross* (New York: Paulist Press, 1990), 81.

20. Thomas à Kempis, *The Imitation of Christ* (Harmondsworth: Penguin, 1952), 88.

21. Julian of Norwich, *Revelations of Divine Love* (Harmondsworth: Penguin, 1966), 67–68.

The Russian Holy Fool

22. Marie-Louise von Franz, "The Process of Individuation," in *Man and His Symbols,* edited by C. G. Jung (New York: Dell Publishers, 1964), 169.

23. Ibid., 161.

24. John Saward, *Perfect Fools* (Oxford: Oxford University Press, 1980), 12.

25. Jim Forest, "Holy Foolishness," in *The Tablet* (23 July 1994), 917.

26. Ibid.

27. John Saward, *Perfect Fools* (Oxford: Oxford University Press, 1980), 12.

28. Ibid., 14.

29. Ibid., 18.

30. Ibid., 20–21.

31. Ibid., 21.

32. Ibid., 22.

33. G. P. Fedotov, *The Russian Religious Mind* (Cambridge: Harper Torchbooks, 1960), 126.

34. Ibid., 123.

35. Cf. Jim Forest, "Holy Foolishness," in *The Tablet* (23 July 1994), 917.

36. Cf. John Saward, *Perfect Fools* (Oxford: Oxford University Press, 1980), 23.

37. Fyodor Dostoevsky, *The Idiot* (Harmondsworth: Penguin, 1955), 530.

38. Cf. Fyodor Dostoevsky, *Crime and Punishment* (New York: Penguin, 1950), 292.

39. Ibid., 7.

40. Jim Forest, "Holy Foolishness," in *The Tablet* (23 July 1994), 918.

41. Anonymous, *The Way of a Pilgrim* (New York: Image Books, 1978), 13.

42. Ibid., 24.

43. Richard Rohr, "Holy Fools. Ushers of the Next Generation in the Church," in *Sojourners* (July 1994), 19.

Holy Foolishness and the Church Today

44. Erich Fromm, *Psychoanalysis and Religion* (New York: Bantam Books, 1950), 33.

45. Thomas Moore, *Care of the Soul. A Guide for Cultivating Depth and Sacredness in Everyday Life* (New York: HarperCollins, 1992), 5.

46. John Kavanaugh, *Following Christ in a Consumer Society* (New York: Orbis Books, 1981), 45.

47. Paul Tillich, *The Courage to Be* (New Haven: Yale University Press, 1952), 46.

48. Etty Hillesum, *An Interrupted Life* (New York: Pantheon Books, 1981), 186.

49. Ibid., 151.

50. Joseph Bernardin, *The Gift of Peace* (Chicago: Loyola Press, 1997), 36.

51. John Kavanaugh, *Following Christ in a Consumer Society* (New York: Orbis Books, 1981), 45.

52. T. S. Eliot, "The Four Quartets," in *The Complete Poems and Plays* (New York: Harcourt, Brace & World, 1971), 136.

53. Oscar Cullman, *Early Christian Worship* (Bristol: Wyndham Hall Press, 1953), 15.

54. Ibid., 12.

55. Thomas Driver, *The Magic of Ritual* (New York: HarperCollins, 1991), 7.

56. Cf. Ibid., 75.

57. Ibid., 11.

58. Ibid., 37.

59. *The Liturgy Documents. A Parish Resource* (Chicago: Liturgy Training Publications, 1980), 7.

60. Euripides, "The Bacchae," in *The Bacchae and Other Plays* (Harmondsworth: Penguin, 1972), 193–194.

61. Parliament of the World's Religions, *The Global Ethic* (Chicago: PWR, 1993), 13.

62. Ibid., 15.

63. Ibid., 22.

64. Ewert Cousins, *Christ of the 21st Century* (Rockport: Element Books, 1992), 3.

65. Cf. Ibid., 5.

66. Ibid., 10.

67. "Nostra Aetate," in *Vatican Council II: Constitutions, Decrees, Declarations,* edited by A. Flannery (New York: Costello Publishing Co., 1996), 569–571.

68. DePaul University, Department of Religious Studies, *Religious Worlds* (Chicago: Kendall-Hunt Publishing Co., 1991), 67.

69. Cf. Langston Hughes, "Harlem," in *The Bedford Introduction to Literature,* edited by M. Meyer (Boston: St. Martin's Press, 1990), 803.

70. Joseph Bernardin, *A Blessing to Each Other: Cardinal Joseph Bernardin and Jewish Catholic Dialogue* (Chicago: Liturgy Training Publications, 1996), 156.

71. Ibid., 137.

72. Eugene Fisher and Leon Klenicki, *From Desolation to Hope: An Interreligious Holocaust Memorial Service* (Chicago: Liturgy Training Publications, 1983), 10.

73. Joseph Bernardin, *A Blessing to Each Other. Cardinal Joseph Bernardin and Jewish Catholic Dialogue* (Chicago: Liturgy Training Publications, 1996), 137.

74. DePaul University, Deparment of Religious Studies, *Religious Worlds* (Chicago: Kendall-Hunt Publishing Co., 1991), 66.

75. Ibid., 68.

76. Eugene Fisher and Leon Klenicki, *From Desolation to Hope: An Interreligious Holocaust Memorial Service* (Chicago: Liturgy Training Publications, 1983), 17.

77. Cf. Ibid., 19.

78. Ibid., 19.

Holy Foolishness and a New Ecclesiology

79. Edward Schillebeeckx, *The Mission of the Church* (New York: Crossroad, 1973), 20.

80. Cf. Ibid.

81. "Gaudium et Spes," in *Vatican Council II: Constitutions, Decrees, Declarations,* edited by A. Flannery (New York:

Costello Publishing Co., 1996), 207.

82. Avery Dulles, *Models of the Church* (New York: Image Books, 1987), 20.

83. Edward Schillebeeckx, *The Mission of the Church* (New York: Crossroad, 1973), 26.

84. Cf. Avery Dulles, *Models of the Church* (New York: Image Books, 1987), 27.

85. Ibid., 32.

86. Cf. Ibid., 28.

87. Ibid., 21.

88. Cf. Ibid., 41.

89. Ibid., 98.

90. Bernard Cooke, *Christian Community: Response to Reality* (New York: Holt, Rinehard and Winston, 1970), 31.

91. Edward Schillebeeckx, *Church: The Human Story of God* (New York: Crossroad, 1990), 59.

92. Cf. Robert Ludwig, *Reconstructing Catholicism for a New Generation* (New York: Crossroad, 1995), 30.

93. Harvey Cox, *The Feast of Fools* (New York: Harper & Row, 1969), 142.

94. John Allen, "Teens Seek More Youth Friendly Liturgies," in *The National Catholic Reporter* (12 December 1997), 3.

95. "Lumen Gentium," in *Vatican Council II: Constitutions, Decrees, Declarations,* edited by A. Flannery (New York: Costello Publishing Co., 1996), 7.

96. Ibid., 52.

97. Avery Dulles, *Models of the Church* (New York: Image Books, 1987), 96.

98. "Lumen Gentium," in *Vatican Council II: Constitutions, Decrees, Declarations,* edited by A. Flannery (New York: Costello Publishing Co., 1996), 50.

99. Joseph Martin, *Foolish Wisdom: Stories, Activities and Reflections from Ken Feit* (San Jose: Resource Publications, 1990), 1.

100. Ibid., 5.

101. Cf. Ibid., 35.

102. Ibid., 44.

103. Ibid., 47.

104. "Presbyterorum Ordinis," in *Vatican Council II: Constitutions, Decrees, Declarations,* edited by A. Flannery (New York: Costello Publishing Co., 1996), 320.

105. Henri Nouwen, *Clowning in Rome: Reflections on Solitude, Celibacy, Prayer and Contemplation* (New York: Image Books, 1979), 10.

106. Ibid., 110.

107. Avery Dulles, *Models of the Church* (New York: Image Books, 1987), 200.

108. Gary MacEoin, "Synod Strives to Make American Church More Roman, Dissenters Say," in *The National Catholic Reporter* (12 December 97), 13.

109. Ibid.

Conclusion

1. Federico Fellini, *La Strada* (Janus Films, 1961).

Topical
Bibliography

Anthropology

Cushing, Frank Hamilton. *Zuni Folk Tales*. Tucson: University of
Arizona Press, 1931.
Eliade, Mircea. *The Sacred and the Profane: The Nature of Religion*.
New York: Harcourt Brace Jovanovich, 1959.
———. *Myth and Reality*. New York: Harper & Row, 1963.
———. *The Myth of the Eternal Return or Cosmos and History*.
Princeton: Princeton University Press, 1954.
———. *Myths, Dreams, and Mysteries*. New York: Harper & Row,
1960.
Frazer, Sir James. *The Golden Bough*. New York: Collier Books,
1922.
Hamilton, Edith. *Mythology*. New York: Mentor Books, 1969.
Radin, Paul. *The Trickster: A Study in American Indian Mythology*.
New York: Schocken Books, 1972.
Rosenberg, Donna, ed. *World Mythology*. Lincolnwood: NTC
Publishing Group, 1994.
Saward, John. *Perfect Fools*. Oxford: Oxford University Press, 1980.
Welsford, Enid. *The Fool: His Social and Literary History*. Gloucester:
Peter Smith, 1966.
Willeford, William. *The Fool and His Scepter*. Evanston:
Northwestern University Press, 1969.

Archetypal Studies

Achterberg, Jeanne. *Imagery in Healing: Shamanism and Modern Medicine.* Boston: Shambhala, 1985.

Campbell, Joseph. *The Portable Jung.* New York: Viking Books, 1971.

———. *The Hero with a Thousand Faces.* Princeton: Princeton University Press, 1949.

———. *The Mythic Imagination.* Princeton: Princeton University Press, 1974.

———. *The Power of Myth.* New York: Doubleday, 1988.

Edinger, Edward. *Ego and Archetype.* New York: Penguin, 1972.

Johnson, Robert. *He: Understanding Masculine Psychology.* New York: Harper & Row, 1989.

———. *Inner Work.* New York: Harper & Row, 1986.

———. *She: Understanding Feminine Psychology.* New York: Harper & Row, 1989.

———. *Owning Your Own Shadow.* New York: HarperCollins, 1991.

———. *Transformation: Understanding the Three Levels of Masculine Consciousness.* New York: HarperCollins, 1991.

———. *We: Understanding the Psychology of Romantic Love.* New York: Harper & Row, 1983.

Jung, C. G., ed. *Man and His Symbols.* New York: Dell Publishers, 1964.

———. "The Concept of the Collective Unconscious." In *The Portable Jung,* edited by Joseph Campbell. New York: Penguin, 1971.

Larsen, Stephen. *The Mythic Imagination.* New York: Bantam Books, 1991.

Miller, David. *Christs: Meditations on Archetypal Images in Christian Theology.* New York: Seabury Press, 1981.

Miller, James. *Myth and Method.* Nebraska: University of Nebraska Press, 1960.

Nietzsche, Friedrich. *On The Genealogy of Morals and Ecce Homo.* New York: Vintage Books, 1967.

Pearson, Carol. *Awakening the Heroes Within.* New York: HarperCollins, 1991.

———. *The Hero Within.* New York: HarperCollins, 1989.

Rank, Otto. *The Myth of the Birth of the Hero.* New York: Vintage Books, 1964.

Vanek, Elizabeth-Anne. "Image Power." *Emmanuel* (April 1990).
Zweig, Connie, and Jeremiah Abrams. *Meeting the Shadow: The Hidden Power of the Dark Side of Human Nature.* New York: G. P. Putnam's, 1991.

Biblical Studies

Alter, Robert, and Frank Kermode, eds. *The Literary Guide to the Bible.* Cambridge: Belknap, 1987.
Bergant, Dianne. *What Are They Saying About Wisdom Literature?* New York: Paulist Press, 1984.
Brown, Raymond. *The Birth of the Messiah.* New York: Doubleday, 1977.
_____. *The Death of the Messiah.* New York: Doubleday, 1994.
Bruce, F. F. *The Hard Sayings of Jesus.* Downers Grove: InterVarsity Press, 1983.
Crossan, John. D. *In Parables: The Challenge of the Historical Jesus.* San Francisco: Harper & Row 1973.
————. *The Historical Jesus: The Life of a Mediterranean Jewish Peasant.* New York: HarperSanFrancisco, 1991.
————. *In Fragments: The Aphorisms of Jesus.* San Francisco: Harper & Row, 1983.
————. *The Dark Interval. Towards a Theology of Story.* Sonoma: Polebridge Press, 1988.
Dodd, C. H. *The Parables of the Kingdom.* New York: Charles Scribner's Sons, 1961.
Fitzmyer, Joseph. *The Biblical Commission's Document: The Interpretation of the Bible in the Church.* Rome: Editrice Pontificio Instituto Biblico, 1995.
Harrington, Wilfred. *A Key to the Parables.* New Jersey: Deus Books, 1964.
Heschel, Abraham. *The Prophets.* New York: Harper & Row, 1962.
Hunter, A. M. *Interpreting the Parables.* London: SCM Press, Ltd., 1960.
Lambrecht, Jan. *Parables of Jesus: Insight and Challenge.* Bangalore: Theological Publications in India, 1976.
Landy, Francis. "Humour as a Tool for Biblical Exegesis." In *On Humour and the Comic in the Hebrew Bible,* edited by Yehuda Radday and Athalya Brenner. Sheffield: Almond Press, 1990.
Mally, Edward. "The Gospel According to Mark." In *The Jerome*

Biblical Commentary, edited by Raymond Brown, Joseph Fitzmyer, and Roland Murphy. Englewood Cliffs: Prentice-Hall, 1968.

McCarthy, Dennis. "Hosea." In *The Jerome Biblical Commentary,* edited by Raymond Brown, Joseph Fitzmyer, and Roland Murphy. Englewood Cliffs: Prentice-Hall, 1968.

Perrin, Norman. *Jesus and the Language of the Kingdom.* Philadelphia: Fortress Press, 1976.

Rollins, Wayne. *Jung and the Bible.* Atlanta: John Knox, 1983.

Sanford, John. *Mystical Christianity: A Psychological Commentary on the Gospel John.* New York: Crossroad, 1995.

Stern, David. *Jewish New Testament Commentary.* Clarksville: Jewish New Testament Publications, Inc., 1992.

Stuhlmueller, Carroll. *Biblical Meditations for Lent.* New York: Paulist Press, 1978.

———. *Psalms I.* Collegeville: The Liturgical Press, 1983.

———. "The Gospel According to Luke." In *The Jerome Biblical Commentary,* edited by Raymond Brown, Joseph Fitzmyer, and Roland Murphy. Englewood Cliffs: Prentice Hall,1968.

Mary Ann Tolbert. *Perspectives on the Parables.* Philadelphia: Fortress Press, 1979.

Christian Spirituality

à Kempis, Thomas. *The Imitation of Christ.* Harmondsworth: Penguin, 1952.

Augustine. *Confessions.* Harmondsworth: Penguin, 1961.

William Barry. *God's Passionate Desire and Our Response.* Notre Dame: Ave Maria Press, 1993.

Bernardin, Joseph. *The Gift of Peace.* Chicago: Loyola Press, 1997.

Bonhoeffer, Dietrich. *The Cost of Discipleship.* New York: Macmillan, 1937.

———. *Letters and Papers from Prison.* New York: Macmillan, 1967.

Bonaventure. *The Soul's Journey into God: The Tree of Life: The Life of St. Francis.* New York: Paulist Press, 1978.

Cox, Harvey. *A Feast of Fools.* New York: Harper & Row, 1969.

Erasmus, Desiderius. *The Praise of Folly.* Princeton: Princeton University Press, 1941.

Fedotov, G. P. *The Russian Religious Mind.* Cambridge: Harper Torchbooks, 1960.

Forest, Jim. "Holy Foolishness." *The Tablet* (23 July 1994).

Maria Hass, Alois. "Schools of Late Medieval Mysticism." In *Christian Spirituality of the High Middle Ages and Reformation,* edited by Jill Rait. New York: Crossroad, 1988.

Hays, Edward. *Holy Fools & Mad Hatters.* Leavenworth: Forest of Peace Books, 1993.

Haughton, Rosemary. *The Transformation of Man.* Springfield: Templegate, 1967.

John of the Cross. *The Collected Works.* Translated by Kiernan Kavanaugh and Otilio Rodriguez. Washington: ICS Publications, 1979.

Julian of Norwich. *Revelations of Divine Love.* Harmondsworth: Penguin, 1966.

Francis Kavanaugh, John. *Following Christ in a Consumer Society.* New York: Orbis Books, 1981.

Küng, Hans. *On Being a Christian.* New York: Doubleday & Co., 1984.

Martin, Joseph. *Foolish Wisdom: Stories, Activities and Reflections from Ken Feit.* San Jose: Resource Publications, 1990.

Nouwen, Henri. *Clowning in Rome: Reflections on Solitude, Celibacy, Prayer and Contemplation.* New York: Image Books, 1979.

Richard, Rohr. "Holy Fools: Ushers of the Next Generation in the Church." *Sojourners* (July 1994).

Schneiders, Sandra. "Scripture and Spirituality." In *Christian Spirituality: Origins to the Twelfth Century,* edited by Bernard McGinn, John Meyendorff, and Jean Leclercq. New York: Crossroads, 1987.

Theresa of Avila. *The Interior Castle.* New York: Paulist Press, 1979.

The Way of a Pilgrim. Translated by Helen Bacovcin. New York: Image Books, 1978.

Underhill, Evelyn. *Essentials of Mysticism.* New York: Dutton, 1960.

Vanek, Elizabeth-Anne. "In the Belly of the Great Fish." *Emmanuel* (March 1994).

———. "Prophetic Ministry: Its Hazards and Blessings." *Today's Parish* (September 1992).

———. "Inner Journeying: The Hero's Quest." *Emmanuel* (April 1992).

———. "Godot and Spiritual Blight." *Emmanuel* (December 1991).

———. "Learning from Mystical Tradition." *Emmanuel* (June 1991).

———. "Mysticism and Contemporary Spirituality." *Emmanuel* (May 1991).

———. "Proclaiming the Subversive Word." *Emmanuel* (September 1990).

———. "Prophetic Silence." *Emmanuel* (December 1989).

———. "The Divine Activity of the Poet." *Currents in Theology and Mission* 13 no. 2 (April 1986).

Walsh, Michael, ed. *Butler's Lives of Patron Saints.* San Francisco: Harper & Row, 1987.

Welsch, John. *When Gods Die: An Introduction to John of the Cross.* New York: Paulist Press, 1990.

Christology

Boff, Leonardo. *Jesus Christ Liberator: A Critical Christology for Our Time.* New York: Orbis Books, 1978.

Miguez Bonino, Jose. *Faces of Jesus: Latin American Christologies.* New York: Orbis Books, 1984.

Borg, Marcus. *Meeting Jesus Again for the First Time: The Historical Jesus and the Heart of Contemporary Faith.* New York: HarperCollins, 1994.

Brown, Raymond. *An Introduction to New Testament Christology.* Mahwah: Paulist Press, 1994.

Congar, Yves. *Jesus Christ.* New York: Herder & Herder, 1966.

Cousins, Ewert. *Christ of the 21st Century.* Rockport: Element Books, 1992.

Cullman, Oscar. *The Christology of the New Testament.* Translated by Shirley C. Guthrie and Charles Hall. Philadelphia: Westminster Press, 1963.

Hahn, Ferdinand. *The Titles of Jesus in Christology: Their History in Early Christianity.* New York: The World Publishing Co., 1969.

Hellwig, Monika. *Jesus, the Compassion of God: New Perspectives on the Tradition of Christianity.* Wilmington: Michael Glazier, 1983.

Kasper, Walter. *Jesus the Christ.* New York: Paulist Press, 1976.

Marxen, Willi. *The Beginnings of Christology.* Philadelphia: Fortress Press, 1979.

Pelikan, Jaroslav. *Jesus through the Centuries.* New York: Harper & Row, 1985.

Sabourin, Leopold. *The Names and Titles of Jesus.* Translated by Maurice Carroll. New York: Macmillan Co., 1967.

Sanders, Jack. *The New Testament Christological Hymns: Their*

Historical and Religious Background. Cambridge: Cambridge University Press, 1971.

Schillebeeckx, Edward. *Jesus and Christ*. New York: Crossroad, 1981.

Schüssler Fiorenza, Elizabeth. *Jesus. Miriam's Child, Sophia's Prophet*. New York: Continuum, 1994.

Schreiter, Robert. *Faces of Jesus in Africa*. New York: Orbis Books, 1991.

Slusser, Gerald. *From Jung to Jesus*. Atlanta: John Knox, 1986.

Sugirtharajah, R. S. *Asian Faces of Jesus*. New York: Orbis Books, 1993.

Ecclesiology

Cooke, Bernard. *Christian Community: Response to Reality*. New York: Holt, Rinehart & Winston,1970.

Cox, Harvey. *Religion in the Secular City*. New York: Simon and Schuster, 1984.

Dulles, Avery. *The Dimensions of the Church*. Westminster: Newman Press, 1967.

————. *Models of the Church*. New York: Image Books, 1987.

Küng, Hans. *The Church*. New York: Image Books, 1976.

Ludwig, Robert. *Reconstructing Catholicism for a New Generation*. New York: Crossroad, 1995.

"Lumen Gentium." In *Vatican Council II: Constitutions, Decrees, Declarations*, edited by Austin Flannery. New York: Costello Publishing Co, 1996.

McBrien, Richard. *Church: The Continuing Quest*. New York: Newman Press, 1970.

————. *The Re-Making of the Church: An Agenda for Reform*. New York: Harper & Row, 1973.

MacEoin, Gary. "Synod Tries To Make American Church More Roman Dissenters Say." *The National Catholic Reporter* (12 December 1997).

Minear, Paul. *Images of the Church in the New Testament*. Philadelphia: Westminster Press, 1960.

"Presbyterorum Ordinis." In *Vatican Council II: Constitutions, Decrees, Declarations*, edited by Austin Flannery. New York: Costello Publishing Co., 1996.

Schillebeeckx, Edward. *Church: The Human Story of God*. New York: Crossroad, 1990.

Zizioulas, John. "The Early Christian Community." In *Christian
Spirituality: Origins to the Twelfth Century,* edited by Bernard
McGinn, John Meyendorff, and Jean Leclercq. New York:
Crossroad, 1987.

Interreligious Dialogue

Bernardin, Joseph. *A Blessing to Each Other: Cardinal Joseph
Bernardin and Jewish Catholic Dialogue.* Chicago: Liturgy
Training Publications, 1996.
Fisher, Eugene, and Leon Klenicki. *From Desolation to Hope: An
Interreligious Holocaust Memorial Service.* Chicago: Liturgy
Training Publications, 1983.
Lefebure, Leo. *The Buddha and the Christ: Explorations in Buddhist
and Christian Dialogue.* New York: Orbis Books, 1993.
"Nostra Aetate." In *Vatican Council II: Constitutions, Decrees,
Declarations,* edited by Austin Flannery. New York: Costello
Publishing Co. 1996.
Parliament of the World's Religions. *The Global Ethic.* Chicago:
PWR, 1993.

Jewish Spirituality

Ausubel, Nathan, ed. *A Treasury of Jewish Folklore.* New York:
Crown Publishers, 1948.
Heschel, Abraham. *Man's Quest for God.* New York: Charles
Scribner's Sons, 1954.
———. *God in Search of Man.* New York: Octagon Books, 1972.
Hillesum, Etty. *An Interrupted Life.* New York: Pantheon Books,
1981.

Literature and Art

Alighieri, Dante. *L' Inferno.* Translated by Dorothy Sayers.
Harmondsworth: Penguin, 1949.
———. *Il Purgatorio.* Translated by Dorothy Sayers.
Harmondsworth: Penguin, 1955.
———. *Il Paradiso.* Translated by Mark Musa. Harmondsworth:
Penguin, 1984.
Aristotle, Horace & Longinus. *Classical Literary Criticism.*
Translated by T. S. Dorsch. Harmondsworth: Penguin, 1965.

Attar, Farid Ud-Din. *The Conference of the Birds.* Translated by
    Afkham Darbandi and Dick Davis. Harmondsworth:
    Penguin, 1986.
Beckett, Samuel. *Waiting for Godot.* London: Faber & Faber, 1971.
Bradley, A. C. *Shakespearean Tragedy.* London: Macmillan & Co.,
    1969.
Courthion, Pierre. *Georges Rouault.* New York: Harry N. Abrams,
    Inc.
Dostoevsky, Fyodor. *Crime and Punishment.* New York: Vintage
    Press, 1950.
————. *The Idiot.* Harmondsworth: Penguin, 1955.
Eliot, T. S. *The Complete Poems and Plays.* New York: Harcourt,
    Brace and World, 1971.
Esslin, Martin. *The Theatre of the Absurd.* Harmondsworth:
    Penguin, 1968.
Euripides. *The Bacchae and Other Plays.* Harmondsworth: Penguin,
    1954.
Gassner, John. *A Treasury of the Theatre.* Vol. 1. New York: Simon
    and Schuster, 1963.
Happe, Peter. *English Mystery Plays: A Selection.* Harmondsworth:
    Penguin, 1975.
Hughes, Langston. "Harlem." In *The Bedford Introduction to
    Literature,* edited by Michael Meyer. Boston: St. Martin's
    Press, 1990.
La Strada. Directed by Federico Fellini. Janus films Inc., 1961.
Luke, Helen. *Dark Wood to White Rose: Journey and Transformation
    in Dante's Divine Comedy.* New York: Parabola Books, 1989.
The Quest of the Holy Grail. Translated by P. M. Matarasso.
    Harmondsworth: Penguin, 1969.
O'Connor, Flannery. *The Complete Stories.* New York: The Noonday
    Press, 1971.
Palgrave, F. T., ed. *The Golden Treasury of the Best Songs and Lyrical
    Poems in the English Language.* London: Oxford University
    Press, 1963.
Patricca, Nicholas. *The Fifth Sun.* Woodstock: The Dramatic
    Publishing Co., 1984.
Perrine, Norman, ed. *Literature. Structure, Sound and Sense.* New
    York: Harcourt Brace Jovanovich, 1988.
Plautus. *The Pot of Gold and Other Plays.* Harmondsworth:
    Penguin, 1965.
Rushdie, Salman. *The Satanic Verses.* New York: Viking Penguin,

Inc., 1988.

Shakespeare, William. *The Complete Works*. New York: Harcourt, Brace & World, 1968.

The Wickerman. Directed by Peter Snell. Media Home Entertainment, 1961.

Vanek, Elizabeth-Anne. *Extraordinary Time*. Canton: Life Enrichment Publishers, 1988.

————. *Woman Dreamer*. Bristol: Wyndham Hall Press, 1989.

————. *Frost and Fire*. Canton: Life Enrichment Publishers, 1985.

————. "Was It Not Enough?" *Emmanuel* (December 1995).

Wagner, Richard. *Parsifal*. London: John Calder Publishers, 1986.

Wordsworth, William. "Ode on Intimations of Immortality From Recollections of Early Childhood." In *The Golden Treasury*. London: Oxford University Press, 1963.

Liturgy

Allen, John. "Teens Seek More Youth-Friendly Liturgies." In *The National Catholic Reporter* (12 December 1997).

Bausch, William. *A New Look At the Sacraments*. Mystic: Twenty-Third Publications, 1988.

Cullman, Oscar. *Early Christian Worship*. Bristol: Wyndham Hall Press, 1953.

Driver, Tom. *The Magic of Ritual: Our Need for Liberating Rites that Transform Our Lives and Our Communities*. New York: HarperCollins, 1991.

The Liturgy Documents: A Parish Resource. Chicago: Liturgy Training Publications, 1980.

Vanek, Elizabeth-Anne. "Eucharist. More Than You Think." *Religion Teacher's Journal* (January 1984).

————. "Festivals of Memory." *Emmanuel* (July / August 1989).

————. "Epiphany, the Magi and Us: Challenging the Status Quo." *Liturgy* 4 no. 3 (December 1984).

————. "Beyond Signs." *Modern Liturgy* (December 1984).

Young, Frances. *The Making of the Creeds*. London: SCM Press, 1991.

Peace and Justice

Day, Dorothy. *The Long Loneliness*. New York: Harper & Row, 1952.

Gioseffi, Daniela. *Women on War*. New York: Simon & Schuster,

1988.
Jeffrey, Paul. "Guatemala Catholics Find the Path to a New Future, Confront Sins of the Past." *The National Catholic Reporter* (13 February 1998).

Psychology

Fowler, James. *Stages of Faith: The Psychology of Human Development and the Quest for Meaning.* New York: HarperSanFrancisco, 1981.
Freud, Sigmund. *The Basic Writings.* New York: The Modern Library, 1938.
Fromm, Eric. *Psychoanalysis and Religion.* New York: Bantam Books, 1950.
Jacobi, Jolande. *The Psychology of C. G. Jung.* New Haven: Yale University Press, 1973.
James, William. *The Varieties of Religious Experience.* New York: Penguin, 1982.
Levine, Stephen. *Who Dies?* New York: Doubleday, 1982.
Malony, Newton, and A. Adams Lovekin. *Glossolalia. Behavioral Science Perspectives on Speaking in Tongues.* New York: Oxford University Press, 1984.
Moore, Thomas. *Care of the Soul: A Guide for Cultivating Depth and Sacredness in Everyday Life.* New York: HarperCollins, 1992.
Scott Peck, M. *The Road Less Travelled.* New York: Simon & Schuster, 1978.
Ulanov, Ann and Barry. *Religion and the Unconscious.* Philadelphia: Westminster Press, 1975.
Viorst, Judith. *Necessary Losses.* New York: Fawcett Gold Medal, 1986.
Von Franz, Marie-Louise. "The Process of Individuation." In *Man and his Symbols,* edited by C. G. Jung. New York: Dell Publishing Co., 1964.

Spiritual Direction

Gratton, Carolyn. *The Art of Spiritual Guidance.* New York: Crossroad, 1993.
May, Gerald. *Care of Mind, Care of Spirit: Psychiatric Dimensions of Spiritual Direction.* New York: HarperSanFrancisco, 1982.
Vanek, Elizabeth-Anne. *Image Guidance: A Tool for Spiritual*

Direction. Mahwah: Paulist Press, 1992.

———. *Image Guidance and Healing*. Mahwah: Paulist Press, 1994.

———. *From Center to Circumference: God's Place in the Circle of Self*. Mahwah: Paulist Press, 1996.

Studies in Comedy

Boston, Richard. *An Anatomy of Laughter*. London: Collins, 1974.

Enck, John, Elizabeth Forter, and Alvin Whitely. *The Comic in Theory and Practice*. New York: Appleton-Century-Crofts, Inc., 1960.

Kronenberger, Louis. *The Thread of Laughter*. New York: Alfred A. Knopf, Inc., 1952.

Towsen, John. *Clowns*. New York: Hawthorne Books Inc., 1976.

Voss, Nelvin. *For God's Sake Laugh!* Atlanta: John Knox Press, 1967.

Theology

Aquinas, Thomas. *Of God and His Creatures*. Westminster: The Carroll Press, 1950.

Congar, Yves. *I Believe in the Holy Spirit*. New York: Crossroad, 1983.

Davies, Brian. *The Thought of Thomas Aquinas*. Oxford: Clarendon Paperbacks, 1992.

Johnson, Elizabeth. *She Who Is: The Mystery of God in Feminist Theological Discourse*. New York: Crossroad, 1992.

Keane, Marie-Henry. "The Spirit of Life." In *Doing Theology in Context: South African Perspectives*, edited by John de Gruchy and C. Villa-Vicencio. New York: Orbis Books, 1995.

Moltmann, Jurgen. *The Crucified God*. Minneapolis: Fortress Press, 1993.

———. *The Trinity and the Kingdom*. Minneapolis: Fortress Press, 1993.

Shea, John. *The Spirit Master*. Chicago: The Thomas More Press, 1987.

Tillich, Paul. *The Courage To Be*. New Haven: Yale University Press, 1952.

Thurnnberg, Lars. "The Human Person As Image of God." In *Christian Spirituality: Origins to the Twelfth Century*, edited by Bernard McGinn, John Meyendorff, and Jean Leclercq. New York: Crossroad, 1987.

Vanek, Elizabeth-Anne. "The God Beyond Images." *Emmanuel* (January 1992).

Varillon, Francis. *The Humility and Suffering of God.* New York: Alba House, 1983.

World Religions

Buddhist Scriptures. Translated by Edward Conze. Harmondsworth: Penguin, 1984.

DePaul University, Department of Religious Studies. *Religious Worlds.* Chicago: Kendall-Hunt, 1991.

Eliade, Mircea, and Ioan Couliano. *The Eliade Guide to World Religions.* New York: HarperCollins, 1991.

McGaa, Ed. *Mother Earth Spirituality: Native American Paths to Healing Ourselves and Our World.* New York: HarperCollins, 1990.

Smith, Huston. *The Religions of Man.* New York: Harper & Row, 1986.

Index

Archetype, 1, 2, 15–18, 27, 35, 39, 47, 57, 92, 128, 171–174, 195

Archetypal Biblical Criticism, 58, 60

Archetype of Self, Jesus, 19, 25–27, 185

Artificial Fools, 43–46, 190

Axial Period, First, 213

Axial Period, Second, 213

Baptism, 73, 164–166, 196

Beatitudes, 96–105, 114, 179, 197

Christology, 1, 7, 8, 12, 13, 54, 132, 175, 176, 210

Christological Titles, 1–4, 12, 13, 130, 225

Christological Titles, Negative, 28, 130, 135, 136

Christ the King, 13, 30, 141, 144

Clowns, 14, 35, 36, 43, 47, 50, 51, 52, 80, 171, 179, 209, 220, 222, 234, 241

Clown Societies, 45

Comedy, 53, 54, 67, 70, 72, 84, 148, 157

Comedy of the Resurrection, 148, 149, 210

Commodity Form of Life, 195, 201, 202, 203, 204, 207, 212, 216, 219

Consciousness, of a Child, 91–96, 196, 201, 240

Consciousness, Transformation of, 27, 49, 90–94, 117, 123, 124, 129, 149, 164, 183, 197, 212, 213

Conventional Wisdom; cf "World's Wisdom"

Court Fools; cf "Jester"

Crucifixion, 4–7, 12, 14, 30, 66, 78, 143, 144, 167, 169, 223

Dark Night, Senses, 23, 25

Dark Night, Spirit, 23, 25

Dark Wood, 22–24

Demons, 75, 77, 120, 131, 135, 147, 161

Devil, 33, 119, 135, 189

Detachment, 18, 20, 24, 121

Dionysus, 151, 173–177, 185, 187, 196, 197, 204, 206, 208, 211, 225

Discipleship, 126, 159, 176, 178, 180–183, 194

Divine Child, 16, 66, 68, 71, 72

Divine Folly, 2, 34, 77, 164, 223

Ecclesiology, 38, 194, 223–230

Eschatological Banquet, 42, 76, 77

Eucharist, 7, 42, 129, 205, 206, 235

Feast of the Ass, 44

Festum Stultorum, 44, 45

Fisher King, 48

Free Will, 58–61

Grace, Cheap, 159, 160, 180, 216

Grace, Costly, 159–160, 180, 215, 216, 240, 241

Global Consciousness, 91, 212, 213, 235–237

Global Ethic, 212

God of Humility, 66

Hero, 16, 67, 69, 70

Heroism, 196, 198

Holocaust, 198, 199, 217, 218, 222

Holy Spirit, 2, 3, 149–159, 161–164, 167, 170, 175, 187, 204

Humiliation of Christ, 4–6, 11, 29, 30, 35, 40, 43, 47, 78, 102, 136, 137, 141, 188

Illumination, 24, 25, 26

Imitation of Christ, 7, 26, 161, 168, 176, 180, 184, 188, 231

Incarnation, 65, 66, 166

Institutional Church, 3, 225, 226, 228–230, 234, 238

Inculturation, 8, 9, 235–237

Individuation, 18, 20, 27, 185

Infancy Narratives, 67–74

Inner Power, 215, 219, 220, 221

Interreligious Dialogue, 214, 215

Iurodivii, 73, 74, 146, 184, 186, 189, 192

Jester; cf "Court Fool" 27, 36, 40–47, 74, 82, 87, 89, 90, 92, 133, 146, 155, 171, 191, 197, 201, 209, 210, 215, 218, 229, 232, 241

Jesus, as "Buddy," 176–185

Jesus as "Blasphemer," 81, 125, 126, 134, 138, 139, 171

Jesus "In Foolish Company," 75–77, 102, 126, 131, 133

Jesus as Healer, 8, 27, 80, 122–130, 209

Jesus, the Lord, 4, 73

Jesus as "Mad," 72, 86–88, 131, 132, 137

Jesus, Man of Sorrows, 137, 142

Jesus, the Messiah, 5, 145, 174

Jesus, Mockery of, 125, 130, 137–146, 171, 201

Jesus, as "Possessed," 86, 87, 125, 131, 135

Jesus, as "Sinner," 71, 81, 86, 87, 134

Jesus, Son of God, 45, 75

Jesus, Son of Man, 5, 6

Jesus, Suffering Servant, 6, 10, 12, 137, 142

Jesus, as Teacher, 8, 27, 90–130

Job, 21–23

Jung, C. G., 15, 18, 19, 39, 44, 185

Kavanah, 110

Kronia, 40, 143

Kyrios, 4, 73

Law, 78–83, 87, 89, 95, 96, 99, 104, 109, 110, 131, 133, 134, 215, 235, 237

Liberation, 80, 123, 124, 126, 129, 139

Liturgical Fooling, 44, 45, 80

Liturgy, 9, 166, 167, 206–212, 229

Lord's Prayer, 104, 120, 179, 197, 206

Magician, 16, 18, 36, 75

Martyr, 16–18, 164, 177

Mary, 28, 70, 71, 74, 197, 198

Mechanistic Living, 17, 172–175

Mock Kings, 40, 141

Models of Church, 224–226

Mosaic Code, 29, 30, 99, 102

Mystical Consciousness, 12, 19–27

Naive Fools, 50, 91, 184, 186

Natural Fools, 43, 44, 190, 191, 239

Parable, 39, 46, 95, 104–114, 174, 197, 208

Paradox, 98, 114–121, 179, 183, 197, 208, 221

Paradox, Way of, 113–119, 170, 204, 205

Parasite, 41, 42, 43, 76

Parliament of the World's Religions, 212

Parsifal, 48, 49

Passion Narratives, 40, 67, 72, 136, 137, 140, 143, 147, 219

Passive Resistance, 215, 220, 221

Pentecost, 151–153

Prayer, 120–122

Priest Fool, 231–234

Prometheus, 172, 174, 195, 198

Prophets, 33, 47, 52, 53, 61, 62–64, 74, 78, 82, 86, 104, 139, 140, 153, 155, 164, 167, 217

Purgation, 21–25

Pyramid of Power, 230, 231, 238

Resurrection, 14

Ritual Fool, 50

Romanization of Church, 229, 235–237

Roman Saturnalia, 39

Rouault, Georges, 10, 11, 171

Russian Holy Fools, 184, 186, 188, 189, 190

Sacean Feast, 40, 143

Sage, 17, 34, 36, 41, 46, 96

Scapegoat, 5, 35, 45–47, 143, 147

Shabbat, 79–89, 131, 134, 215

Shadow, 16, 17, 39, 42, 47, 185, 201

Sisyphus, 172–177, 185, 195, 198, 206, 207, 225

Spiritual Liberation, 25

Suffering of God, 62–65, 169, 170

Symbolic Exegesis, 86

Temple, 83–90

Theology, 3, 9

Torah, 78, 82, 83, 96, 100, 104, 134

Tragedy, 147

Trickster, 16, 29, 30, 35, 37, 38, 40, 42, 43, 50, 54, 71, 100, 106, 146, 171, 179, 184, 241

Trinity, 2, 14, 57, 166–171

Truth Speaking, 36, 46, 47, 74, 90, 175, 190, 218, 232, 233

Unholy Fools, 27, 31, 32, 33

Union with God, 23, 25

Warrior, 17

Wisdom, God's, 3, 11, 13, 14,
18, 33, 55–62, 70, 77, 84, 104,
108, 110, 111, 116, 122, 127, 136,
159, 171, 175, 181, 186, 217

Wisdom, World's, 3, 11, 14,
32, 33, 55–58, 70, 77, 78, 99,
101, 104, 107, 108, 110, 111,
116, 122, 136, 138, 154, 159,
175, 181, 182, 201–203, 205,
212, 216, 217, 233

Sheed & Ward

Other Books of Interest
available at your favorite bookstore

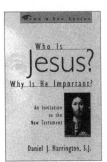

Who Is Jesus? Why Is He Important?
An Invitation to the New Testament
Daniel J. Harrington, S.J.
Who Is Jesus? Why Is He Important? leads readers step-by-step
through the entire New Testament. Father Harrington synthesizes
the best of contemporary scholarship, placing it in dialogue with
deeply personal and pastoral concerns. No matter how familiar you
are with the New Testament — from beginner to professional — this is
a reliable guide that seeks honest answers to complex questions.
199 pp 1-58051-053-1 *$10.95*

Prayers and Fables
Meditating on Aesop's Wisdom
William Cleary
"God Most Knowledgeable, Most Intelligent, Most Wise, can you
help me to win something like $5 million for a $1 investment?" So
begins just one of the quirky prayers based on Aesop's fables in this
witty collection. Cleary has put fifty fables back into verse, and
supplies a brief moral and prayer, bringing the fable to life with
practical application.
180 pp 1-55612-960-2 *$14.95*

Wagering on Transcendence
The Search for Meaning in Literature
Phyllis Carey, Editor
These essays analyze concrete examples of spiritual journeys: from
biography to ecology, from poetry to novels, from philosophy to
stage plays. They explore how nature can be an avenue of
transcendence, how the transforming effects that the search for
meaning can have on the individual, and how transcendence can be
experienced through community.
320 pp 1-55612-982-3 *$24.95*

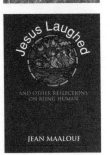

Jesus Laughed and Other Reflections on Being Human
Jean Maalouf
The way of Incarnational spirituality is an on-going dynamic that
gives Jesus, the Incarnate God, a chance to live on and transform the
world again.
160 pp 1-55612-911-4 *$12.95*

SHEED & WARD
An Apostolate of the Priests of the Sacred Heart

30 Amberwood Parkway
Ashland, OH 44805

Email www.bookmasters.com/sheed *Phone* 1-800-266-5564 or *Fax* 419-281-6883